**Oxford Applied Mathemati
and Computing Science Se**

CW01024810

General Editors

J. Crank, H. G. Martin, D. M. Melluish

D. S. JONES
University of Dundee

Elementary information theory

CLARENDON PRESS · OXFORD
1979

Oxford University Press, Walton Street, Oxford OX2 6DP

OXFORD LONDON GLASGOW NEW YORK
TORONTO MELBOURNE WELLINGTON CAPE TOWN
IBADAN NAIROBI DAR ES SALAAM LUSAKA ADDIS ABABA
KUALA LUMPUR SINGAPORE JAKARTA HONG KONG TOKYO
DELHI BOMBAY CALCUTTA MADRAS KARACHI

© D. S. Jones 1979

British Library Cataloguing in Publication Data

Jones, Douglas Samual
   Elementary Information Theory. – (Oxford
   applied mathematics and computing science series.)
   1. Information Theory
   I Title II Series
   001.53'9   Q360   79–40182
   Casebound ISBN 0 19 859636 7
   Paperback ISBN 0 19 859637 5

Typeset by the Universities Press, Belfast
Printed and bound in Great Britain at
The Camelot Press Ltd, Southampton

This book is dedicated
with deep affection to
IVY, HELEN, and PHILIP

Preface

A one term's course on information theory has a number of advantages. It makes relatively few demands on the previous knowledge of the student and so can be placed anywhere convenient in the curriculum. Touching on the structure of language and having applications to computing it is suitable for students with a wide variety of interests. Important theorems can be reached without great effort and yet the techniques are sufficiently testing to stretch the student. The course can be followed, if desired, by more sophisticated units dealing with algebraic coding theory, cryptography, linguistics, error analysis, and optical communication, to choose a few examples.

The course presented in this book is largely self-contained. After a discussion of definitions there is a treatment of elementary coding theory including optimal binary codes. Another chapter deals with the capacity of a channel for discrete sources. Error correcting codes and continuous information are considered in further chapters. Exercises at various levels of difficulty are provided at the ends of chapters. Starred sections indicate topics from which a selection may be made to suit particular requirements.

My thanks are due to my wife Ivy for her continued support and forebearance, and to Mrs. D. Ross for managing to remain cheerful while typing the manuscript.

Dundee   D. S. J.
January 1978

Contents

1 Elements of probability

The theory of information is based on notions drawn from probability. Indeed, some people regard information theory as a branch of applied probability. However, for much of the development the amount of probability theory needed is not large and the brief introduction given in this chapter should suffice for most purposes.

1.1. Probability

The starting point for the mathematical theory of probability is a real or imagined experiment such as tossing a coin, throwing a die, drawing a card from a deck, counting the number of road accidents on a day, tossing a coin ten times, and so on. After the experiment a certain *outcome* is observed, e.g. the coin toss resulted in a head, a 3 was thrown on the die, the ten of hearts was drawn from the pack.

If the number of outcomes of the experiment is finite then *finite probability* is involved; if the number of outcomes is countable then the situation is one of *discrete probability*.

Tossing a coin once is an example of finite probability because there are two possible outcomes, namely heads or tails, provided the coin is not permitted to stand on its edge. Similarly, throwing a die and drawing a card from a pack come within finite probability, there being 6 and 52 possible outcomes in the two cases. If a coin is tossed 10 times there are 1024 possible outcomes and again finite probability is concerned. On the other hand, if the experiment is tossing a coin until a head appears the possible outcomes are

$$H, TH, TTH, TTTH, \ldots$$

where H, T stand for head and tail respectively. Now the number of outcomes is infinite but countable so this experiment comes under the heading of discrete probability.

In advance of the experiment we do not know which outcome will occur, but we associate with an outcome a probability p. It is difficult to define precisely what is meant by p but the following conveys a rough idea. Suppose that the experiment is conducted n times and the particular outcome under consideration occurs f times. Then f/n is expected to approach p as $n \to \infty$.

Since f cannot be less than zero nor exceed n, it follows that p will be positive and lie somewhere between 0 and 1. Because $f = 0$ implies the non-occurrence of an outcome it is usual in discrete probability to interpret $p = 0$ as meaning that a particular outcome cannot occur. Similarly, $p = 1$ is taken to signify that an outcome is certain to occur because, if $f = n$, the same outcome appears after every experiment.

From now on, it will be understood that discrete probability (which includes finite probability) is under discussion unless otherwise is specified.

DEFINITION 1.1a *With each outcome O_n of all possible outcomes $O_1, O_2, \ldots$ of an experiment assume that there is an associated probability $P(O_n)$ which is positive, lies in $[0, 1]$, and is such that*

$$P(O_1) + P(O_2) + \cdots = 1.$$

Making $P(O_n)$ positive and in $[0, 1]$ is in conformity with properties of p described above. The last equation of Definition 1.1a is merely an assertion that it is certain that there must be one outcome from an experiment.

The notation $P(\ )$ will be used extensively to denote the probability of the occurrence of whatever is between the parentheses. Thus, in drawing a card from a pack, $P(2 \text{ of diamonds})$ would mean the probability of picking the two of diamonds.

When the number of outcomes is finite, say n, and there is no reason to suppose that one outcome will appear in preference to any other

$$P(O_1) = P(O_2) = \cdots = P(O_n).$$

It then follows from Definition 1.1a that, in fact,

$$P(O_1) = P(O_2) = \cdots = P(O_n) = 1/n. \tag{1.1.1}$$

An ideal coin should not favour heads or tails and so (1.1.1) implies that

$$P(H) = P(T) = \tfrac{1}{2}.$$

If it should happen that $P(H) = \tfrac{2}{3}$, $P(T) = \tfrac{1}{3}$ the coin would not be ideal but *loaded* or *biased* in favour of heads. It will be assumed that coins are ideal unless otherwise stated.

A perfect die is one in which no face is preferentially treated so that, from (1.1.1),

$$P(1) = P(2) = \cdots = P(6) = \tfrac{1}{6}.$$

It is conventional to assume that in drawing a card from a pack (which contains 52 cards) any one is equally likely to be drawn so that

$$P(8 \text{ of clubs}) = \tfrac{1}{52}.$$

Likewise, in bridge, where the pack is distributed in four hands of 13 cards, it is conventional to regard all distributions as equally likely. The verification of this assumption in bridge would require some 10^{30} experiments with well-shuffled packs and involve millions of man-years.

The probability of an *event E* can be determined once a rule has been provided which says for every possible outcome of an experiment whether or not the event E has occurred. There is an important distinction between outcomes and events. Outcomes are fixed by the experiment and are not within our control. In contrast, events can be chosen to suit our convenience.

DEFINITION 1.1b. *The probability of an event E is the sum of the probabilities of the outcomes in which E occurs.*

For example, if a coin is tossed and E is the tossing of a head

$$P(E) = P(H) = \tfrac{1}{2}.$$

In the experiment of tossing a coin twice, let E be the event that H appears only once. The possible outcomes are HH, HT, TH, TT; and

$$P(E) = P(HT) + P(TH) = \tfrac{1}{4} + \tfrac{1}{4} = \tfrac{1}{2}.$$

When the number of outcomes is finite and they are all equally likely, suppose k of them entail the event E. Then, from (1.1.1) and Definition 1.1b,

$$P(E) = k/n.$$

The probability of any outcome cannot be negative and so $P(E) \geqslant 0$. On the other hand, $p(e) \leqslant P(O_1) + P(O_2) + \cdots$ and so, from Definition 1.1a,

$$0 \leqslant P(E) \leqslant 1. \tag{1.1.2}$$

Of course, $1 - P(E)$ is the probability that E will not occur.

Let E_1 and E_2 be two events. Two new events can be defined from them. $E_1 \cup E_2$ is the event in which *either E_1 or E_2 or both occur*. $E_1 \cap E_2$ is the event in which *both E_1 and E_2 occur*. It may happen that if E_1 occurs, E_2 cannot and vice versa. Then E_1 and E_2 are said to be *mutually exclusive* and

$$P(E_1 \cap E_2) = 0. \qquad (1.1.3)$$

This may be expressed as $E_1 \cap E_2 = 0$ on the understanding that 0 here stands for the null event and $P(0) = 0$.

An important result is given by the following theorem.

THEOREM 1.1.

$$P(E_1 \cup E_2) = P(E_1) + P(E_2) - P(E_1 \cap E_2)$$

and, if E_1 and E_2 are mutually exclusive,

$$P(E_1 \cup E_2) = P(E_1) + P(E_2).$$

Proof. In $P(E_1) + P(E_2)$ any outcome favourable to E_1 is counted once and any outcome favourable to E_2 is counted once. Therefore, outcomes favourable to both are counted twice. Hence, if these are subtracted once, as is done by taking away $P(E_1 \cap E_2)$, the outcomes favourable to either E_1 or E_2 or both are left. The first statement of the theorem is consequently demonstrated. The second assertion follows at once from (1.1.3) for mutually exclusive events.

According to (1.1.2), $P(E_1 \cap E_2) \geq 0$ and so we infer from Theorem 1.1 that

$$P(E_1 \cup E_2) \leq P(E_1) + P(E_2). \qquad (1.1.4)$$

Let $E = E_1 \cup E_2$; then, from (1.1.4),

$$P(E_1 \cup E_2 \cup E_3) = P(E \cup E_3) \leq P(E) + P(E_3)$$

$$\leq P(E_1 \cup E_2) + P(E_3)$$

$$\leq P(E_1) + P(E_2) + P(E_3)$$

from (1.1.4) again. Obviously, the general formula is given by the following corollary.

COROLLARY 1.1.

$$P(E_1 \cup E_2 \cup \cdots) \leq P(E_1) + P(E_2) + \cdots$$

Example 1.1. In the experiment of tossing a coin twice let E_1 be the event that a head appears on the first toss and E_2 the event that a head occurs on the second toss. The possible outcomes are HH, HT, TH, and TT each of which has probability $\frac{1}{4}$ because they are all equally likely. The ones favourable to E_1 are HH and HT so that

$$P(E_1) = \tfrac{1}{4} + \tfrac{1}{4} = \tfrac{1}{2}.$$

Similarly, HH and TH entail E_2; so $P(E_2) = \frac{1}{2}$.

For $E_1 \cup E_2$ the relevant outcomes are HT, TH, and HH while $E_1 \cap E_2$ requires HH. Thus

$$P(E_1 \cup E_2) = \tfrac{3}{4}, \qquad P(E_1 \cap E_2) = \tfrac{1}{4}.$$

These results are consistent with Theorem 1.1 since

$$\tfrac{3}{4} = \tfrac{1}{2} + \tfrac{1}{2} - \tfrac{1}{4}.$$

1.2. Samples

Consider an alphabet of n letters $a_1, a_2, \ldots, a_n$. Pick r of them to form, say, $a_{j_1}, a_{j_2}, \ldots, a_{j_r}$. This is a *sample* of size r. Often the place from where the sample is drawn is called the population.

If each choice of letter in the sample is made from the entire alphabet any particular letter may appear more than once in the sample. This is known as *sampling with replacement* and, almost without exception, is the type of sampling which arises in the theory of information. On the other hand, if a letter once drawn cannot be picked again, the process is *sampling without replacement* and no letter can appear twice or more in a sample. There is no limit to the size of samples with replacement but, in samples without replacement, r cannot exceed n because the population is exhausted when $r = n$.

In sampling with replacement each choice of letter can be made in n ways so that the number of different samples of size r which can be selected is n^r. If each of the samples is equally probable the probability of one particular sample being chosen is $1/n^r$ from (1.1.1). Such a situation is often described as *random sampling*.

For sampling without replacement the first letter can be chosen in n ways. Once it has been selected there are $n-1$ possibilities open to the second letter. After the first and second letters have been fixed there are $n-2$ opportunities for the third. Consequently, the number of samples of size r $(r \le n)$ is $n(n-1) \cdots (n-r+1)$. If the samples are equally probable the probability of one of them is $1/n(n-1) \cdots (n-r+1)$; again the term random sample is employed.

Keep r fixed and let $n \to \infty$. Then $n-j$ is approximately n for $j = 0, \ldots, r-1$ and

$$n(n-1) \cdots (n-r+1) \sim n^r.$$

Thus the two methods of sampling are virtually equivalent for small samples from large populations.

1.3. Conditional probability

The probability of an event can alter as more is learned about it. Suppose a card is drawn from a pack then the probability that it is a queen is $\frac{4}{52} = \frac{1}{13}$. Suppose the further knowledge that the card drawn is a knave, queen, or king is available. Then the probability that it is a queen is $\frac{4}{12}$ or $\frac{1}{3}$. *Conditional probability* is the name given to probability when extra information is at our disposal.

To see how to calculate it consider a population of n people of whom b are blonde and f are female. Let E_1 be the event that a person chosen at random is blonde and E_2 the event that a person chosen at random is female. Then, from Section 1.1,

$$P(E_1) = b/n, \qquad P(E_2) = f/n.$$

Let f_b be the number of females who are blonde. Suppose it is known that the person chosen is female. Then the probability that she is blonde is f_b/f because f_b of the f possible outcomes are favourable. Let us agree to write this as $P(E_1 \mid E_2)$, meaning the probability that a person is blonde knowing that the person is female. Then

$$P(E_1 \mid E_2) = \frac{f_b}{f} = \frac{f_b}{n} \cdot \frac{n}{f} = \frac{P(E_1 \cap E_2)}{P(E_2)}.$$

This formula is the basis of the general definition of conditional probability (Definition 1.3).

DEFINITION 1.3. *If $P(E_1) > 0$ the conditional probability $P(E \mid E_1)$ is defined by*

$$P(E \mid E_1) = \frac{P(E \cap E_1)}{P(E_1)}.$$

$P(E \mid E_1)$ is the conditional probability of the event E given that the event E_1 has occurred.

When $P(E_1) = 0$, $P(E \mid E_1)$ is apparently undefined but in the context in which $P(E_1) = 0$ signifies that E_1 cannot occur it is meaningless to talk about the conditional probability of E when E_1 has occurred.

If Theorem 1.1 is applied to the events $E_1 \cap E$ and $E_2 \cap E$,

$$P(E_1 \cap E \cup E_2 \cap E) = P(E_1 \cap E) + P(E_2 \cap E)$$
$$- P(E_1 \cap E \cap E_2 \cap E).$$

But the event $E_1 \cap E \cup E_2 \cap E$ is the same as $E_1 \cup E_2 \cap E$, and $E_1 \cap E \cap E_2 \cap E$ coincides with $E_1 \cap E_2 \cap E$. Hence

$$P(E_1 \cup E_2 \cap E) = P(E_1 \cap E) + P(E_2 \cap E) - P(E_1 \cap E_2 \cap E).$$

Division by $P(E)$ and use of Definition 1.3 gives

$$P(E_1 \cup E_2 \mid E) = P(E_1 \mid E) + P(E_2 \mid E) - P(E_1 \cap E_2 \mid E).$$

In other words, *Theorem* 1.1 *is unaffected by conditioning on an event.* As a consequence Corollary 1.1 holds under conditioning on an event.

From Definition 1.3

$$P(E_1 \mid E_2 \cap E_3) = \frac{P(E_1 \cap E_2 \cap E_3)}{P(E_2 \cap E_3)} = \frac{P(E_1 \cap E_2 \cap E_3)}{P(E_2 \mid E_3)P(E_3)}$$

whence

$$P(E_1 \cap E_2 \cap E_3) = P(E_1 \mid E_2 \cap E_3)P(E_2 \mid E_3)P(E_3).$$
$$(1.3.1)$$

There is no difficulty in generalizing (1.3.1) to more events, e.g.

$$P(E_1 \cap E_2 \cap E_3 \cap E_4) = P(E_1 \mid E_2 \cap E_3 \cap E_4)P(E_2 \cap E_3 \cap E_4)$$
$$= P(E_1 \mid E_2 \cap E_3 \cap E_4)$$
$$\times P(E_2 \mid E_3 \cap E_4)P(E_3 \mid E_4)P(E_4). \quad (1.3.2)$$

Example 1.3. A carton contains 80 light bulbs of which 20 are defective. A bulb selected at random is found to be defective. What is the probability that a second bulb chosen at random is defective if the first is not replaced?

Let E_1 be the event that the first bulb is defective, E_2 the event that the second bulb is defective. We are asked for $P(E_2 \mid E_1)$.

Given that E_1 occurs there are 19 defective bulbs in 79 and so

$$P(E_2 \mid E_1) = \frac{19}{79}.$$

Since $P(E_1) = \frac{1}{4}$,

$$P(E_2 \cap E_1) = \frac{19}{79} \cdot \frac{1}{4} = \frac{19}{316}$$

which is the probability of two defectives on successive choices before any selection is made.

1.4. Independence

It may happen that the occurrence or otherwise of an event E_2 has no influence on the occurrence of E_1. In that case $P(E_1 \mid E_2) = P(E_1)$ because E_2 conveys no knowledge about E_1. It follows from Definition 1.3 that $P(E_1 \cap E_2) = P(E_1)P(E_2)$ in these circumstances. This is such an important concept that it deserves its own definition.

DEFINITION 1.4. *Two events E_1, E_2 are said to be statistically independent if, and only if,*

$$P(E_1 \cap E_2) = P(E_1)P(E_2).$$

To put it another way, two events are characterized as statistically independent when the probability of their joint occurrence is the product of their separate probabilities.

Example 1.4a. A card is drawn from a pack. The probability that it is a ten is 4/52 or 1/13. The probability that it is a spade is 13/52 or 1/4. The probability that it is the ten of spades is 1/52. Since $1/52 = (1/4)(1/13)$, there is agreement with the idea that the events of drawing a ten and of drawing a spade are statistically independent.

Example 1.4b. In a random permutation of a, b, c, d the event a precedes b is statistically independent of c precedes d.

Example 1.4c. In an experiment the probability that E occurs is p. If the experiment is repeated in an independent way the probability that E will occur on the second experiment is also p.

If E occurs on both experiments, the two cases are statistically independent and so Definition 1.4 implies that the probability of the double occurrence is p^2. Similarly, the probability of r occurrences on r independent experiments is p^r.

When, in r experiments, E occurs only s times $(s \leqslant r)$ the probability of a particular sequence is $p^s(1-p)^{r-s}$ since $1-p$ is the probability of non-occurrence of E on an experiment (Section 1.1). The number of ways in which E can occur s times is the number of ways of selecting s slots from r, i.e. $r!/s!(r-s)!$. Hence Definition 1.1b implies that E can occur exactly s times in r independent experiments with probability

$$\frac{r!}{s!(r-s)!} p^s(1-p)^{r-s}.$$

Note that this is consistent with the preceding paragraph when $s = r$ because $0! = 1$.

Example 1.4d. The probability that a lawyer has a car accident in one year is p_1 and for a miner is p_2. If there are 5 times as many miners as lawyers, find the probability that one person selected at random from the combined group will have an accident in the second year if the person has had one in the first year.

Let E_1, E_2 be the events of an accident in the first and second years respectively. Since the lawyers form $\frac{1}{6}$ of the group and the miners $\frac{5}{6}$

$$P(E_1) = \tfrac{1}{6}p_1 + \tfrac{5}{6}p_2.$$

The probability of a lawyer having an accident in both years is $p_1{}^2$ according to Example 1.4c. For miners the relevant probability is $p_2{}^2$. Hence

$$P(E_1 \cap E_2) = \tfrac{1}{6}p_1{}^2 + \tfrac{5}{6}p_2{}^2.$$

Therefore

$$P(E_2 \mid E_1) = \frac{p_1{}^2 + 5p_2{}^2}{p_1 + 5p_2}$$

is the desired conditional probability.

As a numerical illustration take $p_1 = 0.6$, $p_2 = 0.06$. Then $P(E_1) = 0.15$, $P(E_1 \cap E_2) = 0.063$, $P(E_2 \mid E_1) = 0.42$. Thus, knowing that a person has had an accident one year increases the odds (by almost a factor of 3) that the person will have a second accident, indicating that the person chosen at random has a certain proneness to accidents. This is in contrast to the probability of two successive accidents being quite small when there is no advance knowledge of an accident in one year. Statistical independence is lacking here.

The notion of statistical independence can be extended to more than two events. For example, three events are (mutually) statistically independent if and only if

$$P(E_j \cap E_k) = P(E_j)P(E_k) \qquad (j \neq k)$$
$$P(E_1 \cap E_2 \cap E_3) = P(E_1)P(E_2)P(E_3),$$

i.e. not only are the events independent in pairs but also the probability of the triple is the product of the three probabilities. Similarly, for the independence of four events, they must be independent in pairs, in triples and the probability of the four must be the product of the four probabilities. The generalization to n events is immediate.

1.5. The law of large numbers

In many situations it is convenient to classify the result of an experiment as either a success (S) or a failure (F). What constitutes a success is not of concern but it can be chosen to suit our own purposes. Repeat the experiment until it has been carried out n times, each repetition being independent of the others, and count the number of times that S occurs—say, S_n. Then, if p is the probability of S on a single experiment, the behaviour of S_n is governed by the Law of Large Numbers.

LAW OF LARGE NUMBERS. *Given arbitrarily small $\varepsilon > 0$ and $\delta > 0$, then*

$$P\left(\left|\frac{S_n}{n} - p\right| < \varepsilon\right) > 1 - \delta$$

for sufficiently large n.

This is a standard result which can be found in textbooks on probability and no proof will be given here.

If it were legitimate to place ε and δ equal to zero the law would state that it was certain that S_n/n was p. Because this is illegal the most that the law suggests is that S_n/n approaches p as $n \to \infty$, in conformity with the earlier rough idea of probability in

Section 1.1. But one must not be read more into the law than is actually there. The law is a statement about probability and asserts that it is almost certain for large n that S_n/n will be near p, but not that it is absolutely certain. In other words, S_n/n can fluctuate quite widely from p (and in practice usually does) but only for rare values of n.

Example 1.5. In an infinite decimal let the occurrence of 5 be regarded as a success and any other digit as a failure. If all digits are equally likely $p = 1/10$. Then the law of large numbers says that, of the first n figures, $n/10$ will be 5 with high probability as $n \to \infty$.

Similarly, in an infinite sequence of binary digits, the first n figures will contain pn zeros with high probability as $n \to \infty$ if p is the probability of 0 occurring at any place.

Exercises

1.1. Two dice are thrown. List the possible outcomes of the experiment. Do you think that the sum of two faces is as likely to be 3 as to be 7?

1.2. From five digits 1, 2, 3, 4, 5 one is chosen and then a second selection is made from the remaining four digits. Find the probability that an odd digit will be chosen (a) the first time, (b) the second time, (c) both times.

1.3. Let every permutation of the four symbols a_1, a_2, a_3, a_4 be equally probable. Let E_j be the event that a_j appears in the jth position. Verify that

$$P(E_1 \cup E_3) = P(E_1) + P(E_3) - P(E_1 \cap E_3).$$

1.4. Two dice are thrown. E_1 is the event that the sum of the faces is odd. E_2 is the event that at least one 1 is thrown. Describe $E_1 \cup E_2$ and $E_1 \cap E_2$; find their probabilities.

1.5. A coin is tossed until the same result appears twice in succession. With every possible outcome requiring n tosses associate the probability $1/2^n$. Find the probability that the experiments ends (a) before the sixth toss, (b) after an even number of tosses.

1.6. How many different sets of initials can be formed if every person has one surname and (a) exactly two forenames, (b) at most two forenames. Deduce that in case (b) some people have the same initials in a town of 20 000 inhabitants.

1.7. Three dice are thrown. If no two faces are the same, what is the probability that one is a 3?

1.8. The probability that a man will live 10 more years is 0.4 and the probability that his wife will live 10 more years is 0.5. Find the probability (a) they will both live for 10 years, (b) at least one will live for 10 years, (c) neither will live for 10 years.

1.9. Of three cards one is marked 1 on both sides, one has 0 on both sides, and the third has 1 on one side and 0 on the other. A card is selected at random and found to have 1 on one side. What is the probability that there is 1 on the other side?

1.10. A television advertisement for perfume is seen by 40 per cent of the nation. If the probability is 0.1 that a person who sees the advertisement buys the perfume what is the probability that a person picked at random will have seen the advertisement and bought the perfume?

1.11. The probability that a child is born a boy is $\frac{1}{2}$ and the probability that a family has exactly k children is p_k with $p_0 + p_1 + \cdots = 1$. What is the probability that a family has boys but no girls? If it is known that the family has no girls, what is the probability that it has only one child?

1.12. In Exercise 1.11, $p_k = ap^k$ for $k \geqslant 1$, a being a positive constant and $0 < p < 1$. Show that the probability that a family contains m boys $(m \geqslant 1)$ is $2ap^m/(2-p)^{m+1}$. Given that a family includes at least one boy, what is the probability there are two or more?

1.13. Blondes are always on time for appointments, redheads are always late, and brunettes toss a coin for each appointment to decide whether to be prompt or late. The numbers of blondes, redheads, and brunettes are in the ratio $1:1:2$. If a female arrives on time what is the probability that she is (a) blonde, (b) redhead, (c) brunette. If she arrives promptly for three successive appointments, what is the probability that she is a brunette?

1.14. The events $E_1, E_2, \ldots, E_n$ are statistically independent and $P(E_k) = p_k$. Find the probability that none of the events occurs.

2 Basic concepts

Before introducing some of the definitions of information theory, it is desirable to remove one possible cause of misapprehension. Possible combinations of the letters a, n, and t are tan, ant, nat. These words may have meaning and significance for readers but their impact on individuals will vary, depending on the reader's subjective reaction. Subjective information conveyed in this way is impossible to quantify in general. Therefore the meaning of groups of symbols is excluded from the theory of information; each symbol is treated as an entity in its own right and how any particular grouping is interpreted by an individual is ignored. Information theory is concerned with how symbols are affected by various processes but not with information in its most general sense.

2.1. Self-information

Let S be a system of events $E_1, E_2, \ldots, E_n$ in which $P(E_k) = p_k$ with $0 \le p_k \le 1$ and

$$p_1 + p_2 + \cdots + p_n = 1.$$

Then we introduce the following definition

DEFINITION 2.1. *The self-information of the event E_k is written $I(E_k)$ and defined by*

$$I(E_k) = -\log p_k.$$

The base of the logarithm is not specified in the definition. For most of our work it will not matter what base is chosen since a change of base merely alters the scale of units. The most common bases encountered are 2 and e. With base 2, I is measured in *bits* (an abbreviation of binary digits) whereas, in base e, the units of I are *nats* (to indicate that a natural logarithm is involved). The number of nats is 0.693 times the number of bits. Normally, no special choice of base will be made (other than requiring it to exceed unity) but when the base 2 is employed this will be shown by writing $\log_2$ or by appending the word bits at an appropriate place. A natural logarithm will always be written as ln.

When $p_k = \frac{1}{2}$, $-\log_2 p_k = 1$ and $I(E_k) = 1$ bit so that 1 bit of information occurs on the choice of one from two equally likely possibilities. The base of 2 is therefore especially apposite for dealing with binary digits and can therefore be expected to be important in applications to computing and coding.

Tables of logarithms to the base 2 are available but if they are not to hand calculations can be carried out by observing that

$$\log_2 x = \frac{\log_{10} x}{\log_{10} 2} = \frac{\ln x}{\ln 2} = \ln x \log_2 e. \qquad (2.1.1)$$

In general,

$$\log_a x = \ln x / \ln a \qquad (2.1.2)$$

and, since the restriction $a > 1$ has been imposed above, $\ln a > 0$ so that the logarithms which arise will always be positive multiples of the natural logarithm. This fact will be used frequently in subsequent analysis.

The smaller p_k is, the larger $I(E_k)$ is. This is in harmony with our feeling that, the rarer an event is, the more information is conveyed by its occurrence.

Example 2.1a. A letter is chosen at random from the English alphabet. Since there are 26 possibilities

$$I = -\log_2 \frac{1}{26} = 4.7 \text{ bits}$$

is the measure of information in the choice.

Example 2.1b. A binary number of m digits is chosen at random. Each digit of the number can be picked in two different ways so that there are 2^m equally probable possibilities. Hence

$$I = -\log_2 \frac{1}{2^m} = m \text{ bits.}$$

Thus m bits of information are needed to specify a sequence of m binary digits.

Example 2.1c. 64 points are arranged in a square grid. Let E_j, F_k be the events that a point picked at random is in the jth column, kth row respectively. Then

$$P(F_j) \cdot P(F_k) = \tfrac{1}{8}$$

and

$$I(E_j) = 3 \text{ bits}, \qquad I(F_k) = 3 \text{ bits}$$

so that being told that the point is in the jth column provides 3 bits of information and the same amount comes from being informed that it is in the kth row. The knowledge that it is in both the jth column and kth row means that the point is one from 64 equally likely possibilities, i.e.

$$I(E_j \cap F_k) = -\log_2 \frac{1}{64} = 6 \text{ bits.}$$

Consequently,

$$I(E_j \cap F_k) = I(E_j) + I(F_k) \tag{2.1.3}$$

which reflects the fact that being in rows or columns are independent events.

The formula (2.1.3) is not peculiar to Example 2.1c but holds whenever there is statistical independence. Suppose that S consists of the events $E_j \cap F_k$ where $P(E_j) = p_j$ $(p_1 + \cdots + p_n = 1)$ and $P(F_k) = q_k$ $(q_1 + \cdots q_m = 1)$. Then if E_j and F_k are statistically independent for all j and k,

$$P(E_j \cap F_k) = p_j q_k$$

by Definition 1.4. Hence

$$\begin{aligned}
I(E_j \cap F_k) &= -\log p_j q_k = -\log p_j - \log q_k \\
&= I(E_j) + I(F_k) \qquad (j = 1, \ldots, n; \, k = 1, \ldots, m)
\end{aligned} \tag{2.1.4}$$

by Definition 2.1.

2.2. Entropy

A function f has the value f_k associated with the event E_k of the system S. Then $E(f)$, the *expectation* or *average* or *mean* of f, is defined by

$$E(f) = \sum_{k=1}^{n} p_k f_k.$$

This notion enables us to introduce the following definition.

DEFINITION 2.2. *The entropy of S, called H(S), is the average of the self-information, i.e.*

$$H(S) = E(I) = -\sum_{k=1}^{n} p_k \log p_k.$$

Since p_k may be zero, $p_k \log p_k$ could be indeterminate in this definition so, when $p_k = 0$, the value zero is assigned to $p_k \log p_k$.

The letter H is used in honour of Boltzmann who first defined a measure of this type (in the statistical mechanics of gases) and designated it as H.

It has already been pointed out that the self-information of an event increases as its uncertainty grows. Therefore the entropy may be regarded as a *measure of uncertainty*. Properties of the entropy which substantiate this point of view will now be derived.

Firstly, note that $\log p_k \leq 0$ for $0 < p_k \leq 1$ and so $H(S) \geq 0$. Thus, the entropy can never be negative. It may, however, be zero.

Let $p_1 = 1$, $p_2 = \cdots = p_n = 0$. The convention on the meaning of $p_k \log p_k$ when $p_k = 0$ removes all terms from the sum in Definition 2.2, except $p_1 \log p_1$ which disappears because $\log 1 = 0$. Hence, in this case, $H(S) = 0$. Of course there is certainty in this case because the event E_1 must occur. Conversely, $H(S) = 0$ implies that $p_k \log p_k = 0$ for all k so that p_k is either 0 or 1. But only one p_k can be unity since their sum must be 1. Hence, *the entropy vanishes if, and only if, there is complete certainty:*

The entropy is positive or zero but there is a limit to how large it can be. To demonstrate this we first prove a theorem that will have many applications later.

THEOREM 2.2a. *For $x > 0$*

$$\ln x \leq x - 1$$

with equality only when $x = 1$.
Proof. For $0 < t \leq 1$, $1/t \geq 1$. Therefore, integration over a positive interval supplies

$$\int_x^1 dt/t \geq \int_x^1 dt$$

for $0 < x \leq 1$. Evaluating the integrals provides the inequality of the theorem when $0 < x \leq 1$.

If $t \geq 1$, $1/t \leq 1$ and

$$\int_1^x dt/t \leq \int_1^x dt$$

for $x \geq 1$. Again the stated inequality is verified.

Finally, since $1/t$ does not equal 1 unless $t = 1$, strict inequality must occur unless $x = 1$. But, when $x = 1$, both sides of the relation vanish and the theorem is proved.

We are now in a position to demonstrate the following theorem.

THEOREM 2.2b. $H(S) \leq \log n$ *with equality only when* $p_1 = p_2 = \cdots = p_n = 1/n$.
Proof. Assume firstly that no p_k is zero. Then, by Theorem 2.2a,

$$\sum_{k=1}^n p_k \ln \frac{1}{np_k} \leq \sum_{k=1}^n p_k \left(\frac{1}{np_k} - 1\right) \leq \sum_{k=1}^n \left(\frac{1}{n} - p_k\right) \leq 1 - 1 \leq 0. \tag{2.2.1}$$

Hence

$$-\sum_{k=1}^n p_k \ln p_k \leq \sum_{k=1}^n p_k \ln n \leq \ln n. \tag{2.2.2}$$

As remarked in Section 2.1, ln can be converted to log by multiplying by a suitable positive constant. Since multiplication by a positive constant does not invalidate an inequality

$$-\sum_{k=1}^n p_k \log p_k \leq \log n$$

or

$$H(S) \leq \log n. \tag{2.2.3}$$

Since every p_k is positive, equality will arise only if it does for every term in (2.2.1) which requires, on account of Theorem 2.2a, $1/np_k = 1$ for all k. The theorem is therefore proved for non-zero probabilities.

If a probability, say p_j, is zero $p_j \ln p_j n = 0$ and

$$p_j \ln \frac{1}{np_j} < \frac{1}{n} - p_j. \tag{2.2.4}$$

Thus (2.2.1) continues to hold and the upper bound on $H(S)$ then follows from (2.2.2). However, the inequality (2.2.4) prevents equality in (2.2.3). The proof is finished.

When all the events are equally probably, the most uncertainty prevails as to which event will occur. It is therefore satisfactory that the entropy should be a maximum in such a situation. The fact that $H(S)$ is a maximum when the events are equally uncertain but zero when there is certainty provides some justification for considering entropy as a measure of uncertainty.

2.3. Mutual information

Quite often the connections between two systems are under consideration and a definition of information which takes note of this fact is desirable. Let S_1 be a system with events $E_1, \ldots, E_n$, the associated probabilities being $p_1, \ldots, p_n$ with $p_j \geq 0$, $\sum_{j=1}^{n} p_j = 1$. Let S_2 be a system with events $F_1, \ldots, F_m$ with probabilities $q_1, \ldots, q_m$, $q_k \geq 0$, $\sum_{k=1}^{m} q_k = 1$. Observe that the possibility of different numbers of events in the two systems has been allowed for.

The connection between the two systems is obtained by specifying

$$P(E_j \cap F_k) = p_{jk} \qquad (j = 1, \ldots, n; k = 1, \ldots, m)$$

subject to $p_{jk} \geq 0$,

$$\sum_{j=1}^{n} \sum_{k=1}^{m} p_{jk} = 1. \tag{2.3.1}$$

Equation (2.3.1) is, of course, a statement that one event from S_1 and one event from S_2 must occur.

The p_{jk}, p_j, and q_k are related. If k is given every one of its possible values the set $E_j \cap F_k$ will contain all combinations in which E_j can occur. It follows from Definition 1.1b that

$$p_j = P(E_j) = \sum_{k=1}^{m} P(E_j \cap F_k) = \sum_{k=1}^{m} p_{jk}. \tag{2.3.2}$$

Remark that, on account of (2.3.1), $\sum_{j=1}^{n} p_j = 1$ as it should. Similarly,

$$q_k = P(F_k) = \sum_{j=1}^{n} P(E_j \cap F_k) = \sum_{j=1}^{n} p_{jk} \tag{2.3.3}$$

and $\sum_{k=1}^{m} q_k = 1$. By virtue of Definition 1.3

$$P(E_j \mid F_k) = P(E_j \cap F_k)/P(F_k) = p_{jk}/q_k, \tag{2.3.4}$$

$$P(F_k \mid E_j) = p_{jk}/p_j. \tag{2.3.5}$$

The effect of conditioning is specified in the following definition.

Definition 2.3a. *The conditional self-information* $I(E_j \mid F_k)$ *of* E_j *given that* F_k *has occurred and the conditional entropy* $H(S_1 \mid S_2)$ *are defined by*

$$I(E_j \mid F_k) = -\log P(E_j \mid F_k) = -\log(p_{jk}/q_k),$$

$$H(S_1 \mid S_2) = \sum_{j=1}^{n} \sum_{k=1}^{m} p_{jk} I(E_j \mid F_k) = -\sum_{j=1}^{n} \sum_{k=1}^{m} p_{jk} \log(p_{jk}/q_k).$$

The conditional self-information is the natural analogue of the self-information, based on the conditional probability instead of the probability. Conditional entropy is likewise an analogue of entropy, obtained by taking the average of the conditional self-information over all pairs of events, one from each system. In conformity with the convention already adopted for entropy a term in $H(S_1 \mid S_2)$ in which $p_{jk} = 0$ is omitted. No trouble will arise from the vanishing of a q_k because then (2.3.3) implies that $p_{jk} = 0$ for $j = 1, \ldots, n$ and the term will be omitted anyway. Similar considerations will apply to entropies defined subsequently but it will be understood that the convention is being followed without explicit mention of the fact.

Definition 2.3b. *The mutual information* $I(E_j, F_k)$ *between the events* E_j *and* F_k *is defined by*

$$I(E_j, F_k) = \log \frac{P(E_j \cap F_k)}{P(E_j)P(F_k)} = \log \frac{p_{jk}}{p_j q_k}.$$

The mutual information $I(S_1, S_2)$ *between* S_1 *and* S_2 *is defined by*

$$I(S_1, S_2) = \sum_{j=1}^{n} \sum_{k=1}^{m} p_{jk} I(E_j, F_k) = \sum_{j=1}^{n} \sum_{k=1}^{m} p_{jk} \log \frac{p_{jk}}{p_j q_k}.$$

The use of the same notation for both events and systems should cause no confusion because the argument should make it clear which type is being considered.

The interchange of E_j and F_k in the logarithm of the mutual information leaves it unaltered. The adjective mutual is therefore reasonable and suggests that $I(E_j, F_k)$ is a measure of the information in the joint occurrence of E_j and F_k. As a result of

Definitions 2.3b, 2.3a, and 2.1

$$I(E_j, F_k) = -\log P(E_j) + \log P(E_j \mid F_k) = I(E_j) - I(E_j \mid F_k)$$

which may be interpreted as saying that the mutual information is the self-information of E_j less the conditional self-information given F_k. If E_j and F_k are statistically independent $I(E_j, F_k) = 0$ which is fair since neither event would be expected to pass on any information about the other in such circumstances.

The mutual information between systems is the average of the mutual information between events. Before examining its properties it is helpful to bring in another average, the *joint entropy*, according to the following definition.

DEFINITION 2.3c. *The joint entropy $H(S_1 \cap S_2)$ is defined by*

$$H(S_1 \cap S_2) = -\sum_{j=1}^{n} \sum_{k=1}^{m} p_{jk} \log p_{jk}.$$

Clearly $H(S_1 \cap S_2) \geq 0$. Also

$$H(S_1 \cap S_2) = -\sum_{j=1}^{n} \sum_{k=1}^{m} p_{jk} \left(\log \frac{p_{jk}}{q_k} + \log q_k \right)$$

$$= H(S_1 \mid S_2) - \sum_{k=1}^{m} q_k \log q_k$$

from Definition 2.3a and (2.3.3). Hence

$$H(S_1 \cap S_2) = H(S_1 \mid S_2) + H(S_2). \tag{2.3.6}$$

Division by p_j instead of q_k leads to

$$H(S_1 \cap S_2) = H(S_2 \mid S_1) + H(S_1). \tag{2.3.7}$$

Further

$$I(S_1, S_2) = \sum_{j=1}^{n} \sum_{k=1}^{m} p_{jk} \left(\log \frac{p_{jk}}{q_k} - \log p_j \right)$$

$$= H(S_1) - H(S_1 \mid S_2) \tag{2.3.8}$$

when note is taken of (2.3.2). Similarly

$$I(S_1, S_2) = H(S_2) - H(S_2 \mid S_1). \tag{2.3.9}$$

The combination of (2.3.8) and (2.3.6) gives a result which may be called Theorem 2.3a.

THEOREM 2.3a. $I(S_1, S_2) = H(S_1) + H(S_2) - H(S_1 \cap S_2)$.

The similarity of the structure of Theorem 2.3a to Theorem 1.1 will be remarked. Since $H(S_1 \cap S_2) \geq 0$ an analogue to Corollary 1.1 is

$$I(S_1, S_2) \leq H(S_1) + H(S_2),$$

i.e. *the mutual information of two systems cannot exceed the sum of their separate entropies.* This is to be expected since some of the uncertainty about S_2 will, in general, be uncertainty about S_1 as well.

Observe also that the interchange of S_1 and S_2 makes no difference to the right-hand side in Theorem 2.3a so that $I(S_1, S_2) = I(S_2, S_1)$ and the term mutual is again seen to be relevant.

If each event E_j is statistically independent of every event F_k this may be conveniently summarized as S_1 is statistically independent of S_2. When S_1 is statistically independent of S_2

$$p_{jk} = p_j q_k \qquad (j = 1, \ldots, n; k = 1, \ldots, m) \qquad (2.3.10)$$

according to Definition 1.4. Moreover, $I(E_j, F_k) = 0$ and so $I(S_1, S_2) = 0$ may be inferred from Definition 2.3b. This is as it should be since the occurrence of an event in S_2 tells us nothing about the events of S_1. From Theorem 2.3a

$$H(S_1 \cap S_2) = H(S_1) + H(S_2),$$

i.e. *the joint entropy of two statistically independent systems is the sum of their separate entropies.*

In general, the specification of S_2 would be expected to reduce the uncertainty about S_1, Confirmation is forthcoming from Theorem 2.3b.

THEOREM 2.3b. $H(S_1 \mid S_2) \leq H(S_1)$ *with equality only if* S_1 *and* S_2 *are statistically independent.*

Proof. When all p_{jk} are positive, Theorem 2.2a enables the statement

$$\sum_{j=1}^{n} \sum_{k=1}^{m} p_{jk} \ln \frac{p_j q_k}{p_{jk}} \leq \sum_{j=1}^{n} \sum_{k=1}^{m} p_{jk} \left(\frac{p_j q_k}{p_{jk}} - 1 \right) \leq 1 - 1 \leq 0$$

from (2.3.1). Multiplication by the appropriate positive constant then supplies

$$-\sum_{j=1}^{n}\sum_{k=1}^{m} p_{jk} \log \frac{p_{jk}}{q_k} \leqslant -\sum_{j=1}^{n}\sum_{k=1}^{m} p_{jk} \log p_j \leqslant -\sum_{j=1}^{n} p_j \log p_j$$

from (2.3.2). The inequality of the theorem follows immediately. Equality can occur only if $p_j q_k / p_{jk} = 1$, i.e. (2.3.10) is satisfied or S_1 and S_2 are statistically independent.

If a p_{jk} is zero, $p_{jk} \ln(p_j q_k / p_{jk}) \leqslant p_j q_k - p_{jk}$ since the left-hand side is zero by convention and again the inequality is satisfied. Now equality is possible only if one at least of p_j and q_k is zero and then $p_{jk} = p_j q_k$ trivially. The proof is terminated.

COROLLARY 2.3b. $I(S_1, S_2) \geqslant 0$, *with equality only when S_1 and S_2 are statistically independent.*
Proof. This is an immediate consequence of (2.3.8) and Theorem 2.3b.

The mutual information $I(S_1, S_2)$ can be visualized from another point of view. It has just been seen that, when S_1 and S_2 are statistically independent, $I(S_1, S_2) = 0$. On the other hand, when S_1 and S_2 have the same number of events and are tightly coupled in the sense that $P(F_j | E_j) = 1$ for all j, $P(F_k | E_j) = 0$ for $k \neq j$ from (2.3.3)–(2.3.5). Hence $H(S_2 | S_1) = 0$ and $H(S_1 | S_2)$ also vanishes. Therefore, (2.3.8) and (2.3.9) imply that $I(S_1, S_2) = H(S_1) = H(S_2)$ or S_2 carries the same average information as S_1. This is only to be expected since the tight coupling makes S_1 and S_2 as good as identical.

If S_1 corresponds to letters being produced by a source and S_2 the letters which are observed after transmission, $I(S_1, S_2)$ gives a measure of the average information per letter after transmission. In the case of tight coupling this is the same as the average information per letter of the source; no errors have been committed in transmission. The worst situation is when transmission is so bad that S_1 and S_2 are statistically independent; then $I(S_1, S_2) = 0$ indicating that after transmission no information is available about the source. In general, there will be some loss of information during transmission, quantified by the amount by which $I(S_1, S_2)$ falls short of $H(S_1)$.

In this context formula (2.3.8) can be interpreted as stating that the mutual information is the information available from the source S_1 less the uncertainty as to what was sent after observation following transmission. Equally well, it can be thought of, via

(2.3.9), as the information received less that part of it caused by imperfections in transmission. The version of Theorem 2.3a expresses the mutual information as the sum of the information received and that of the source less the joint entropy which is a convenient point of view in some applications.

Example 2.3a. The symbols 0 and 1 are being transmitted along a channel. The probability that a symbol which is 0 at the beginning ends up as 0 is $1-\varepsilon$ ($0 \leqslant \varepsilon \leqslant 1$) while the probability that it ends up as 1 is ε. Similarly, 1 is unaltered with probability $1-\varepsilon$ and changes to 0 with probability ε. Such a channel is known as a *binary symmetric channel with crossover probability ε*. It is illustrated diagrammatically in Fig. 2.3.1.

Let S_1 be the input with $E_1 = 0$, $E_2 = 1$ and S_2 the output with $F_1 = 0$, $F_2 = 1$. Then the probabilities given are

$$P(F_1 \mid E_1) = 1-\varepsilon, \qquad P(F_2 \mid E_1) = \varepsilon,$$
$$P(F_1 \mid E_2) = \varepsilon, \qquad P(F_2 \mid E_2) = 1-\varepsilon.$$

Suppose that

$$P(E_1) = p_1, \qquad P(E_2) = p_2 = 1 - p_1.$$

Then

$$p_{11} = P(E_1 \cap F_1) = P(F_1 \mid E_1)P(E_1) = (1-\varepsilon)p_1,$$
$$p_{12} = P(E_1 \cap F_2) = \varepsilon p_1,$$
$$p_{21} = P(E_2 \cap F_1) = \varepsilon p_2, \qquad p_{22} = P(E_2 \cap F_2) = (1-\varepsilon)p_2.$$

Hence, from (2.3.3),

$$q_1 = P(F_1) = p_{11} + p_{21} = \varepsilon + (1-2\varepsilon)p_1,$$
$$q_2 = P(F_2) = p_{12} + p_{22} = \varepsilon + (1-2\varepsilon)p_2.$$

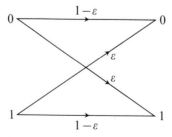

FIG. 2.3.1. The binary symmetric channel with crossover probability ε.

If the inputs are equally probable $p_1 = p_2 = \frac{1}{2}$ and then $q_1 = q_2 = \frac{1}{2}$ so that the outputs are equally probable. This result is not surprising in view of the completely symmetrical nature of the arrangement.

Continuing with the case of equally probable inputs

$$I(E_1, F_1) = \log 2(1 - \varepsilon) = I(E_2, F_2),$$
$$I(E_1, F_2) = \log 2\varepsilon = I(E_2, F_1).$$

For very small ε the reception of 0 makes it highly likely that 0 was sent. Indeed, $I(E_1, F_1)$ is positive for tiny ε, becoming 1 bit when $\varepsilon = 0$, corresponding to absolute certainty. As ε increases from zero, $I(E_1, F_1)$ decreases, indicating the growing lack of certainty as to which binary digit was sent.

On the other hand, $I(E_2, F_1)$ is negative for small ε suggesting that the idea that a 1 was sent when a 0 is received should be mistrusted.

An assessment of the overall situation is provided by the entropy

$$H(S_2) = -\tfrac{1}{2} \log \tfrac{1}{2} - \tfrac{1}{2} \log \tfrac{1}{2} = 1 \text{ bit.}$$
$$H(S_2 \mid S_1) = -\tfrac{1}{2}(1 - \varepsilon)\log(1 - \varepsilon) - \tfrac{1}{2}\varepsilon \log \varepsilon$$
$$- \tfrac{1}{2}\varepsilon \log \varepsilon - \tfrac{1}{2}(1 - \varepsilon)\log(1 - \varepsilon)$$
$$= -(1 - \varepsilon)\log(1 - \varepsilon) - \varepsilon \log \varepsilon.$$

As ε increases from 0 to $\frac{1}{2}$, $H(S_2 \mid S_1)$ increases (as may be checked by taking a derivative with respect to ε) from 0 to 1 bit whereas $H(S_2)$ stays constant. On account of (2.3.9), $I(S_1, S_2)$ falls from 1 bit to 0. That there should be no effective transference of information when $\varepsilon = \frac{1}{2}$ may appear startling at first sight. However, the uncertainty in the output when $\varepsilon = \frac{1}{2}$ is unaffected by any knowledge of the input and we should do as well by tossing an ideal coin to decide what output symbol was received.

When ε increases from $\frac{1}{2}$ to 1, $H(S_2 \mid S_1)$ drops back to zero and $I(S_1, S_2)$ rises to 1. That there should be certainty about the position when $\varepsilon = 1$ is acceptable because we are sure that the output symbol is the opposite of that which was sent. This reveals that when an information measure signifies certainty it does not necessarily mean that what is observed is true but merely that a correct identification can be made with certainty.

Example 2.3b. The following messages may be sent over a binary symmetric channel with crossover probability ε:

$$M_1 = 00, \qquad M_2 = 01, \qquad M_3 = 10, \qquad M_4 = 11$$

and they are equally probable at the input. What is the mutual information between M_1 and the first output digit being 0? What additional mutual information is conveyed by the knowledge that the second output digit is also 0?

The probability that the input is M_1 and the first output digit is 0 is

$$P(M_1 \cap 0) = P(0 \mid M_1)P(M_1) = (1-\varepsilon)\tfrac{1}{4}.$$

Definition 2.3b gives

$$I(M_1, 0) = \log \frac{(1-\varepsilon)\frac{1}{4}}{\frac{1}{4} \cdot \frac{1}{2}} = 1 + \log(1-\varepsilon) \text{ bits}$$

which steadily diminishes with increasing ε.

For the output 00 we have

$$P(M_1 \cap 00) = P(00 \mid M_1)P(M_1) = \tfrac{1}{4}(1-\varepsilon)^2$$

and

$$I(M_1, 00) = 2 + 2\log(1-\varepsilon) \text{ bits.}$$

The extra mutual information is $1 + \log(1-\varepsilon)$ bits.

2.4. More than two systems

Two systems are sometimes insufficient to cope with the matter in hand and definitions for greater numbers of systems are desirable. Three systems will be sufficient to indicate how the extension goes. Let them be S_1, S_2, and S_3 with corresponding events E_j, F_k, and G_l. The fundamental probability is that for the simultaneous occurrence of E_j in S_1, F_k in S_2, and G_l in S_3, namely $P(E_j \cap F_k \cap G_l)$ which is, naturally, a non-negative number subject to

$$\sum_j \sum_k \sum_l P(E_j \cap F_k \cap G_l) = 1 \tag{2.4.1}$$

the summation for each index being over all the events in the relevant system. All other probabilities can be deduced. For instance

$$P(E_j \cap F_k) = \sum_l P(E_j \cap F_k \cap G_l), \qquad (2.4.2)$$

$$P(E_j) = \sum_k \sum_l P(E_j \cap F_k \cap G_l) = \sum_k P(E_j \cap F_k), \qquad (2.4.3)$$

$$\sum_j P(E_j) = 1, \qquad \sum_j \sum_k P(E_j \cap F_k) = 1 \qquad (2.4.4)$$

the last two results following at once from (2.4.1).

The first definition is given below.

DEFINITION 2.4a. *The mutual information for events* $I(E_j \cap F_k, G_l)$ *and for systems* $I(S_1 \cap S_2, S_3)$ *are defined by*

$$I(E_j \cap F_k, G_l) = \log \frac{P(E_j \cap F_k \cap G_l)}{P(E_j \cap F_k)P(G_l)},$$

$$I(S_1 \cap S_2, S_3) = \sum_j \sum_k \sum_l P(E_j \cap F_k \cap G_l) \log \frac{P(E_j \cap F_k \cap G_l)}{P(E_j \cap F_k)P(G_l)}.$$

The definition for events is entirely consistent with Definition 2.3b. Indeed, if E_j and F_k in Definition 2.3b are replaced by $E_j \cap F_k$ and G_l respectively Definition 2.4a is recovered. An averaging process over all combinations of events supplies the definition for systems.

DEFINITION 2.4b. *The mutual information between* E_j *and* F_k *conditioned on* G_l *is defined by*

$$I(E_j, F_k \mid G_l) = \log \frac{P(E_j \cap F_k \mid G_l)}{P(E_j \mid G_l)P(F_k \mid G_l)}.$$

The mutual information between S_1 *and* S_2 *conditioned on* S_3 *is*

$$I(S_1, S_2 \mid S_3) = \sum_j \sum_k \sum_l P(E_j \cap F_k \cap G_l) \log \frac{P(E_j \cap F_k \mid G_l)}{P(E_j \mid G_l)P(F_k \mid G_l)}.$$

The conditional mutual information is the same as the unconditioned in Definition 2.3b except that conditional probability replaces probability. Any term in $I(S_1, S_2 \mid S_3)$ in which $P(E_j \cap F_k \cap G_l) = 0$ is excluded from the summation.

If

$$P(E_j \cap F_k \mid G_l) = P(E_j \mid G_l)P(F_k \mid G_l) \qquad (2.4.5)$$

for all j, k, and l such that $P(G_l) \neq 0$, S_1 and S_2 are said to be *statistically independent when conditioned on* S_3.

THEOREM 2.4a. $I(S_1, S_2 \mid S_3) \geq 0$ *with equality only when* S_1 *and* S_2 *are statistically independent when conditioned on* S_3.

Comparison of the theorem with Corollary 2.3b may be made and we see that the mutual information between two systems is non-negative whether or not there is conditioning on a third. Furthermore, some kind of statistical independence is always required for the mutual information to vanish.

Proof. Writing $\sum'$ to denote the omission of a term in which $P(E_j \cap F_k \cap G_l) = 0$ we have

$$\sum_j{}' \sum_k{}' \sum_l{}' P(E_j \cap F_k \cap G_l) \ln \frac{P(E_j \mid G_l) P(F_k \mid G_l)}{P(E_j \cap F_k \mid G_l)}$$

$$\leq \sum_j{}' \sum_k{}' \sum_l{}' P(E_j \cap F_k \cap G_l) \left\{ \frac{P(E_j \mid G_l) P(F_k \mid G_l)}{P(E_j \cap F_k \mid G_l)} - 1 \right\}$$

$$\leq \sum_j{}' \sum_k{}' \sum_l{}' P(E_j \cap F_k \cap G_l) \left\{ \frac{P(E_j \cap G_l) P(F_k \cap G_l)}{P(E_j \cap F_k \cap G_l) P(G_l)} - 1 \right\}$$

by means of Theorem 2.2a. At first glance the $P(G_l)$ in the denominator would seem troublesome if it vanished. However, from (2.4.3), $P(G_l) = 0$ enforces $P(E_j \cap F_k \cap G_l) = 0$ for all E_j and F_k in S_1 and S_2 respectively; so the apparently awkward term has already been removed from the summation.

Now, taking advantage of (2.4.1), we have

$$\sum_j{}' \sum_k{}' \sum_l{}' P(E_j \cap F_k \cap G_l) = \sum_j \sum_k \sum_l P(E_j \cap F_k \cap G_l) = 1$$

because the additional terms are all zero. Also

$$\sum_j{}' P(E_j \cap G_l) = \sum_j{}' \sum_k P(E_j \cap F_k \cap G_l)$$

$$= \sum_j \sum_k P(E_j \cap F_k \cap G_l) = P(G_l)$$

from (2.4.1) and (2.4.3). Similarly

$$\sum_k{}' P(F_k \cap G_l) = P(G_l), \qquad \sum_l{}' P(G_l) = 1.$$

In consequence an upper bound for our left-hand side is zero. Converting the natural logarithm to log by multiplication by a positive constant, we deduce $-I(S_1, S_2 \mid S_3) \leq 0$ as required.

Equality demands that

$$P(E_j \cap G_l)P(F_k \cap G_l) = P(E_j \cap F_k \cap G_l)P(G_l)$$

for all j, k, l such that $P(E_j \cap F_k \cap G_l) \neq 0$. Because $P(G_l) \neq 0$ for such l, (2.4.5) is verified and the theorem is proved.

There is a further property which is of considerable interest. From Definition 2.4a

$$
\begin{aligned}
I(S_1 \cap S_2, S_3) &= \sum_j \sum_k \sum_l P(E_j \cap F_k \cap G_l) \\
&\quad \times \left\{ \log \frac{P(E_j \cap G_l)}{P(E_j)P(G_l)} + \log \frac{P(E_j)P(E_j \cap F_k \cap G_l)}{P(E_j \cap F_k)P(E_j \cap G_l)} \right\} \\
&= \sum_j \sum_l P(E_j \cap G_l) \log \frac{P(E_j \cap G_l)}{P(E_j)P(G_l)} \\
&\quad + \sum_j \sum_k \sum_l P(E_j \cap F_k \cap G_l) \log \frac{P(F_j \cap G_l \mid E_j)}{P(F_k \mid E_j)P(G_l \mid E_j)} \\
&= I(S_1, S_3) + I(S_2, S_3 \mid S_1) \qquad\qquad (2.4.6)
\end{aligned}
$$

by means of (2.4.2) and Definitions 2.3b and 2.4b. Interchanging S_1 and S_2 makes no difference to the left-hand side of (2.4.6) and so

$$I(S_1 \cap S_2, S_3) = I(S_2, S_3) + I(S_1, S_3 \mid S_2). \qquad (2.4.7)$$

Subtraction of (2.4.7) from (2.4.6) leads to

THEOREM 2.4b.

$$I(S_1, S_3) = I(S_2, S_3) + I(S_1, S_3 \mid S_2) - I(S_2, S_3 \mid S_1).$$

Exchanging S_1 and S_3 has no effect on $I(S_1, S_3)$ and so Theorem 2.4b implies

$$I(S_1, S_3) = I(S_1, S_2) + I(S_1, S_3 \mid S_2) - I(S_1, S_2 \mid S_3). \qquad (2.4.8)$$

If S_1 and S_3 are statistically independent when conditioned on S_2, $I(S_1, S_3 \mid S_2) = 0$ from Theorem 2.4a. It may also be inferred from Theorem 2.4a that $I(S_2, S_3 \mid S_1) \geqslant 0$ and $I(S_1, S_2 \mid S_3) \geqslant 0$. Hence Theorem 2.4b and (2.4.8) supply the Data Processing Theorem.

DATA PROCESSING THEOREM. *If S_1 and S_3 are statistically independent when conditioned on S_2, then*

$$I(S_1, S_3) \leqslant I(S_2, S_3), \qquad I(S_1, S_3) \leqslant I(S_1, S_2).$$

Moreover, Corollary 2.3b enables one to say that $I(S_1, S_3) \geq 0$ so that a deduction from Theorem 2.4b is given in the Convexity Theorem.

CONVEXITY THEOREM. *If S_1 and S_3 are statistically independent when conditioned on S_2, then*

$$I(S_2, S_3) \geq I(S_2, S_3 \mid S_1).$$

The implications of the Convexity Theorem will be of importance in a later chapter, but the significance of the Data Processing Theorem can be gathered from the following considerations. Let the input data be S_1 which reappears, after processing, as S_2 (Fig. 2.4.1). S_2 is used as input to another processor whose output is S_3. Then

$$P(E_j \cap F_k) = P(F_k \mid E_j)P(E_j) \tag{2.4.9}$$

where, since one F_k is present whatever E_j is input,

$$\sum_k P(F_k \mid E_j) = 1. \tag{2.4.10}$$

Furthermore, any G_l must be initiated by some F_k, so that

$$P(E_j \cap F_k \cap G_l) = P(G_l \mid F_k)P(F_k \mid E_j)P(E_j) \tag{2.4.11}$$

with

$$\sum_l P(G_l \mid F_k) = 1. \tag{2.4.12}$$

By virtue of (2.4.10)–(2.4.12) and $\sum_j P(E_j) = 1$ we deduce that

$$\sum_j \sum_k \sum_l P(E_j \cap F_k \cap G_l) = 1$$

so that the probabilities anticipated from (2.4.11) for two successive processors are consistent with (2.4.1). Moreover, division of (2.4.11) by $P(F_k)$, when it is non-zero, followed by use of (2.4.9) leads to

$$P(E_j \cap G_l \mid F_k) = P(G_l \mid F_k)P(E_j \mid F_k),$$

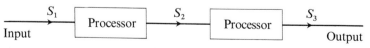

FIG. 2.4.1. Illustration of Data Processing Theorem for a cascade of processors.

i.e. in the arrangement of Fig. 2.4.1, S_1 and S_3 are statistically independent when conditioned on S_2.

The first part of the Data Processing Theorem shows that the mutual information between input and output can never exceed the mutual information between the output and intermediary. Likewise, the second part demonstrates that the mutual information between input and output cannot exceed that between input and intermediary. Thus the mutual information between input and output tends to decrease as the number of processors augments. To put it another way, data processing may transform the data to a more useful form but it cannot create new information and, in fact, may reduce the amount of information available before processing. Remembering a set of figures by their mean and standard deviation may be easy on the memory but information in the original set has been lost by the reduction to two numbers.

The valuable conclusion has been reached that *data processing cannot increase the amount of information in the data.*

2.5. Uniqueness theorem

The properties of information and entropy that have been set forth in the preceding sections are sufficient to convince one that the definitions are sound ones on which to base further study. The object of this section is to demonstrate that no other definition than Definition 2.2 is possible if certain plausible hypotheses are adopted.

Subsequently, $f(p_1, \ldots, p_n)$ will be a continuous function of its arguments in which $p_k \geq 0$ $(k = 1, \ldots, n)$ and $\sum_{k=1}^{n} p_k = 1$. The conditions to be met by f are set out in the following hypothesis.

HYPOTHESIS. *For every positive integer n,*
   (a) *f takes its largest value for* $p_k = 1/n$,
   (b) *f is unaltered if an impossible event is added to the system, i.e. if n is changed to* $n+1$ *and* $p_{n+1} = 0$

$$f(p_1, \ldots, p_n, 0) = f(p_1, \ldots, p_n),$$

   (c)

$$f(p_1, \ldots, p_j, \ldots, p_k, \ldots, p_n) = f(p_1, \ldots, p_j + p_k, \ldots, 0, \ldots, p_n)$$
$$+ (p_j + p_k) f\left(\frac{p_j}{p_j + p_k}, \frac{p_k}{p_j + p_k}, 0, \ldots, 0\right).$$

The justification for the inclusion of the various elements in the Hypothesis when f is to be a measure of uncertainty can be seen from the following sentiments. (a) The most uncertainty can be expected when all events in the system are equally probable. (b) An impossible event can never occur so that its presence cannot affect the uncertainty. (c) This is the most difficult to comprehend and a small example will make a stepping stone to the general exposition. Suppose there are three events E_1, E_2, E_3 with associated probabilities $\frac{1}{2}, \frac{1}{3}, \frac{1}{6}$ respectively (Fig. 2.5.1). The events may be proceeded to directly with the apposite probabilities as in Fig. 2.5.1(a). Alternatively, we may choose between E_1 and the pair E_2 and E_3 with probability $\frac{1}{2}$ for each choice (Fig. 2.5.1(b)). If E_1 turns up the process stops but if the pair E_2 and E_3 arises then E_2 is chosen with probability $\frac{2}{3}$ and E_3 with probability $\frac{1}{3}$. The net result is that E_1, E_2, and E_3 end up in the compound experiment with the same probabilities as in the original and so the uncertainty should be the same whichever route is traversed. This is what (c) says.

In the general compound experiment any E_i except the particular pair E_j, E_k has associated probability p_i. E_j and E_k are grouped together with probability $p_j + p_k$. If the group is chosen on the first stage, then E_j is picked with probability $p_j/(p_j + p_k)$ and E_k with probability $p_k/(p_j + p_k)$. The verification that the compound experiment is equivalent to the original is straightforward because

$$P(E_i) = p_i \qquad (i \neq j, k),$$
$$P(E_j) = P(\text{group chosen and } E_j \text{ picked})$$
$$= P(E_j \text{ picked} \mid \text{group chosen})P(\text{group chosen})$$
$$= \frac{p_j}{p_j + p_k} \cdot (p_j + p_k) = p_j,$$
$$P(E_k) = p_k.$$

The uncertainty of the compound experiment is to be the same as that of the original, which stands on the left-hand side of (c). The uncertainty of the first stage is the first term on the right-hand side of (c). There is no further uncertainty unless the group is chosen; the uncertainty within the group is the second f on the right-hand side of (c). Since the choice of the group occurs with

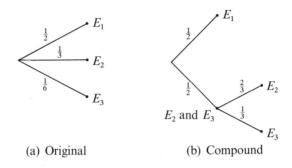

(a) Original   (b) Compound

FIG. 2.5.1. Compound experiment equivalent to original.

probability $p_j + p_k$ the second term on the right-hand side has to be added to achieve the total uncertainty of the compound experiment.

UNIQUENESS THEOREM. *When f fulfils the Hypothesis*

$$f(p_1, \ldots, p_n) = -C \sum_{k=1}^{n} p_k \log p_k$$

where C is a positive constant.

Proof. When $p_1 = \cdots = p_n = 1/n$ we write $g(n)$ for f, i.e.

$$g(n) = f\left(\frac{1}{n}, \frac{1}{n}, \ldots, \frac{1}{n}\right).$$

It is convenient to derive a general attribute of f before commencing the detailed proof. Let r of the arguments of f be p. The intention is to combine them by means of (c) of the Hypothesis. Since their precise location is unimportant in (c) they can be placed in any convenient position and it will simplify the notation to put them at the end. Now

$$f(p_1, \ldots, p_{n-r}, p, \ldots, p) = f(p_1, \ldots, p_{n-r}, p, \ldots, p, 2p, 0)$$
$$+ 2pf(\tfrac{1}{2}, \tfrac{1}{2}, 0, \ldots, 0)$$

by (c). From (b)

$$f(p_1, \ldots, p_{n-r}, p, \ldots, p) = f(p_1, \ldots, p_{n-r}, p, \ldots, p, 2p, 0) + 2pf(\tfrac{1}{2}, \tfrac{1}{2})$$
$$= f(p_1, \ldots, p_{n-r}, p, \ldots, 3p, 0, 0)$$
$$+ 3pf(\tfrac{1}{3}, \tfrac{2}{3}) + 2pf(\tfrac{1}{2}, \tfrac{1}{2})$$

by (c) and (b) again. Continuing this process we obtain

$$f(p_1, \ldots, p_{n-r}, p, \ldots, p) = f(p_1, \ldots, p_{n-r}, rp)$$
$$+ rpf\left(\frac{1}{r}, 1 - \frac{1}{r}\right) + \cdots + 2pf(\tfrac{1}{2}, \tfrac{1}{2}).$$

$$(2.5.1)$$

Apply (2.5.1) to $g(n)$ with $p = 1/n$ and $r = n - 1$. Then

$$g(n) = f\left(\frac{1}{n}, 1 - \frac{1}{n}\right) + \left(1 - \frac{1}{n}\right)f\left(\frac{1}{n-1}, 1 - \frac{1}{n-1}\right) + \cdots + \frac{2}{n}f(\tfrac{1}{2}, \tfrac{1}{2}).$$

Inserting this in (2.5.1) we have

$$f(p_1, \ldots, p_{n-r}, p, \ldots, p) = f(p_1, \ldots, p_{n-r}, rp) + rpg(r)$$
$$(2.5.2)$$

which is the general result sought.

Turning to the proof of the theorem the case of equal probabilities is first taken. From (b) of the Hypothesis

$$g(n) = f\left(\frac{1}{n}, \ldots, \frac{1}{n}, 0\right) \quad \text{(with } n+1 \text{ entries)}$$

$$\leq f\left(\frac{1}{n+1}, \ldots, \frac{1}{n+1}, \frac{1}{n+1}\right) \quad \text{(with } n+1 \text{ entries)}$$

on account of (a). Hence

$$g(n) \leq g(n+1),$$

i.e. g is a non-decreasing function of its argument.

If m is a positive integer

$$g(r^m) = f\left(\frac{1}{r^m}, \ldots, \frac{1}{r^m}\right)$$

with r^m entries in f. Combine the last r of these by (2.5.2) with $p = 1/r^m$; there results

$$g(r^m) = f\left(\frac{1}{r^m}, \ldots, \frac{1}{r^m}, \frac{1}{r^{m-1}}\right) + \frac{1}{r^{m-1}} g(r)$$

with $r^m - r$ entries of $1/r^m$ in f. Coalesce another r of these and then

$$g(r^m) = f\left(\frac{1}{r^m}, \ldots, \frac{1}{r^{m-1}}, \frac{1}{r^{m-1}}\right) + \frac{2}{r^{m-1}} g(r).$$

Doing this until all the $1/r^m$ have been amalgamated we obtain

$$g(r^m) = g(r^{m-1}) + g(r).   \tag{2.5.3}$$

Applying (2.5.3) to itself we have

$$g(r^m) = g(r^{m-2}) + 2g(r) = g(r) + (m-1)g(r) = mg(r).$$
$$\tag{2.5.4}$$

If $g(r)$ were negative, increasing m in (2.5.4) would force g to be a decreasing function of its argument contrary to what has already been established. Consequently, $g(r)$ is positive, the possibility of its being zero for all arguments being obviously of no interest.

Let r, m, and s be positive integers chosen arbitrarily. Fix t as that positive integer such that

$$s^t \leq r^m \leq s^{t+1}.   \tag{2.5.5}$$

Because g is non-decreasing

$$g(s^t) \leq g(r^m) \leq g(s^{t+1})$$

and then (2.5.4) implies

$$tg(s) \leq mg(r) \leq (t+1)g(s).$$

The positivity of g now enforces

$$\frac{t}{m} \leq \frac{g(r)}{g(s)} \leq \frac{t+1}{m}.   \tag{2.5.6}$$

But, because of (2.5.5),

$$\frac{t}{m} \leq \frac{\log r}{\log s} \leq \frac{t+1}{m}.   \tag{2.5.7}$$

The combination of (2.5.6) and (2.5.7) gives

$$-\frac{1}{m} \leq \frac{g(r)}{g(s)} - \frac{\log r}{\log s} \leq \frac{1}{m}.$$

The arbitrary nature of m permits it to be made as large as desired and one is forced to the conclusion that

$$\frac{g(r)}{g(s)} = \frac{\log r}{\log s}.$$

Because this holds for arbitrary r and s there is no alternative but

$$g(r) = C \log r \qquad (2.5.8)$$

for some constant C. Indeed, by fixing s and allowing r to vary we could make the identification $C = g(s)/\log s$. Since g is positive, (2.5.8) requires C to be positive and the theorem is proved for equal probabilities.

Suppose now that the probabilities are rational numbers. By reducing them to a common denominator we can write $p_k = m_k/M$ ($k = 1, \ldots, n$) where m_k and M are positive integers such that $\sum_{k=1}^n m_k = M$. If f has M entries

$$f\left(\frac{1}{M}, \ldots, \frac{1}{M}\right) = f\left(\frac{1}{M}, \ldots, \frac{m_n}{M}\right) + \frac{m_n}{M} g(m_n)$$

by (2.5.2) with $p = 1/M$ and $r = m_n$. Again

$$f\left(\frac{1}{M}, \ldots, \frac{1}{M}\right) = f\left(\frac{1}{M}, \ldots, \frac{m_{n-1}}{M}, \frac{m_n}{M}\right) + \frac{m_{n-1}}{M} g(m_{n-1}) + \frac{m_n}{M} g(m_n)$$

$$= f\left(\frac{m_1}{M}, \ldots, \frac{m_n}{M}\right) + \frac{m_1}{M} g(m_1) + \cdots + \frac{m_n}{M} g(m_n)$$

whence $\qquad (2.5.9)$

$$f(p_1, \ldots, p_n) = g(M) - p_1 g(m_1) - \cdots - p_n g(m_n).$$

By virtue of (2.5.8)

$$f(p_1, \ldots, p_n) = C(\log M - p_1 \log m_1 - \cdots - p_n \log m_n)$$

$$= -C \sum_{k=1}^n p_k \log p_k$$

since $\sum_{k=1}^n p_k = 1$. The theorem is therefore proved for rationals which are non-zero. If one of them, say p_j, is zero the term in j disappears from (2.5.9) and therefore from the final summation in accordance with our convention.

The theorem, having been demonstrated for rationals, holds for general probabilities by the continuity of f and the proof is terminated.

The choice of the positive constant C is a matter of personal convenience and determines the scale of operation. In this book the simplest selection of $C = 1$ has been made.

Exercises

⌐ 2.1. You are told that, when a pair of dice were rolled, the sum of the faces was (a) 2, (b) 7. How much information is there in the two messages?

2.2.   After a perfect shuffle of a pack of cards all orders of the cards are equally probable. How much information is contained in the message that a certain order has occurred?

   In a cutting shuffle the pack is first cut at a random place into two decks A and B. A new pack is formed in steps by selecting either the top card of A or the top card of B at each stage, all ways of choosing the cards from A and B being equally probable. Show that less than 5 cutting shuffles cannot possibly produce a perfect shuffle.

2.3. In the system S the probabilities p_1 and p_2 where $p_2 > p_1$ are replaced by $p_1 + \varepsilon$ and $p_2 - \varepsilon$ respectively under the proviso $0 < 2\varepsilon < p_2 - p_1$. Prove that $H(S)$ is increased. (This is yet another indication that entropy may be regarded as a measure of uncertainty.)

/ 2.4. If 25 per cent of all girls are blondes and 75 per cent of all blondes have blue eyes, how much additional information do you get by being told that a blue-eyed girl is blonde, given that 50 per cent of all girls have blue eyes?

2.5. The N events of the system S are such that $p_k = k^{-\alpha}(\sum_{j=1}^{N} j^{-\alpha})^{-1}$ with $0 \leqslant \alpha < 1$. Assuming that

$$\sum_{j=1}^{N} j^{-\alpha} = \int_{1}^{N} t^{-\alpha}\,dt + O(1)$$

prove that, as $N \to \infty$,

$$H(S) = \log N - \frac{\alpha}{1-\alpha}\log e + O(1).$$

2.6. In Exercise 2.5, $\alpha = 1$. Prove that a first approximation to $H(S)$ is $\frac{1}{2}\log N$ as $N \to \infty$. The next term involves $\log \ln N$. (*Zipf's law* asserts that the distribution of words in one person's vocabulary is of this type, the most frequently used words having the larger probabilities.)

/ 2.7. In a binary symmetric channel with crossover probability 0.01 find the mutual information (a) between 1 transmitted and a 1 received, (b) between a 1 transmitted and a 0 received. Show that the mutual information between S_1 and S_2 is 0.92 bits.

2.8. The following messages may be despatched over a binary symmetric channel with crossover probability $\ast$.

$$M_1 = 0000, \qquad M_2 = 0011, \qquad M_3 = 0101, \qquad M_4 = 0110,$$
$$M_5 = 1001, \qquad M_6 = 1010, \qquad M_7 = 1100, \qquad M_8 = 1111$$

and they are equally probable at the input. What is the mutual information between M_1 and the first output digit being 0? How much additional mutual information is conveyed by the knowledge that the second, third, and fourth output digits are also 0?

2.9. An alphabet consists of 8 consonants and 8 vowels, all equally probable. A consonant is always identified correctly but only half the vowels are identified correctly, the other half being mistaken for different vowels, all vowels being involved in errors to the same extent. Show that average information per letter in a sequence is 2.8 bits.

2.10. Of the letters A, B, C, D half are received in error, the errors being equally spread among the others. Show that the information per letter is 0.21 bits assuming A, B, C, D are equally probable at input.

2.11. S_1 consists of the events $E_1, \ldots, E_n$ with $P(E_j) = p_j$ $(j \neq n)$, $P(E_n) = \alpha$ where $0 < \alpha < 1$. S_2 consists of $E_1, \ldots, E_{n-1}$ with $P(E_j) = p_j(1-\alpha)^{-1}$ for $j = 1, \ldots, n-1$. Prove that

$$H(S_1) = \alpha \log(1/\alpha) - (1-\alpha)\log(1-\alpha) + (1-\alpha)H(S_2)$$

and deduce that

$$H(S_1) \leq \alpha \log(1/\alpha) - (1-\alpha)\log(1-\alpha) + (1-\alpha)\log(n-1).$$

2.12. In S_1 the events $E_1, \ldots, E_n$ have probabilities $P(E_j) = p_j$ whereas, in S_2, $P(E_k) = q_k$. Prove that

$$\sum_{k=1}^{n} p_k \log(p_k/q_k) \geq 0, \qquad \sum_{k=1}^{n} p_k^2/q_k \geq 1.$$

2.13. In Exercise 2.12, $q_i = \sum_{j=1}^{n} a_{ij}p_j$ where the numbers a_{ij} are non-negative for all i, j and

$$\sum_{j=1}^{n} a_{ij} = 1 \ (i = 1, \ldots, n), \ \sum_{i=1}^{n} a_{ij} = 1 (j = 1, \ldots, n).$$

Prove that the entropy of S_2 is never less than that of S_1, being equal if and only if $q_1, \ldots, q_n$ is a rearrangement of $p_1, \ldots, p_n$.

2.14. Prove that $H(S_1 \mid S_2) \geq 0$.

2.15. Prove that

$$I(S_1, S_2 \cap S_3) = I(S_1, S_2) + I(S_1, S_3 \mid S_2)$$

and use this to obtain another proof of (2.4.8).

2.16. In the *cascade* of Fig. 2.4.1, F_i and F_j are said to be equivalent if $P(E_k \mid F_i) = P(E_k \mid F_j)$ for all k. Show that $I(S_1, S_2) = I(S_1, S_3)$ if and only if, for each G_l, $P(G_l \mid F_i) > 0$ and $P(G_l \mid F_j) > 0$ imply that F_i and F_j are equivalent.

Deduce that the presence of S_2 destroys no information about S_1 provided that non-equivalent events in S_2 are never compared.

3 Coding theory

3.1. Memoryless sources

Imagine that the set of letters $a_1, \ldots, a_N$ acts as a source for messages. At each unit of time the source is visualized as producing one of the letters so that the message consists of a sequence of letters drawn from the set, i.e. there is sampling with replacement. The messages are composed of letters in a generalized sense since here the terminology of letters encompasses numbers, mathematical signs, Morse or, indeed, any convenient distinguishable symbols.

Each time that the source generates a letter it may be postulated that the probability of the production of a particular letter is the same as on all other occasions and that successive letters are statistically independent. The source then has no recollection of the letters it has sent previously and at each unit of time conducts an independent experiment to decide on the letter to put forward. The source is then called *discrete and memoryless*. The assumption of a discrete memoryless source simplifies the analysis substantially but practical sources may not comply with it. For example, in written English an article on jelly is likely to contain the letter j far more times than it would turn up on a page of newsprint. There is also a certain amount of dependence in that the letter u nearly always follows q. Nevertheless, the discrete memoryless source may be thought of as a first, if rough, approximation over medium time intervals and a source will be treated as of this type unless otherwise is stated.

The letters from the source are frequently transformed into code, e.g. the conversion of a computer program into combinations of binary digits, the sending of a message by Morse code. In the Morse code the letter E is denoted by $\cdot$, Q by $---\cdot-$, and B by $-\cdot\cdot\cdot$; the codes corresponding to the various source letters are not all of the same length. In general, such codes are referred to as *variable-length codes*. They can be inconvenient when the source produces letters at a fixed rate and the encoding has to be done at a fixed rate but they may possess other advantages as will be seen.

Fixed-length codes are those in which every code word has the same length. Teletypes in which each of 32 symbols is represented by 5 binary digits form an example of fixed-length coding.

3.2. Fixed-length codes

A message consists of a sequence of letters from the source. It will therefore be helpful to concentrate on source sequences of n letters. If the source alphabet is $a_1, \ldots, a_N$ each slot of the source sequence can be filled in N different ways and so there are N^n possible source sequences of length n.

The number of letters in the code alphabet will be taken as M so as to allow for the source and code alphabets containing different numbers of symbols. All code words have the same number of letters in fixed-length coding which is the subject of this section. Let there be m letters in a code word. Then the number of different code words available is M^m.

To pinpoint a source sequence from a code word each source sequence of length n must correspond to its own distinctive code word. This is not possible unless there are at least as many code words as there are source sequences of length n, i.e. $M^m \geqslant N^n$ or

$$m \geqslant n \log N / \log M \qquad (3.2.1)$$

which sets a minimum to the length of code words for unique identification of the source sequence.

Example 3.2. Each letter of the English alphabet is converted to binary representation by fixed-length coding. What is the minimum length of a code word?

In this case $N = 26$, $n = 1$, and $M = 2$ so that (3.2.1) gives $m \geqslant \log_2 26 \geqslant 4.7$. A fractional code letter is not permissible so that the minimum length of a code word is 5 letters.

The inequality (3.2.1) is violated if less than $\log N / \log M$ code letters are assigned to each source letter. Then it may not be feasible to decode a source sequence from a code word. In spite of this, improvement on (3.2.1) can be achieved if an arbitrarily small error in decoding is accepted.

A typical source sequence will be denoted by $u_1, u_2, \ldots, u_n$ where u_j stands for the letter which occupies the jth slot. For example, in the source sequence a_1, a_1, a_7, u_2 we have $u_3 = a_7$ but, in a_2, a_3, a_1, a_3, we have $u_3 = a_1$. Let the probability that the source produces a_k at a particular unit of time be p_k. Associated with the probability is the source entropy $H(U) = -\sum_{k=1}^{N} p_k \log p_k$, the letter U being adopted in place of S because a typical element of the sequence is being denoted by u_j.

It might happen that $p_k = 0$. The letter a_k would then never be selected from the source and no loss would be incurred by deleting it from the alphabet. It will be assumed that such deletion is carried out so that only positive values of the probabilities need be considered.

If the typical source sequence $u_1, \ldots, u_n$ is abbreviated as $\mathbf{u}$, one can state the following theorem.

SOURCE SEQUENCE PARTITION THEOREM. *Given $\varepsilon > 0$ and $\delta > 0$, the source sequences can be divided into two groups when n is sufficiently large. The probability $P(\mathbf{u})$ of the occurrence of a sequence $\mathbf{u}$ in the first group satisfies*

$$\left| \frac{\log P(\mathbf{u})}{n} + H(U) \right| < \delta.$$

The sum of the probabilities of all sequences in the second group is less than ε.

The requirement for n to be sufficiently large means that the theorem is essentially concerned with long sequences of source letters.

Proof. The law of large numbers (Section 1.5) suggests that the letter a_k will occur about np_k times in a long source sequence of n letters because the occurrence of a_k can be treated as a success and its non-occurrence as a failure. Despite the law of large numbers the letter a_k will not actually arise on np_k occasions in a particular sequence but some other number of times, say n_k. The sequences are now divided into those where the law of large numbers is a good guide and those where it is less satisfactory. Specifically, the source sequences are split into two groups G_1, G_2:

G_1 contains every sequence $\mathbf{u}$ in which

$$|n_k/n - p_k| < \eta \quad \text{for} \quad k = 1, \ldots, N; \qquad (3.2.2)$$

G_2 consists of all other sequences.

The positive number η is at our disposal and the intention is to make it sufficiently small for G_1 to have the properties of the first group described in the theorem.

Equivalent to (3.2.2) when **u** is in G_1 is

$$n_k/n = p_k + \theta_k \eta \qquad (3.2.3)$$

where $|\theta_k| < 1$. Also

$$P(\mathbf{u}) = p_1{}^{n_1} p_2{}^{n_2} \cdots p_N{}^{n_N}$$

because a_1 occurs n_1 times, a_2 appears n_2 times, ... and the elements of the sequence are statistically independent (cf. Example 1.4c). Since no p_k is zero

$$\begin{aligned}
\log P(\mathbf{u}) &= \sum_{k=1}^{N} n_k \log p_k \\
&= \sum_{k=1}^{N} n(p_k + \theta_k \eta)\log p_k
\end{aligned}$$

or

$$\frac{\log P(\mathbf{u})}{n} + H(U) = \eta \sum_{k=1}^{N} \theta_k \log p_k.$$

Hence

$$\left| \frac{\log P(\mathbf{u})}{n} + H(U) \right| \leqslant \eta \sum_{k=1}^{N} |\theta_k| \, |\log p_k| < \eta \sum_{k=1}^{N} |\log p_k|.$$

The sum on the right-hand side is a definite finite quantity since every p_k is positive and N is finite. Therefore, if η is chosen as $\delta/\sum_{k=1}^{n} |\log p_k|$ the inequality of the theorem is satisfied for **u** in G_1.

If **u** is in G_2 there is at least one j such that

$$|n_j/n - p_j| \geqslant \eta. \qquad (3.2.4)$$

Let E_j be said to occur when (3.2.4) holds. Then $P(E_j)$ is the sum of the probabilities of all the sequences in which (3.2.4) is true. Now the sum of the probabilities of all sequences in G_2 is $P(E_1 \cup E_2 \cup \cdots \cup E_n)$ and, by Corollary 1.1,

$$P(E_1 \cup \cdots \cup E_N) \leqslant \sum_{j=1}^{N} P(E_j)$$

$$\leqslant N \max_{j} P(|n_j/n - p_j| \geqslant \eta).$$

The number η has been fixed and so, by the law of large numbers, n can be made sufficiently big for

$$\max_j P(|n_j/n - p_j| \geq \eta) \leq \varepsilon/N.$$

Hence G_2 has the attribute of the second group in the theorem and the proof is complete.

The Source Sequence Partition Theorem enables an estimate of the number of sequences in G_1 to be made. For definiteness, the base of logarithms will be taken as 2. Then, if $\mathbf{u}$ is in G_1,

$$2^{-n\{\delta + H(U)\}} < P(\mathbf{u}) < 2^{n\{\delta - H(U)\}}. \tag{3.2.5}$$

Now if N_G is the number of sequences in G_1, $N_G \min P(\mathbf{u})$ cannot exceed the sum of the probabilities of the sequences in G_1 and so $N_G \min P(\mathbf{u}) \leq 1$. It follows from (3.2.5) that

$$N_G < 2^{n\{H(U)+\delta\}}. \tag{3.2.6}$$

On the other hand, every sequence is in either G_1 or G_2 and hence the sum of the probabilities of the sequences in G_1 is not less than $1 - \varepsilon$, i.e. $1 - \varepsilon \leq N_G \max P(\mathbf{u})$ and (3.2.5) supplies

$$N_G > (1 - \varepsilon)2^{n\{H(U)-\delta\}}. \tag{3.2.7}$$

The value of N_G is fairly tightly circumscribed by (3.2.6) and (3.2.7). The smallness of ε and δ indicates that N_G is not far off $2^{nH(U)}$.

Suppose that the length of a code word satisfies

$$(m/n)\log M \geq H(U) + \delta.$$

The number of code words is then greater than N_G by (3.2.6) and a different code word can be assigned to each sequence of G_1. At worst, only the sequences of G_2 will not receive separate code words. Thus P_0, the probability that a source sequence does not have its own characteristic code word, satisfies $P_0 \leq \varepsilon$.

Conversely, if

$$(m/n)\log M < H(U) - 2\delta$$

there are insufficient code words to cover G_1. In fact, the sum of the probabilities of sequences in G_1 for which code words can be provided cannot surpass

$$2^{n\{H(U)-2\delta\}} \max P(\mathbf{u}) \leq 2^{-n\delta}.$$

Now $1 - P_0 \leq 2^{-n\delta}$ which implies that $P_0 \to 1$ as $n\delta \to \infty$.

If we allow $\delta \to 0$, perhaps like $1/n^{\frac{1}{2}}$, we can summarize these results in the following theorem.

SOURCE CODING THEOREM. *If P_0 is the probability that a source sequence does not correspond to a distinctive code word, when $(m/n)\log M \geqslant H(U)$, P_0 can be made arbitrarily small by taking n large enough. If the inequality is not satisfied P_0 becomes arbitrarily close to 1 as $n \to \infty$.*

The maximum entropy per letter of a code word cannot be greater than $\log M$ by Theorem 2.2b and so that the maximum entropy per code word is $m \log M$. We cannot hope to achieve unique decodability unless the code has more entropy than the source and so we cannot expect to reduce m below its value in the Source Coding Theorem. For this theorem asserts that there is a code in which the code letters have maximum entropy (and code words of minimum length) and decoding error is negligible. Shortening the code words is bound to introduce error.

A mechanism for constructing the code, when m is not less than the minimum of the Source Coding Theorem, is to enumerate all the sequences in G_1. Allot each one a different code word. All the sequences in G_2 are represented by the same code word. The Source Coding Theorem then guarantees that negligible error will be committed when the source sequences are long enough.

Although the Source Coding Theorem shows the existence of a code with useful properties it has the defect of demanding long sequences. Long sequences necessitate long times of transmission, which tend to be costly. Therefore a balance has to be struck between the expenses one is prepared to meet and the errors of transmission that can be tolerated.

3.3. Variable-length codes

In a variable-length code the length of the code word for the source letter a_k may be different from that of the code word for a_j. To allow for this possibility, the number of letters in the code word corresponding to a_k is denoted by l_k; sometimes l_k is called the length of the code word.

Example 3.3. The letters of the source are four in number and their associated probabilities are shown in Table 3.3 below.

TABLE 3.3. *Four possible binary codes for a source of four letters*

Source letter	$P(a_k)$	Code A	Code B	Code C	Code D
a_1	0.5	0	0	0	0
a_2	0.25	0	1	10	01
a_3	0.125	1	00	110	011
a_4	0.125	10	11	111	0111

Coding by means of binary digits $(M = 2)$ can be carried out in many ways; four alternatives are shown in Table 3.3.

Decoding with variable-length code words has a feature which is not present in fixed-length coding. In fixed-length coding we know that after each m letters of a code sequence we have reached the end of a code word. Therefore, the only source of error in decoding, with perfect transmission, is when two source sequences have the same code word. But, in variable-length coding, some method of recognizing the code word is required. For example, in Code A of Table 3.3, is a received 10 to be taken as a_4 or $a_3 a_2$? In Code B, is 00 to be identified with a_3 or $a_1 a_1$? Note that interjecting an extra space does not resolve this difficulty because that is equivalent to adding an extra symbol to the code.

A formal definition for decodability is given below.

DEFINITION 3.3a. *A code is uniquely decodable if, for each source sequence of finite length, the sequence of code letters does not coincide with the sequence of code letters for any other source sequence.*

Codes A and B are not uniquely decodable. Code D is, the arrival of 0 signalling the start of a code word and all code words being different.

One type of coding is of particular importance in aiming for unique decodability. To set the scene let X_k be a code word of length l_k which has the letters $x_1, x_2 \cdots x_{l_k}$. Any beginning sequence $x_1, x_2, \ldots, x_j$ with $1 \le j \le l_k$ is called a *prefix* of X_k. Now introduce Definition 3.3b.

DEFINITION 3.3b. *A prefix condition code is one in which no code word is the prefix of any other code word.*

Code A is not a prefix condition code because 1, the code word for a_3, is a prefix for a_4. Code B is not a prefix condition code because 0, the code word for a_1, is a prefix for a_3. Code D is not a prefix condition code because a_2 is a prefix for a_3 and a_4. However, Code C is a prefix condition code.

Any sequence of code words from a prefix condition code is uniquely decodable. Working from the beginning of a code word we know at once when the end of a code word has been reached because that code word cannot be the prefix of any other. For instance, the sequence 11010011010 in Code C can be split as 110,10,0,110,10 and decoded as $a_3a_2a_1a_3a_2$.

Not every uniquely decodable code is a prefix condition code because Code D is uniquely decodable though it is not a prefix condition code. Later on it will be seen, however, that a uniquely decodable code can always be converted to a prefix condition code.

The advantage of the prefix condition code is that decoding can be accomplished without delay because the end of a code word can be recognized immediately and subsequent parts of the message do not have to be observed before decoding is commenced.

A simple way of building a prefix condition code is by drawing a tree. For the sake of illustration the derivation of Code C will be described. Starting from the root (Fig. 3.3.1), the first choice is between 0 and 1. Suppose 0 is selected. This is distinguished by a

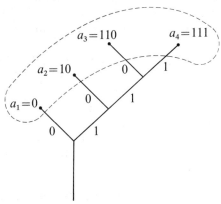

FIG. 3.3.1. The tree for a prefix condition code.

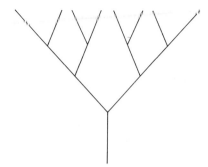

FIG. 3.3.2. The full tree.

heavy dot and becomes one code word. Then proceed up the 1 branch and make another selection between 0 and 1. Supposing it to be 0 we obtain the code word 10. Carry on in this manner until at the last stage both branches are chosen providing that sufficient code words have been created. Since the path from the root to each code word is completely different, the prefix condition must be satisfied.

A full tree in which both branches are drawn at every node (Fig. 3.3.2) contains all possible code words, separate ones corresponding to different nodes. Thus a prefix condition code can always be represented by a tree.

The correspondence between source letters and code words in a prefix condition code can be made in an arbitrary fashion but, in the interest of economy, the shorter code words should be allocated to the more frequently occurring source letters. For this reason, 0 in Code C is chosen for a_1 and 10 for a_2.

When the code alphabet possesses M letters the same principles are adopted but now there are M branches at each node of the tree. Nodes at the correct level to match the code words of shortest length desired are elected to supply the code words and no further code words are permitted via these nodes. The exercise is repeated for the code words which are next in length and so on.

The procedure can be carried out systematically and the most frequently used source-letters allocated to the shortest code words. Divide the source letters into M subsets making the probability of each subset as close to $1/M$ as feasible. Assign a different code letter for each subset. (In code C two subsets of probability $\frac{1}{2}$ are desired and they are a_1, $a_2+a_3+a_4$; the first group is assigned 0 and the second 1.) For any subset with a single member the process is terminated; each of the other subsets is split into M subsets with probability as near to $1/M^2$ as possible and each of the new subsets is assigned a different code letter. (In Code C the process is terminated for a_1 which gets the code word 0 while $a_2+a_3+a_4$ is split as a_2, a_3+a_4 two groups with probability $\frac{1}{4}$ of which the first is assigned 0.) Continue in this fashion until the source letters are exhausted. (In Code C, a_2 terminates after two steps with the code word 10 whereas a_3 and a_4 require a further step to reach 110 and 111 respectively.) If the splitting can be achieved so that, at every stage, all subsets are equally probable then clearly $P(a_k) = 1/M^{l_k}$.

The quantities $1/M^{l_k}$ have an important role to play in general as can be seen from the following theorem.

KRAFT'S THEOREM. *A prefix condition code exists for code words of lengths $l_1, l_2, \ldots, l_N$ if, and only if,*

$$\sum_{k=1}^{N} 1/M^{l_k} \leq 1.$$

Since $M \geq 2$, the inequality in Kraft's Theorem can always be satisfied by making the l_k large enough. Therefore, the valuable conclusion can be drawn that a prefix condition code can always be achieved by having the code words long enough.

Proof. Draw the full tree which has M branches coming from every node. (See Fig. 3.3.3 for the case when $M = 3$. There are M nodes of order 1, M^2 of order 2, ..., M^k of order k, etc.) Each node gives rise to a code word, those of order 1 supplying the M

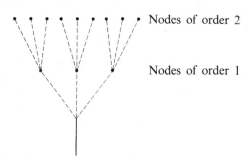

FIG. 3.3.3. The full tree when $M = 3$.

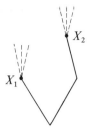

$$\text{FIG. 3.3.4. Selection of nodes as code words.}$$

code words of 1 letter, those of order 2 the M^2 code words of 2 letters and so forth.

Arrange the source letters so that $l_1 \le l_2 \le \cdots \le l_N$; this can be done by relabelling the source letters and working with the new labels.

Pick any node of order l_1, say X_1, as the first code word. Eliminate all the branches leaving X_1 (Fig. 3.3.4). Since there are M^{l_1} nodes of order l_1, this procedure removes a fraction $1/M^{l_1}$ of the tree beyond the l_1 level. Choose any node of order l_2, which has not been eliminated, as X_2, the second code word. Excise all the branches from X_2. The total fraction removed now is not above $1/M^{l_1} + 1/M^{l_2}$.

Repetition of the process leads to the situation that, after determination of the code word X_k $(k < N)$, at most the fraction $\sum_{j=1}^{k} 1/M^{l_j}$ has been removed. By the given inequality this fraction is less than 1 and so nodes are still available for further code words. Therefore the procedure can be taken as far as X_N, provided that the tree extends to nodes of order l_N. By construction the prefix condition is complied with and so the satisfaction of the given inequality warrants the existence of a prefix condition code.

Conversely, any given prefix condition code can be embedded in the full tree which has nodes of order equal to the largest of the lengths of the code words. A terminal node of order l_k (i.e. one of the nodes in the prefix condition code) has stemming from it a fraction $1/M^{l_k}$ of the full tree beyond that level. But the branches stemming from the terminal nodes are disjoint on account of the prefix condition. Hence their fractions can sum to at most 1 and the proof of the theorem is complete.

Kraft's Theorem does *not* assert that any code which satisfies the inequality therein must be a prefix condition code. In fact, Code D of Table 3.3 is a counter-example to any such assertion because it satisfies Kraft's inequality and yet is not a prefix condition code. Nevertheless, there is a prefix condition code with no longer lengths than Code D, namely Code C. Nor is the prefix condition code of the theorem unique because the interchange of 0 and 1 in Code C would manufacture a different prefix condition code with the same lengths.

The relation between Codes C and D is a particular case of the following theorem.

THEOREM 3.3. *If a code is uniquely decodable with code words of lengths $l_1, \ldots, l_N$ then the inequality of Kraft's Theorem is satisfied.*

Proof. Let r be any positive integer. Then

$$\left(\sum_{k=1}^{N} 1/M^{l_k} \right)^r = \sum_{k_1=1}^{N} \frac{1}{M^{l_{k_1}}} \cdot \sum_{k_2=1}^{N} \frac{1}{M^{l_{k_2}}} \cdot \cdots \cdot \sum_{k_r=1}^{N} \frac{1}{M^{l_{k_r}}}$$

$$= \sum_{k_1=1}^{N} \sum_{k_2=1}^{N} \cdots \sum_{k_r=1}^{N} \frac{1}{M^{l_{k_1}+l_{k_2}+\cdots+l_{k_r}}}$$

because a finite number of terms can always be rearranged without affecting their sum. Now $l_{k_1} + l_{k_2} + \cdots + l_{k_r}$ is the number of code letters in some sequence of r code words. As $k_1, \ldots, k_r$ vary all possible sequences of r code words are generated. Let r_i be the number of sequences of r code words which contain i letters. There cannot be less than 1 letter nor more than rl_{max} letters, where l_{max} is the greatest of $l_1, \ldots, l_N$, in r code words. Hence

$$\left(\sum_{k=1}^{N} 1/M^{l_k} \right)^r = \sum_{i=1}^{rl_{max}} \frac{r_i}{M^i} .$$

The code is uniquely decodable so that all sequences of r code words with a total of i letters must be distinct, i.e. r_i cannot exceed the maximum number of different sequences of i letters which is M^i. Hence

$$\sum_{k=1}^{N} 1/M^{l_k} \leq \left(\sum_{i=1}^{rl_{max}} 1 \right)^{1/r} \leq (rl_{max})^{1/r}.$$

Allowing $r \to \infty$, the right-hand side tends to unity and the theorem is proved.

If Theorem 3.3 and Kraft's Theorem are combined there results the following corollary.

COROLLARY 3.3. *Any uniquely decodable code can be replaced by a prefix condition code without changing any of the lengths of the code words.*

3.4. Average length of a code word

Some idea of the length of message involving many source letters can be obtained from the average length $\bar{l}$ of a code word. The average is defined as at the beginning of Section 2.2 by

$$\bar{l} = \sum_{k=1}^{N} p_k l_k.$$

A source sequence of n letters would then be expected to initiate a code sequence of about $n\bar{l}$ letters. For this reason $\bar{l}$ is sometimes known as the *compression coefficient*.

Reasonably tight bounds on $\bar{l}$ are provided by the following theorem.

VARIABLE-LENGTH CODING THEOREM. *For any uniquely decodable code*

$$\bar{l} \geq H(U)/\log M.$$

Code words can always be chosen to satisfy the prefix condition and

$$\bar{l} < \frac{H(U)}{\log M} + 1.$$

Proof. Substituting the appropriate definitions we have

$$H(U) - \bar{l} \log M = -\sum_{k=1}^{M} (p_k \log p_k + p_k l_k \log M)$$

$$= \sum_{k=1}^{N} p_k \log \frac{1}{p_k M^{l_k}}. \tag{3.4.1}$$

Now, by Theorem 2.2a,

$$\sum_{k=1}^{N} p_k \ln \frac{1}{p_k M^{l_k}} \leq \sum_{k=1}^{N} p_k \left(\frac{1}{p_k M^{l_k}} - 1 \right) \leq \sum_{k=1}^{N} \frac{1}{M^{l_k}} - 1 \tag{3.4.2}$$

since the sum of the probabilities is unity. The unique decodability of the code implies, via Theorem 3.3, that the right-hand side of (3.4.2) cannot exceed zero. Applying (3.4.2), multiplied by a suitable positive constant, to (3.4.1) leads to $H(U) - \bar{l} \log M \leq 0$. Division by the positive quantity $\log M$ gives the inequality in the first part of the theorem.

Remark that equality occurs only if $p_k = 1/M^{l_k}$ for $k = 1, \ldots, N$.

In the second part of the theorem only the probabilities p_k of the source are given and it has to be shown that lengths can be found for the code words complying with the stated conditions. The choice to be made for l_k will be that dictated by

$$1/M^{l_k} \leq p_k < 1/M^{l_k-1}, \tag{3.4.3}$$

for $k = 1, \ldots, N$. From (3.4.3)

$$\sum_{k=1}^{N} 1/M^{l_k} \leq \sum_{k=1}^{N} p_k \leq 1$$

so that Kraft's Theorem ensures that there is a prefix condition code with the chosen lengths.

Moreover, the logarithm is an increasing function of its argument so that, by virtue of (3.4.3),

$$\sum_{k=1}^{N} p_k \log p_k < \sum_{k=1}^{N} p_k \log(1/M^{l_k-1})$$
$$< \sum_{k=1}^{N} p_k(1-l_k)\log M$$
$$< (1-\bar{l})\log M$$

which can be rearranged to give the upper bound on $\bar{l}$. The proof is finished.

A prefix condition code is uniquely decodable. Therefore the lower bound of the theorem also applies to lengths selected according to (3.4.3). Consequently for any given source, a code can be discovered which is uniquely decodable and whose average length is fixed to within one code letter.

If the code alphabet is binary ($M = 2$) and the base of logarithms is 2, the Variable-length Coding Theorem has the implication that average length of code words cannot be less than the entropy of the source and may exceed it by at most one digit.

Accordingly, the source entropy is a fair estimate of the average length of code word. Then (3.4.3) suggests that $-\log_2 p_k$ is a guide to the number of digits in the code word corresponding to a_k. The higher the information associated with a_k, or the rarer its occurrence, the longer is the code word attached to it. Whether this can be improved on will be examined in the next section.

3.5. Optimal coding

Specifying the code word length by (3.4.3) goes some way to assuring the shortest possible code messages by placing short code words against frequently occurring source letters, but does not guarantee that a more efficient code cannot be devised and, in any event, does not lay down the detailed structure of the code. In this section binary coding will be studied with the target of reducing $\bar{l}$ as much as possible. *Optimal coding* can be regarded as achieved if any other set of code words has an $\bar{l}$ which is at least as large.

Relabelling the source letters if necessary we can assume that $P(a_1) \geqslant P(a_2) \geqslant \cdots \geqslant P(a_N)$. The corresponding code words are then denoted by $X_1, \ldots, X_N$, their respective lengths being $l_1, \ldots, l_N$.

The first stage of optimal coding rests on the following theorem.

THEOREM 3.5a. *For a given source there is an optimal (uniquely decodable) binary code in which the least likely code words X_{N-1} and X_N have the same lengths and differ only in the last digit, X_{N-1} ending in 0 and X_N in 1.*
Proof. Consider a code in which $l_N < l_i$ for some i. If the code words X_i and X_N are interchanged, the change in $\bar{l}$ is

$$p_i l_N + p_N l_i - p_i l_i - p_N l_N = (p_i - p_N)(l_N - l_i).$$

Since $p_i \geqslant p_N$ the right-hand side cannot be positive. Hence, any code can be modified to make l_N the maximum code-word length without increasing $\bar{l}$.

Corollary 3.3 makes sure that any uniquely decodable code can be transformed to a prefix condition code without alteration of the lengths of code words. Therefore, it will be sufficient to find an optimum of prefix condition codes since that will coincide with an optimum of uniquely decodable codes. An optimal prefix condition code in which l_N is largest must possess another code word differing from X_N only in the last digit. Otherwise, the last digit of X_N could be dropped without violating the prefix condition. If X_j is the word of the same length as X_N, interchange X_j and X_{N-1}. From the above, this cannot increase $\bar{l}$. The theorem has now been demonstrated, the allocation of 0 to X_{N-1} and 1 to X_N being merely fix ideas.

Theorem 3.5a indicates how the last digits of the longest code words are settled and it remains to invent the rule for designating the earlier digits. To this end consider a source which has the letters $a'_1, a'_2, \ldots, a'_{N-1}$ and associated probabilities defined by

$$P(a'_k) = P(a_k) \qquad (k \leqslant N-2)$$
$$= P(a_{N-1}) + P(a_N) \qquad (k = N-1).$$

This reduced source will be signified by U' to distinguish it from the original source U; in general, primed quantities will refer to U'. Obviously, any code for U' which satisfies the prefix condition can be converted into a prefix condition code for U by adding, to the end of X'_{N-1}, 0 for X_{N-1} and 1 for X_n, and leaving other code words alone.

The key to a systematic technique is given in the following theorem.

THEOREM 3.5b. *If a prefix condition code is optimal for U', it is also optimal for U.*
Proof. According to the rule for transition from a prefix condition code for U' to one for U

$$l_k = l'_k \qquad (k \leqslant N-2)$$
$$= l'_{N-1} + 1 \qquad (k = N-1, N).$$

Consequently

$$\bar{l} = \sum_{k=1}^{N-2} p_k l'_k + (p_{N-1} + p_N)(l'_{N-1} + 1)$$
$$= \bar{l}' + p_{N-1} + p_N.$$

The quantity $p_{N-1} + p_N$ is independent of the code so that a minimum of $\bar{l}'$ entails a minimum of $\bar{l}$. The code is, by construction, consistent with Theorem 3.5a and the proof is terminated.

The problem has thereby been reduced to discovering the optimum for U' with its $N-1$ letters. Application of Theorem

3.5a to U' will deal with its two longest code words and the next step is reduction to U'' with $N-2$ letters. Theorem 3.5b enables us to contemplate only the optimum for U''. Proceeding in this way we eventually arrive at a source with only two letters for which the optimal code is 0 for one and 1 for the other.

This method of working systematically upwards from the least likely source letters is known as the *Huffman coding procedure*. It is capable of being programmed effectively for a digital computer.

Example 3.5. The five letters of a source have the following probabilities:

Letter	$P(a_k)$
a_1	0.3
a_2	0.25
a_3	0.25
a_4	0.1
a_5	0.1

The two least probable letters are a_4 and a_5 so that, in a Huffman code, their last digits are 0 and 1 respectively. In the reduced source

a_1'	0.3
a_2'	0.25
a_3'	0.25
a_4'	0.2

The least probable letters are a_4' and, say, a_3'. To a_3' is allocated 0 and to a_4', 1; this means, in view of the rule for going from U' to U, that a_4 is going to end 10 and a_5 11.

At the next step the probabilities are

a_1''	0.3
a_2''	0.25
a_3''	0.45

Now a_1'' and a_2'' have the digits 0 and 1 respectively, and, at the final stage,

a_1'''	0.55
$a_2'''(=a_3'')$	0.45

so that a_1''' gets 0 and a_2''' 1.

Tracing back our steps we find that a_1 was allotted 0 from a_1''', 0 from a_1'' and no other digits. Similarly 1 comes to a_3 from a_2''' and 0 from a_3'. Continuing in this manner, we obtain the code

$$a_1 = 00, \qquad a_2 = 01, \qquad a_3 = 10, \qquad a_4 = 110, \qquad a_5 = 111.$$

The average length of a code word is given by

$$\bar{l} = 2(0.3) + 2(0.25) + 2(0.25) + 3(0.1) + 3(0.1) = 2.2.$$

The code is optimal in the sense that no other uniquely decodable code can shorten $\bar{l}$. It is not, however, unique. For instance, 0 and 1 could be interchanged or a_2', instead of a_3', taken with a_4'.

The entropy of the source is 2.18 bits so that $\bar{l}$ does not conflict with the bounds in the Variable-length Coding Theorem. The optimal $\bar{l}$ is quite an improvement on the upper bound without succeeding in matching the lower bound where it must fail because the probabilities do not meet the special conditions for equality.

The Huffman procedure can be adapted to code alphabets in which $M > 2$ but it is substantially more complicated because, although there is a theorem similar to Theorem 3.5a in all respects, the direct analogue to Theorem 3.5b is not valid.

3.6. Sources with memory

The sources discussed so far have all been memoryless and successive letters have come forth with statistical independence. It was pointed out in Section 3.1 that statistical independence may not be realized by some practical sources. It would therefore widen the range of the theory usefully if some allowance for dependence could be made. Some generalization in this direction is, indeed, possible and the objective of the next sections is to give an indication of the sort of progress that can be made towards this goal.

The source alphabet is still assumed to have the finite number of letters $a_1, \ldots, a_N$ but now the source is imagined to generate two-sided infinite sequences instead of finite sequences. A typical two-sided infinite sequence is $(\ldots, u_{-1}, u_0, u_1, \ldots)$ where each u_j represents a choice from $a_1, \ldots, a_N$. The presence of statistical dependence means that a complete description of the probability is available only when $P(u_{j+1} \cap u_{j+2} \cap \cdots \cap u_{j+m})$ is known for all sequence lengths m, all starting points j, and all possible choices of the us. Some simplifying assumption is therefore desirable and we shall turn to this point in the next section. In the meantime, the notation will be abbreviated by replacing $\cap$ by a comma except when confusion might arise thereby. Thus the above probability will be written as $P(u_{j+1}, u_{j+2}, \ldots, u_{j+m})$.

The letter in the jth slot of a sequence will be visualized as being drawn from a system U_j containing the letters $a_1, \ldots, a_N$ and a typical choice is u_{jk}. Here the first suffix designates the slot and the second, which can run from 1 to N, specifies which of the letters $a_1, \ldots, a_N$ has been selected. Thus the mutual information between letters in successive slots, with conditioning by a third, is from Definition 2.4b

$$I(u_{1j}, u_{2k} \mid u_{3l}) = \log \frac{P(u_{1j} \cap u_{2k} \mid u_{3l})}{P(u_{1j} \mid u_{3l})P(u_{2k} \mid u_{3l})}$$

and, similarly,

$$I(U_1, U_2 \mid U_3) = \sum_{j=1}^{N} \sum_{k=1}^{N} \sum_{l=1}^{N} P(u_{1j}, u_{2k}, u_{3l})I(u_{1j}, u_{2k} \mid u_{3l}).$$

By Theorem 2.4a, $I(U_1, U_2 \mid U_3) \geqslant 0$.

Likewise

$$I(u_{1j} \mid u_{3l}) = -\log P(u_{1j} \mid u_{3l}),$$

$$I(u_{1j} \mid u_{2k} < u_{3l}) = -\log P(u_{1j} \mid u_{2k} \cap u_{3l})$$

so that

$$I(u_{1j}, u_{2k} \mid u_{3l}) = I(u_{1j} \mid u_{3l}) - I(u_{1j} \mid u_{2k} \cap u_{3l}).$$

In harmony with Definition 2.3a

$$H(U_1 \mid U_3) = \sum_{j=1}^{N} \sum_{k=1}^{N} \sum_{l=1}^{N} P(u_{1j}, u_{2k}, u_{3l})I(u_{1j} \mid u_{3l}), \quad (3.6.1)$$

$$H(U_1 \mid U_2 \cap U_3) = \sum_{j=1}^{N} \sum_{k=1}^{N} \sum_{l=1}^{N} P(u_{1j}, u_{2k}, u_{3l})I(u_{1j} \mid u_{2k} \cap u_{3l}).$$
$$(3.6.2)$$

In fact, the summation with respect to k can be carried out in (3.6.1); it replaces $P(u_{1j}, u_{2k}, u_{3l})$ by $P(u_{1j}, u_{3l})$ and leaves only the summation over j and l. From (3.6.2) and (3.6.1)

$$H(U_1 \mid U_3) - H(U_1 \mid U_2 \cap U_3) = I(U_1, U_2 \mid U_3).$$

Since the right-hand side is non-negative it follows that

$$H(U_1 \mid U_3) \geqslant H(U_1 \mid U_2 \cap U_3) \tag{3.6.3}$$

from which may be deduced that additional conditioning (by U_2) cannot increase the entropy.

These notions may be generalized to an arbitrary finite number of systems.

DEFINITION 3.6. *The conditional and joint entropies are defined by*

$$H(U_1 \mid U_2 \cap U_3 \cap \cdots \cap U_r) = -\sum_{j=1}^{N} \cdots \sum_{t=1}^{N} P(u_{1j}, u_{2k}, \ldots, u_{rt})$$
$$\times \log P(u_{1j} \mid u_{2k} \cap \cdots \cap u_{rt}),$$

$$H(U_1 \cap U_2 \cap \cdots \cap U_r) = -\sum_{j=1}^{N} \cdots \sum_{t=1}^{N} P(u_{1j}, \ldots, u_{rt})$$
$$\times \log P(u_{1j}, \ldots, u_{rt}).$$

According to (1.3.2)

$$P(u_{1j}, \ldots, u_{rt}) = P(u_{rt} \mid u_{1j} \cap \cdots \cap u_{r-1,s}) P(u_{1j} \cap \cdots \cap u_{r-1,s}).$$

Hence

$$H(U_1 \cap U_2 \cap \cdots \cap U_r) = -\sum_{j=1}^{N} \cdots \sum_{t=1}^{N} P(u_{1j}, \ldots, u_{rt})$$
$$\times \{\log P(u_{rt} \mid u_{1j} \cap \cdots \cap u_{r-1,s})$$
$$+ \log P(u_{1j} \cap \cdots \cap u_{r-1,s})\}.$$

Since $\sum_{t=1}^{N} P(u_{1j}, \ldots, u_{rt}) = P(u_{1j}, \ldots, u_{r-1,s})$ we conclude that

$$H(U_1 \cap U_2 \cap \cdots \cap U_r) = H(U_r \mid U_1 \cap U_2 \cap \cdots \cap U_{r-1})$$
$$+ H(U_1 \cap U_2 \cap \cdots \cap U_{r-1}). \tag{3.6.4}$$

Another version of (3.6.4) is obtained by using (1.3.2) in the form

$$P(u_{1j}, \ldots, u_{rt}) = P(u_{1j}) P(u_{2k} \mid u_{1j})$$
$$\times P(u_{3l} \mid u_{1j} \cap u_{2k}) \cdots P(u_{rt} \mid u_{1j} \cap \cdots \cap u_{r-1,s}).$$

The same considerations as led to (3.6.4) now result in

$$H(U_1 \cap U_2 \cap \cdots \cap U_r) = H(U_1) + H(U_2 \mid U_1) + \cdots$$
$$+ H(U_r \mid U_1 \cap \cdots \cap U_{r-1}). \tag{3.6.5}$$

By thinking of $U_1 \cap U_2 \cap \cdots \cap U_v$ $(v < r)$ as U_1 in (3.6.5) we obtain

$$
\begin{aligned}
H(U_1 \cap U_2 \cap \cdots \cap U_r) = {} & H(U_1 \cap \cdots \cap U_v) \\
& + H(U_{v+1} \mid U_1 \cap \cdots \cap U_v) \\
& + H(U_{v+2} \mid U_1 \cap \cdots \cap U_{v+1}) \\
& + \cdots + H(U_r \mid U_1 \cap \cdots \cap U_{r-1}).
\end{aligned}
$$

$$(3.6.6)$$

These relations have been derived for equal numbers of events in $U_1, U_2, \ldots$ because that is the situation relevant to subsequent investigations but they are equally valid when the numbers of events are different.

3.7. Stationary sources

The analysis is much simplified if it is assumed that the probabilities associated with the sequence $(\ldots, u_{-1}, u_0, u_1, \ldots)$ are unaltered if the sequence is shifted to the left by one slot to become $(\ldots, u_0, u_1, u_2, \ldots)$. In other words, the probability description does not change on alteration of the origin of the sequence. Another way of interpreting this property is to say that the probability of a particular sequence occupying the slots 1 to r is the same as the probability of that sequence being in the slots $j+1$ to $j+r$ for any integer j, e.g.

$$P(u_1 = a_2, u_2 = a_3, u_3 = a_1) = P(u_{j+1} = a_2, u_{j+2} = a_3, u_{j+3} = a_1)$$

for any integer j. A source which has this property is said to be *stationary*. Only stationary sources will be considered hereafter.

The joint entropy measures the content of a sequence of r letters. This suggests the following definition.

DEFINITION 3.7. $H_r(U)$, *the entropy per letter in a source sequence of r letters, is defined by*

$$H_r(U) = \frac{1}{r} H(U_1 \cap U_2 \cap \cdots \cap U_r).$$

The entropy per letter of the source, $H_\infty(U)$, is defined by

$$H_\infty(U) = \lim_{r \to \infty} H_r(U).$$

Statistical independence of $U_1, U_2, \ldots, U_r$ (cf. the end of Section 1.4) entails, via Theorem 2.3b and (3.6.5),

$$H_r(U) = \frac{1}{r}\{H(U_1) + H(U_2) + \cdots + H(U_r)\} = H(U_1)$$

since all the entropies are the same in our case. Also $H_\infty(U) = H(U_1)$. Thus our definition of entropy per letter is in agreement with that which has already been employed for statistically independent sources.

The definition of H_r would not be affected if any other r consecutive slots were seized on instead of the ones indicated, on account of the stationarity of the source. However, the definition of H_∞ is deficient in the absence of a proof that the limit exists. This defect will now be remedied.

THEOREM 3.7. *For a discrete stationary source with* $H_1(U) < \infty$,
   (a) $H(U_r \mid U_1 \cap U_2 \cap \cdots \cap U_{r-1})$ *does not increase as* r *increases*,
   (b) $H_r(U) \geqslant H(U_r \mid U_1 \cap U_2 \cap \cdots \cap U_{r-1})$,
   (c) $H_r(U)$ *does not increase with* r,
   (d) $H_\infty(U)$ *exists and* $H_\infty(U) = \lim_{r \to \infty} H(U_r \mid U_1 \cap U_2 \cap \cdots \cap U_{r-1})$.
Proof. The stationarity of the source requires

$$H(U_{r-1} \mid U_1 \cap U_2 \cap \cdots \cap U_{r-2}) = H(U_r \mid U_2 \cap U_3 \cap \cdots \cap U_{r-1}).$$

It has been observed in the preceding section that additional conditioning does not increase the entropy. So, after conditioning the right-hand-side on U_1,

$$H(U_{r-1} \mid U_1 \cap U_2 \cap \cdots \cap U_{r-2}) \geqslant H(U_r \mid U_1 \cap U_2 \cap \cdots \cap U_{r-1})$$

which proves part (a).

Further, from (3.6.5),

$$rH_r(U) = H(U_1) + H(U_2 \mid U_1) + \cdots + H(U_r \mid U_1 \cap \cdots \cap U_{r-1})$$
$$\geqslant rH(U_r \mid U_1 \cap \cdots \cap U_{r-1})$$

by virtue of part (a). Thus (b) is proved.

From (3.6.4)

$$rH_r(U) = H(U_r \mid U_1 \cap \cdots \cap U_{r-1}) + H(U_1 \cap \cdots \cap U_{r-1})$$
$$= H(U_r \mid U_1 \cap \cdots \cap U_{r-1}) + (r-1)H_{r-1}(U)$$

by Definition 3.7. Application of part (h) gives

$$rH_r(U) \leq H_r(U) + (r-1)H_{r-1}(U)$$

or

$$H_r(U) \leq H_{r-1}(U),$$

and (c) is established.

Consequently, $H_r(U)$ is non-increasing with r, bounded below because $H_r(U) \geq 0$ and above since $H_1(U) < \infty$. Therefore $\lim_{r \to \infty} H_r(U)$ exists as a finite number between 0 and $H_1(U)$. The first half of (d) is thereby proved.

With regard to the second half of (d), (3.6.6) provides

$$(r+j)H_{r+j}(U) = H(U_1 \cap \cdots \cap U_{r-1}) + H(U_r \mid U_1 \cap \cdots \cap U_{r-1})$$
$$+ \cdots + H(U_{r+j} \mid U_1 \cap \cdots \cap U_{r+j-1})$$

for an arbitrary positive integer j. Applying part (a) to all terms on the right-hand side except the first we obtain

$$(r+j)H_{r+j}(U) \leq H(U_1 \cap \cdots \cap U_{r-1})$$
$$+ (j+1)H(U_r \mid U_1 \cap \cdots \cap U_{r-1}).$$

Divide by j and let $j \to \infty$, keeping r fixed. Then, from the known existence of H_∞,

$$H_\infty(U) \leq H(U_r \mid U_1 \cap \cdots \cap U_{r-1}) \leq H_r(U)$$

from part (b). Letting $r \to \infty$, $H_r \to H_\infty$ and the proof of the theorem is complete.

Theorem 3.7 shows not only that H_∞, as specified in Definition 3.7, exists but also that the entropy per letter of the source is the limit as $r \to \infty$ of the entropy associated with the rth slot conditioned on the preceding $r-1$ slots.

Having established that Definition 3.7 is sound we can enunciate the following theorem.

VARIABLE-LENGTH STATIONARY SOURCE CODING THEOREM. *For any uniquely decodable set of code words, the average number $\bar{l}$ of code letters per source letter in source sequences of length n satisfies*

$$\bar{l} \geq H_n(U)/\log M.$$

It is always possible to encode so that the prefix condition holds and

$$\bar{l} < \frac{H_n(U)}{\log M} + \frac{1}{n}.$$

For any $\delta > 0$ *and a stationary source, n can be chosen large enough for*

$$\frac{H_\infty(U)}{\log M} \leqslant \bar{l} \leqslant \frac{H_\infty(U)}{\log M} + \delta.$$

Proof. In the Variable-length Coding Theorem single letters from the source were considered. Suppose they were replaced by sequences of n letters. The entropy would then become $nH_n(U)$ and the average length of the code $n\bar{l}$. So the theorem would assert

$$\frac{nH_n(U)}{\log M} \leqslant n\bar{l} < \frac{nH_n(U)}{\log M} + 1.$$

Division by n supplies all but the last part of the current theorem.

Allowing $n \to \infty$, we obtain the final statement and the proof is terminated.

One conclusion of the theorem is that encoding source sequences of n letters rather than individual letters can reduce the average number of code symbols per source letter but the improvement can be at most one symbol. Also demonstrated is that, in binary coding of a stationary source, H_∞ is the number of binary digits per source letter required on average for encoding.

The two variable-length coding theorems resemble one another, displaying a satisfactory interrelationship between dependence and independence. It is not so straightforward, unfortunately, to cope with dependence in the source sequence theorem and a new concept has to be introduced for progress; discussion is deferred to the next section.

3.8. Ergodic sources

Denote the sequence $(\ldots, u_{-1}, u_0, u_1, \ldots)$ by u. A new sequence, to be designated Tu, is formed from u shifting every element of u one slot to the left. In other words, if v is the new sequence so that $v = Tu$, then $v_j = u_{j+1}$ for every integer j. From v the sequence Tv can be formed; if $w = Tv$, then $w_j = v_{j+1} = u_{j+2}$. It is convenient to write Tv as T^2u and the meaning of higher powers of T is evident. For instance, $v = T^r u$ will signify $v_j = u_{j+r}$ for every integer j.

Let $f_r(u)$ be a function which depends only on the source letters which occupy slots $j = 1, \ldots, r$, i.e. $f_r(u)$ is a function only of $u_1, \ldots, u_r$. In stationary sources the r consecutive slots may be placed at any convenient point. The function $f_r(Tu)$ or $f_r(v)$ will depend only on $v_1, \ldots, v_r$, i.e. only on $u_2, \ldots, u_{r+1}$. When it is desired to exhibit explicitly the elements of u in f_r it will be written as $f_r(u_{1j}, u_{2k}, \ldots, u_n)$ for example.

A discrete stationary source is said to be *ergodic* if, and only if,

$$\lim_{L \to \infty} \frac{1}{L} \sum_{l=1}^{L} f_r(T^l u) = \sum_{j=1}^{N} \cdots \sum_{t=1}^{N} P(u_{1j}, \ldots, u_n) f_r(u_{1j}, \ldots, u_n)$$

(3.8.1)

for all $r \geqslant 1$, all f_r for which the right-hand side is finite and for all sequences u though a set of probability zero can be excluded if so wished.

The right-hand side of (3.8.1) is independent of any particular sequence being, in fact, the average of f_r. The left-hand side must, therefore, be independent of any particular sequence u for which it is calculated though, since a set of probability zero may be excepted, this statement need only be true with probability 1. Note that, since infinite sequences are under consideration, probability 1 does not carry with it the implication of certainty.

An apparently less restricted definition of ergodicity is possible. Select a specific sequence of source letters, say $u_1', u_2', \ldots, u_r'$. Define F_r by

$$F_r(u) = 1 \quad \text{for} \quad u_j = u_j' \quad (j = 1, \ldots, r)$$
$$= 0 \quad \text{otherwise.}$$

Then, if (3.8.1) holds with F_r in place of f_r, the source is ergodic. While this definition requires verification of (3.8.1) only for a special choice of f_r and therefore seemingly allows more freedom it can be shown that the two definitions are actually equivalent. For a proof of the equivalence the reader should consult texts on ergodicity.

The second form of the definition indicates that a given sequence of source letters occurs in a long message about as many times as the product of the length of the message and the probability of the given sequence. There is thus some kinship with the law of large numbers. Successive appearances of a particular sequence tend to reveal a degree of independence. So an ergodic source is an attempt to model the circumstances in which the production of a letter depends upon the previous ones, but the dependence decays fairly rapidly as the antecedent recedes. Such behaviour may be anticipated in several practical situations.

The fundamental theorem for ergodic sources is given by the following theorem.

SHANNON–MCMILLAN THEOREM. *For a given sequence* $u_{1j}, \ldots, u_{nt}$ *from a discrete stationary ergodic source in which* $H_1(U) < \infty$, *there is an integer* $n_0(\varepsilon, \delta)$ *for arbitrary given* $\varepsilon > 0$ *and* $\delta > 0$ *such that*

$$P\left\{ \left| \frac{\log P(u_{1j}, \ldots, u_{nt})}{n} + H_\infty(U) \right| > \delta \right\} < \varepsilon$$

for $n \geq n_0(\varepsilon, \delta)$.

The theorem was first proved by Shannon for a particular kind of source and, in full generality, by McMillan in 1953.

Proof. The proof of this theorem is complicated. In essence, the aim is to establish results for a manageable entity (called Q_m below) and then show that this entity is not too far from the desired probability of a sequence.

Define Q_m for $1 \leq m \leq n$ by

$$Q_m = P(u_{1j}, \ldots, u_{mp}) P(u_{m+1,q} \mid u_{1j} \cap \cdots \cap u_{mp})$$
$$\times P(u_{m+2,r} \mid u_{2k} \cap \cdots \cap u_{m+1,q}) \cdots$$
$$P(u_{nt} \mid u_{n-m} \cap \cdots \cap u_{n-1,s}). \quad (3.8.2)$$

Now $\sum_{q=1}^{N} P(u_{m+1,q} \mid u_{1j} \cap \cdots \cap u_{mp}) = 1$ because some u_{m+1} must be chosen whatever the previous letters. An alternative argument is

$$\sum_{q=1}^{N} P(u_{m+1,q} \mid u_{1j} \cap \cdots \cap u_{mp})$$
$$= \sum_{q=1}^{N} P(u_{1j}, \ldots, u_{m+1,q}) / P(u_{1j}, \ldots, u_{mp})$$
$$= P(u_{1j}, \ldots, u_{mp}) / P(u_{1j}, \ldots, u_{mp})$$
$$= 1.$$

Therefore by summing (3.8.2) first with respect to t, then with respect to s and so on we obtain

$$\sum_{j=1}^{N} \cdots \sum_{t=1}^{N} Q_m = 1 \qquad (3.8.3)$$

for each m. Thus Q_m has some of the attributes of a probability.

If $P(u_{1j}, \ldots, u_{mp}) = 0$ the probability of selecting the particular sequence is zero and so there is unit probability that $P(u_{1j}, \ldots, u_{mp}) \neq 0$. Hence, we can assert that

$$\lim_{n \to \infty} \frac{1}{n} \log P(u_{1j}, \ldots, u_{mp}) = 0 \qquad (3.8.4)$$

with probability 1.

The function $\log P(u_{\tau\theta} \mid u_{\tau-m,\alpha} \cap \cdots \cap u_{\tau-1,\eta})$ involves only a sequence of $m+1$ letters and

$$\sum_{\alpha=1}^{N} \cdots \sum_{\theta=1}^{N} P(u_{\tau-m,\alpha}, \ldots, u_{\tau\theta}) \log P(u_{\tau\theta} \mid u_{\tau-m,\alpha} \cap \cdots \cap u_{\tau-1,\eta})$$
$$= -H(U_{m+1} \mid U_1 \cap \cdots \cap U_m). \quad (3.8.5)$$

Stationarity has been invoked to permit the particular sequence of slots on the right-hand side of (3.8.5). The conditional entropy is finite by Theorem 3.7 because of the assumption that $H_1(U) < \infty$. This means that the right-hand side of (3.8.1) is finite when f is identified with $\log P$ and so (3.8.1) can be applied with this f because the source is ergodic. Putting $L = n - m$, we have

$$\lim_{n \to \infty} \frac{1}{n-m} \sum_{\tau=m+1}^{n} \log P(u_{\tau\theta} \mid u_{\tau-m,\alpha} \cap \cdots \cap u_{\tau-1,\eta})$$
$$= -H(U_{m+1} \mid U_1 \cap \cdots \cap U_m) \quad (3.8.6)$$

with probability 1, because each increase of τ by a unit corresponds to an application of T.

Now

$$\lim_{n \to \infty} (\log Q_m)/n = \lim_{n \to \infty} \left\{ \frac{1}{n} \log P(u_{1j}, \ldots, u_{mp}) \right.$$
$$\left. + \frac{1}{n} \sum_{\tau=m+1}^{n} P(u_\tau \mid u_{\tau-m} \cap \cdots \cap u_{\tau-1}) \right\}$$
$$= -H(U_{m+1} \mid U_1 \cap \cdots \cap U_m) \qquad (3.8.7)$$

with probability 1, on account of (3.8.4) and (3.8.6) since $\lim_{n \to \infty} n/(n-m) = 1$.

The formula (3.8.7) bears some resemblance to that being sought. Had all the conditioning sequences in (3.8.2) started at u_1, Q_m would have been the same as the desired probability $P(u_1, \ldots, u_n)$ but then there would have been difficulty in applying ergodicity. Notwithstanding, Q_m is not far off what we are looking for, as will now be shown. In the course of the analysis, *Chebyshev's inequality* (Exercise 3.1) will be required. This inequality states that if $g(E_k)$ is a non-negative real number for each of the events $E_1, \ldots, E_r$ of a system then

$$P\{g(E_j) \geqslant \delta\} \leqslant \sum_{k=1}^{r} P(E_k)g(E_k)/\delta \qquad (3.8.8)$$

for any $\delta > 0$ and $j = 1, \ldots, r$.

An application of Chebyshev's inequality gives

$$P\left\{\left|\log \frac{Q_m}{P(u_{1j}, \ldots, u_{nt})}\right| > n\varepsilon\right\} \leqslant \frac{1}{n\varepsilon} \sum_{j=1}^{N} \cdots \sum_{t=1}^{N} P(u_{1j}, \ldots, u_{nt})$$
$$\times \left|\log \frac{Q_m}{P(u_{1j}, \ldots, u_{nt})}\right|. \qquad (3.8.9)$$

If $z \geqslant 1$, $|\ln z| = \ln z$ and, from Theorem 2.2a,

$$|\ln z| + \ln z = 2 \ln z \leqslant 2(z-1) \leqslant 2z.$$

Therefore

$$|\ln z| \leqslant 2z - \ln z. \qquad (3.8.10)$$

On the other hand, if $0 < z \leqslant 1$, $|\ln z| = -\ln z$ and so (3.8.10) is true. Hence (3.8.10) is valid for $z > 0$.

Since $\log z = \log e \cdot \ln z$, (3.8.10) shows that the right-hand side of (3.8.9) does not exceed

$$\frac{\log e}{n\varepsilon} \sum_{j=1}^{N} \cdots \sum_{t=1}^{N} P(u_{1j}, \ldots, u_{nt})\left\{\frac{2Q_m}{P(u_{1j}, \ldots, u_{nt})} - \ln \frac{Q_m}{P(u_{1j}, \ldots, u_{nt})}\right\}$$
$$= \frac{\log e}{n\varepsilon}\left\{2 - \sum_{j=1}^{N} \cdots \sum_{t=1}^{N} P(u_{1j}, \ldots, u_{nt}) \ln \frac{Q_m}{P(u_{1j}, \ldots, u_{nt})}\right\}$$

from (3.8.3). The evaluation of the last term follows from the incorporation of (3.8.2) so that

$$\sum_{j=1}^{N} \cdots \sum_{t=1}^{N} P(u_{1j}, \ldots, u_{nt}) \log \frac{Q_m}{P(u_{1j}, \ldots, u_{nt})}$$

$$= \sum_{j=1}^{N} \cdots \sum_{t=1}^{N} P(u_{1j}, \ldots, u_{nt})\{\log P(u_{1j}, \ldots, u_{mp})$$

$$- \log P(u_{1j}, \ldots, u_{nt})$$

$$+ \log P(u_{m+1,q} \mid u_{1j} \cap \cdots \cap u_{mp})$$

$$+ \log P(u_{m+2,r} \mid u_{2k} \cap \cdots \cap u_{m+1,q})$$

$$+ \cdots + \log P(u_{nt} \mid u_{n-m} \cap \cdots \cap u_{n-1,s})\}$$

$$= nH_n(U) - mH_m(U) - H(U_{m+1} \mid U_1 \cap \cdots \cap U_m)$$

$$- H(U_{m+2} \mid U_2 \cap \cdots \cap U_{m+1})$$

$$- \cdots - H(U_n \mid U_{n-m} \cap \cdots \cap U_{n-1})$$

on account of Definition 3.7. The source is stationary and so

$$H(U_n \mid U_{n-m} \cap \cdots \cap U_{n-1}) = \cdots$$
$$= H(U_{m+2} \mid U_2 \cap \cdots \cap U_{m+1})$$
$$= H(U_{m+1} \mid U_1 \cap \cdots \cap U_m).$$

Combining together all these resuls we deduce from (3.8.9) that

$$P\left\{ \left| \frac{1}{n} \log Q_m - \frac{1}{n} \log P(u_{1j}, \ldots, u_{nt}) \right| > \varepsilon \right\}$$

$$\leq \frac{1}{\varepsilon} \left[\frac{2}{n} \log e - \frac{m}{n} \{H_n(U) - H_m(U)\} + \left(\frac{m}{n} - 1 \right) \{H_n(U) - H_\infty(U)\} \right.$$

$$\left. + \left(1 - \frac{m}{n} \right) \{H(U_{m+1} \mid U_1 \cap \cdots \cap U_m) - H_\infty(U)\} \right].$$

Let $m \to \infty$; this forces $n \to \infty$ because $m \leq n$. From Theorem 3.7 both H_n and H_m tends to H_∞ and so does $H(U_{m+1} \mid U_1 \cap \cdots \cap U_m)$ by Theorem 3.7(d). Therefore the right-hand side tends to zero as $m \to \infty$ and can be made smaller than any desired quantity by making m large enough.

Choose m so large that, for any $n > m$,

$$P\left\{ \left| \frac{1}{n} \log Q_m - \frac{1}{n} \log P(u_{1j}, \ldots, u_{nt}) \right| > \varepsilon \right\} \leq \delta \quad (3.8.11)$$

and, at the same time,

$$|H(U_{m+1} \mid U_1 \cap \cdots \cap U_m) - H_\infty(U)| < \varepsilon. \qquad (3.8.12)$$

Having fixed m we can, by virtue of (3.8.7), select n_0 so that

$$P\left\{ \left| \frac{1}{n} \log Q_m + H(U_{m+1} \mid U_1 \cap \cdots \cap U_m) \right| > \varepsilon \right\} \leqslant \delta \qquad (3.8.13)$$

for $n \geqslant n_0$.

But

$$\left| \frac{1}{n} \log P(u_{1j}, \ldots, u_{nt}) + H_\infty(U) \right|$$

$$\leqslant \left| \frac{1}{n} \log P(u_{1j}, \ldots, u_{nt}) - \frac{1}{n} \log Q_m \right|$$

$$+ \left| \frac{1}{n} \log Q_m + H(U_{m+1} \mid U_1 \cap \cdots \cap U_m) \right|$$

$$+ |H_\infty(U) - H(U_{m+1} \mid U_1 \cap \cdots \cap U_m)|$$

$$\leqslant \left| \frac{1}{n} \log P(u_{1j}, \ldots, u_{nt}) - \frac{1}{n} \log Q_m \right|$$

$$+ \left| \frac{1}{n} \log Q_m + H(U_{m+1} \mid U_1 \cap \cdots \cap U_m) \right| + \varepsilon$$

on account of (3.8.12). Consequently $\left| \frac{1}{n} \log P + H_\infty \right| > 3\varepsilon$ only if

at least one of the events $\left| \frac{1}{n} \log P - \frac{1}{n} \log Q_m \right| > \varepsilon$ and

$\left| \frac{1}{n} \log Q_m + H(U_{m+1} \mid U_1 \cap \cdots \cap U_m) \right| > \varepsilon$ takes place. There-fore, the probability of this inequality cannot be greater than the sum of the probabilities of these two events by Theorem 1.1. Accordingly, (3.8.11) and (3.8.13) supply

$$P\left\{ \left| \frac{1}{n} \log P(u_{1j}, \ldots, u_{nt}) + H_\infty(U) \right| > 3\varepsilon \right\} \leqslant 2\delta$$

for $n \geqslant n_0$ and the theorem is proved.

The Shannon-McMillan theorem can be interpreted as saying that the sequences for which $\frac{1}{n} \log P + H_\infty$ is not small can be grouped so that their total probability is arbitrarily small and can be regarded as the group G_2 of the Source Sequence Partition Theorem though now the source has memory. The same route as travelled in proving the Source Coding Theorem may now be traversed and we have the following theorem.

MEMORY SOURCE CODING THEOREM. *The Source Coding Theorem remains valid for a stationary ergodic source provided that $H(U)$ is replaced by $H_\infty(U)$.*

In view of this theorem the discussion of coding after the Source Coding Theorem is also applicable to sources with memory, so long as they are stationary and ergodic. The reaching of such a satisfactory state of affairs is a convenient point to break off the discussion of coding.

Exercises

3.1. A system consists of the events $E_1, \ldots, E_r$ and the function g is such that $g(E_k)$ is a non-negative real number for $k = 1, \ldots, r$. Prove that

$$P\{g(E_i) \geq \delta\} \leq \sum_{k=1}^{r} P(E_k)g(E_k)/\delta.$$

[Hint: If E_l is a typical event for which $g(E_l) \geq \delta$, $\sum_l P(E_l) \leq \sum_l P(E_l)g(E_l)/\delta$.]

3.2. A source produces statistically independent binary digits with probabilities $P(0) = \frac{3}{4}$, $P(1) = \frac{1}{4}$. Find n_0 such that

$$P\left\{\left|\frac{1}{n}\log_2 P(\mathbf{u}) + H(U)\right| \geq 0.05\right\} \leq 0.01$$

for $n \geq n_0$. [Exercise 3.1 can be used if desired.]

3.3. Two codes for a source of four letters are:

Letter	p_k	Code A	Code B
a_1	0.4	1	1
a_2	0.3	01	10
a_3	0.2	001	100
a_4	0.1	000	1000

Determine for each code (a) whether it is a prefix condition code, (b) if it is uniquely decodable, (c) the mutual information between the source letter being a_1 and the first symbol of the code word being 1.

3.4. The letters of a source are arranged so that $P(a_j) \geq P(a_k)$ for $k > j \geq 1$. Define $q_1 = 0$ and

$$q_i = \sum_{k=1}^{i-1} P(a_k)$$

for $i > 1$. Convert q_i to its binary decimal (e.g. $\frac{1}{2}$, $\frac{1}{4}$, and $\frac{5}{8}$ become $100\ldots$, $0100\ldots$, $10100\ldots$ respectively) and then truncate this decimal after the smallest number of digits which is not less than the self-information $I(a_i)$. Assign this truncated decimal as the code word for a_i.

Prove that the code satisfies the prefix condition and that $H(U) \leq \bar{l} < H(U) + 1$.

3.5. Show that Kraft's Theorem and Theorem 3.3 remain valid as $N \to \infty$. What is the implication for the Variable-length Coding Theorem when the source entropy is finite?

3.6. A discrete memoryless source has N letters and an entropy of $H(U)$ bits. It is encoded from an alphabet of 3 symbols. The code satisfies the prefix condition and the average length of a code word is $H(U)/\log_2 3$. Show that the probability of occurrence of a source letter is 3^{-r} where r is a positive integer which can depend on the source letter.

Deduce that N is odd.

3.7. A source has six letters with probabilities of occurrence 0.3, 0.2, 0.15, 0.15, 0.1, 0.1. Construct an optimal binary Huffman code and find the average length of a code word.

3.8. Repeat Exercise 3.7 when the probabilities are 0.25, 0.2, 0.2, 0.15, 0.1, 0.1.

3.9. Repeat Exercise 3.7 when the source has seven letters with probabilities 0.3, 0.25, 0.15, 0.1, 0.1, 0.05, 0.05.

3.10. When a sequence of n letters from the source of Exercise 3.7 is encoded the number of code letters is M_n. What happens to M_n/n as $n \to \infty$?

3.11. Repeat Exercise 3.10 for the sources of Exercises 3.8 and 3.9.

3.12. Each letter from a source of N letters occurs with the same probability and is coded by an optimal binary Huffman code. What are the lengths of the code words when (i) $N = 2^j$, (ii) $N = 1 + 2^j$, j being a positive integer?

Generalize your result to the case $N = 2^j \nu$ where $1 \leq \nu < 2$ and prove that the average length of a code word is $j + 2 - 2/\nu$.

3.13. With the notation of Theorem 3.5b, prove that

$$\bar{l} - H(U) \geq \bar{l}' - H(U').$$

3.14. Of n pennies, $N-1$ are known to have the same weight whereas the Nth may be heavier or lighter. A balance is available on which the weights of two groups of pennies may be compared. Find the maximum value of N for which it has been found in m weighings which is the odd penny and whether it is heavier or lighter.

Contemplate generalizing this problem when you have a centrifuge balance which is capable of telling you when one of three groups of pennies is out of balance.

3.15. Prove that

$$H(U_1 \cap U_2 \cap U_3) - H(U_1 \cap U_2) \leqslant H(U_1 \cap U_3) - H(U_1).$$

3.16. If $I(U_1, U_2 \mid U_3) = 0$ prove that $H(U_1 \mid U_3) \leqslant H(U_1 \mid U_2)$.

3.17. For a discrete stationary source define $K_s(U)$ by

$$K_s(U) = \frac{1}{s} H(U_{2s} \cap U_{2s-1} \cap \cdots \cap U_{s+1} \mid U_s \cap \cdots \cap U_1).$$

Show that, when $H_1(U) < \infty$, $\lim_{s \to \infty} K_s(U) = \lim_{r \to \infty} H_r(U) = H_\infty(U)$.

3.18. Denote a two-sided infinite sequence by u. A set of sequences is said to be *invariant* if Tu is a member of the set when u is. If u_0 is a fixed sequence prove that the set comprised of the sequences u_0, Tu_0, $T^2u_0, \ldots, T^{-1}u_0$, $T^{-2}u_0, \ldots$ is invariant. [Another definition of an ergodic source is that every invariant set has either probability 1 or probability 0.]

3.19. A source has two parts A and B. A contains the letter a_1 and B has the letters a_2 and a_3. A choice is first made between A and B by tossing an ideal coin, with heads for A and tails for B. Once A or B has been chosen the source produces an infinite sequence from it but, if B is selected, the letters a_2 and a_3 are picked with equal probability. Source sequences of n letters are coded into binary by putting 0 for a_1 and using code words of length $n+1$ for each of the 2^n sequences involving a_2 and a_3. Show that $\bar{l}$ is minimized by this coding.

Use Exercise 3.18 to demonstrate that the source is not ergodic.

3.20. The sequence $(\ldots, u_{-1}, u_0, u_1, \ldots)$ is drawn from a binary stationary ergodic source. The even digits $\ldots, u_{-2}, u_0, u_2, \ldots$ are statistically independent equally probable binary digits. With probability $\frac{1}{2}$, $u_{2j+1} = u_{2j}$ for all integers j, and with probability $\frac{1}{2}$, $u_{2j-1} = u_{2j}$ for all j. The pair $u_{2j}u_{2j+1}$ is encoded by the rule $00 \to 0$, $11 \to 10$, $01 \to 110$, $10 \to 111$. Prove that, with probability $\frac{1}{2}$, the number of code letters per source letter in a long sequence tends to $\frac{3}{4}$ and, with probability $\frac{1}{2}$, tends to 9/8.

4 Channels

4.1. Introduction

The preceding chapter has dealt with the translation of messages from a source into code. The objective of communication is to pass these coded messages on. They may be transmitted through the air by radio waves, or sent by telephone cable, or dispatched by optical means, or transmitted between two parts of a computer by means of a link, or printed in a book or newspaper. The precise mechanism is immaterial in a general theory and any device by which a signal is transmitted whether it be radio, optical fibre, or book will be called a *channel*. Thus the general structure of a communication system will be that shown in Fig. 4.1.1 where the possibility that the recipient may have to decode the output of the channel has been allowed for. In its simplest form it consists of reading a book, coping with any misprints which have occurred.

The channel is determined as soon as one can say what input signals it will accept, what output it will feed to the decoder, and the relation between input and output. The determination of these characteristics will depend upon the particular mechanism of transmission. How they are found is outside the scope of this book. We shall merely suppose that they can be unearthed and are of the type that will now be described.

It will be assumed that the input comprises sequences of letters from a finite alphabet. Were that alphabet not the same as that of the coder an additional coder would have to be inserted between the coder and channel in Fig. 4.1.1. But then the combination of the two coders could be regarded as a single coder. There is therefore no loss of generality in supposing that the input alphabet of the channel is the output alphabet of the coder.

Similarly, the output will be assumed to consist of sequences of letters from a finite alphabet, which may also be taken as the input alphabet of the decoder. The output alphabet of the channel may not be the same as its input though often it will be.

If to each letter a of the input there corresponds a unique

FIG. 4.1.1. Elements of a communication system.

letter *b* of the output, the channel is said to be *noiseless*. Then the reception of *b* enables one to make the unequivocal identification that the input letter was *a*. No mistakes are being made in transmission.

When the transmission is not totally reliable, an input letter may result in a different output letter on different occasions. The channel is then called *noisy*. Most channels are noisy in practice since there are few if any modes of transmission which do not introduce errors, albeit infrequently. A noisy channel is characterized by the probability that a given output letter stems from an input letter. Sometimes the output letter depends upon a sequence of input letters in which case the channel is said to possess *memory*. Only channels without memory will be considered here.

4.2. Capacity of a memoryless channel

Let the input alphabet be denoted by A and contain the letters $a_1, \ldots, a_n$. Denote the output alphabet by B and its letters, which need not be the same in number as the input, by $b_1, \ldots, b_r$. A memoryless channel is now completely specified by giving $P(b_s \mid a_k)$, i.e. the probability of output b_s when the input is a_k, for $s = 1, \ldots, r$ and $k = 1, \ldots, n$. Whatever the input there will always be an output letter and so

$$\sum_{s=1}^{r} P(b_s \mid a_k) = 1. \qquad (4.2.1)$$

The probabilities $P(b_s \mid a_k)$ which indicate how the transition from input to output takes place will be named *transition probabilities*.

The transition probabilities $P(b_k \mid a_k)$ are usually close to one in printing books and a little less in newspaper reproduction. For fading radio signals they can deviate appreciably from unity.

The probability of the output letter being b_s is the sum of the probabilities of the events favourable to this occurrence and so is given by

$$P(b_s) = \sum_{k=1}^{n} P(b_s \mid a_k) P(a_k) = \sum_{k=1}^{n} P(b_s \cap a_k). \qquad (4.2.2)$$

It is therefore a function of the input probabilities and the channel transition probabilities.

The mutual information between input and output of the channel is, by Definition 2.3b,

$$I(A, B) = \sum_{k=1}^{n} \sum_{s=1}^{r} P(b_s \cap a_k) \log \frac{P(b_s \mid a_k)}{P(b_s)}.$$

Mention has been made in Section 2.3 that the mutual information assesses now much of the content of the input is reflected in the output and that the larger it is the more nearly the input can be extracted from the output (tight coupling being noiseless in the channel context). Therefore, it will be advantageous to make the mutual information as large as possible. For any particular channel the transition probabilities are fixed and so only the input probabilities can be manipulated. On account of (4.2.2) the output probabilities will vary at the same time. The best that can be achieved over all input probabilities represents the capacity of the channel.

Write $P(a_k) = p_k$. Then introduce the following definition.

DEFINITION 4.2. *The capacity C of a memoryless channel is defined by*

$$C = \max I(A, B),$$

the maximum being taken over all possible input probabilities $p_1, \ldots, p_n$ while the transition probabilities $P(b_s \mid a_k)$ are held fixed.

It is therefore necessary to find those p_k, satisfying $p_k \geq 0$ and $\sum_{k=1}^{n} p_k = 1$, which make $I(A, B)$ a maximum. The maximum must exist because a continuous function is being considered in a finite domain of variables. To find it, however, necessitates solving a non-linear optimization problem in several variables.

The standard method of tackling maxima and minima when the variables are constrained is to introduce Lagrange's multipliers. Therefore, consider $I(A, B) - \lambda \sum_{i=1}^{n} p_i$ when λ is a Lagrange multiplier and take a derivative with respect to p_k. In the process, it must be remembered that $P(b_s)$ depends on p_k via (4.2.2).

Consequently

$$\frac{\partial}{\partial p_k} \log P(b_s) = \left\{ \frac{\partial}{\partial p_k} \ln P(b_s) \right\} \log e = \frac{P(b_s \mid a_k)}{P(b_s)} \log e.$$

Thus the equations for a stationary point are

$$\sum_{s=1}^{r} P(b_s \mid a_k) \log \frac{P(b_s \mid a_k)}{P(b_s)} - \sum_{i=1}^{n} \sum_{s=1}^{r} P(b_s \mid a_i) p_i$$

$$\times \frac{P(b_s \mid a_k)}{P(b_s)} \log e - \lambda = 0$$

for $k = 1, \ldots, n$. Since $\sum_{i=1}^{n} P(b_s \mid a_i) p_i = P(b_s)$ from (4.2.2), (4.2.1) entails

$$\sum_{s=1}^{r} P(b_s \mid a_k) \log \frac{P(b_s \mid a_k)}{P(b_s)} = \lambda + \log e \qquad (4.2.3)$$

as the equations to be satisfied for $k = 1, \ldots, n$ at a maximum of $I(A, B)$.

If the equations (4.2.3) have a solution $p_1^m, \ldots, p_n^m$ multiply (4.2.3) by p_k^m and the sum for $k = 1, \ldots, n$. Since $\sum_{k=1}^{n} p_k^m = 1$, there results

$$C = \lambda + \log e. \qquad (4.2.4)$$

Thus the capacity of the channel coincides with the right-hand side of (4.2.3).

It may transpire that at the maximum of $I(A, B)$ one or more p_j are zero. Then (4.2.3) may not be fulfilled when $k = j$. Instead the inequality

$$\sum_{s=1}^{r} P(b_s \mid a_j) \log \frac{P(b_s \mid a_j)}{P(b_s)} \leq \lambda + \log e \qquad (4.2.5)$$

must then be complied with. However, (4.2.4) continues to be valid because the p_j^m which multiplies (4.2.5) in the derivation of (4.2.4) is zero.

The problem of finding the capacity of a channel has therefore been reduced to finding p_k such that (4.2.3) is satisfied for every k for which $p_k \neq 0$ and (4.2.5) for every j for which $p_j = 0$. It does not matter how p_k is arrived at so long as these conditions are verified.

The proof of this statement is deferred to the next section. In the meantime some examples are given of the capacities of various channels.

Example 4.2a. In the binary symmetric channel of Fig. 4.2.1 take $a_1 = 0$, $a_2 = 1$, $b_1 = 0$, $b_2 = 1$. Then

$$P(b_1 \mid a_1) = P(b_2 \mid a_2) = 1 - \varepsilon,$$
$$P(b_2 \mid a_1) = P(b_1 \mid a_2) = \varepsilon$$

and

$$P(b_1) = (1 - \varepsilon)p_1 + \varepsilon p_2,$$
$$P(b_2) = \varepsilon p_1 + (1 - \varepsilon)p_2.$$

Either by calculating $I(A, B)$ and taking derivatives with respect to p_1, p_2 or by quoting (4.2.3) we reach

$$(1 - \varepsilon)\log \frac{1 - \varepsilon}{P(b_1)} + \varepsilon \log \frac{\varepsilon}{P(b_2)} = \lambda + \log e, \qquad (4.2.6)$$

$$\varepsilon \log \frac{\varepsilon}{P(b_1)} + (1 - \varepsilon)\log \frac{1 - \varepsilon}{P(b_2)} = \lambda + \log e. \qquad (4.2.7)$$

Subtraction of (4.2.7) from (4.2.6) gives

$$(1 - \varepsilon)\log \frac{P(b_2)}{P(b_1)} + \varepsilon \log \frac{P(b_1)}{P(b_2)} = 0$$

which implies, if $\varepsilon \neq \frac{1}{2}$, that $P(b_1) = P(b_2)$. Hence $p_1 = p_2$ and both must be $\frac{1}{2}$ to make their sum unity. Substitution of these values

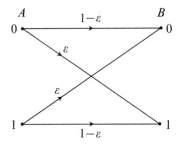

Fig. 4.2.1. The binary symmetric channel.

into the left-hand side of (4.2.6) or (4.2.7), coupled with (4.2.4), supplies

$$C = 1 + \varepsilon \log_2 \varepsilon + (1 - \varepsilon)\log_2(1 - \varepsilon) \text{ bits.}$$

Actually, the symmetry of the arrangement of Fig. 4.2.1 would suggest trying $p_1 = p_2 = \frac{1}{2}$. Then, the equality of the left-hand sides of (4.2.6) and (4.2.7) would signify that they gave capacity.

This latter argument would also apply when $\varepsilon = \frac{1}{2}$ but now the capacity is zero. By virtue of Corollary 2.3b, $I(A, B)$ is zero for all inputs and it may easily be checked that the left-hand sides of (4.2.6) and (4.2.7) are both zero for all inputs. In this case the output never conveys any information about the input. It is also an illustration of the fact that the input probabilities corresponding to capacity need not be unique.

Example 4.2b. The input alphabet consists of two letters $a_1 = 0$, $a_2 = 1$ and the output has three letters $b_1 = 0$, $b_2 = 1$, $b_3 = 2$, the transition probabilities being as shown in Fig. 4.2.2. Again, symmetry suggests that the input letters should not be differentially treated. Therefore try $p_1 = \frac{1}{2}$, $p_2 = \frac{1}{2}$. Then

$$P(b = 0) = \tfrac{1}{2}(1 - \varepsilon),$$
$$P(b = 1) = \varepsilon,$$
$$P(b = 2) = \tfrac{1}{2}(1 - \varepsilon).$$

The left-hand side of (4.2.3) becomes for $k = 1$

$$(1 - \varepsilon)\log \frac{1 - \varepsilon}{\frac{1}{2}(1 - \varepsilon)} + \varepsilon \log \frac{\varepsilon}{\varepsilon}$$

and the same is obtained for $k = 2$. Thus the criteria for a

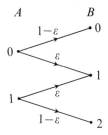

FIG. 4.2.2. Output alphabet larger than the input.

maximum are met and

$$C = 1 - \varepsilon \text{ bits.}$$

It will be noticed that the entropy of the input can be as high as 1 bit and so there are inputs whose entropy exceeds the capacity of the channel. In that eventuality errors in transmission cannot be avoided.

Example 4.2c. The input alphabet has three letters $a_1 = 0$, $a_2 = 1$, $a_3 = 2$ and the output two letters $b_1 = 0$, $b_2 = 1$ with the transition probabilities of Fig. 4.2.3. The uncertainty attached to a_2 compared with the certainty of a_1 and a_3 suggests that a_2 should be avoided. Therefore, try $p_1 = p_3 = \frac{1}{2}$, $p_2 = 0$. Then

$$P(b_1) = \tfrac{1}{2} = P(b_2).$$

The left-hand side of (4.2.3) for $k = 1$ is

$$\log \frac{1}{\frac{1}{2}}$$

and for $k = 3$ also but, for $k = 2$, is

$$\tfrac{1}{2} \log \frac{\frac{1}{2}}{\frac{1}{2}} + \tfrac{1}{2} \log \frac{\frac{1}{2}}{\frac{1}{2}} = 0.$$

Consequently, (4.2.3) is not satisfied for all k. However, $p_2 = 0$ and so only (4.2.5) need be true for $k = 2$. This is, indeed, so with $\lambda + \log e = \log 2$. Thus the choice of input probabilities meets the conditions for a maximum and $C = 1$ bit.

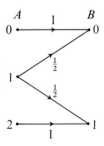

FIG. 4.2.3. Output alphabet smaller than the input.

4.3. Convexity

The proof that the stated criteria are necessary and sufficient for capacity to be achieved rests on the Convexity Theorem of Section 2.4, but it requires a little manoeuvring to reach a position where it can be applied.

Let $p_1^{(0)}, \ldots, p_n^{(0)}$ and $p_1^{(1)}, \ldots, p_n^{(1)}$ be two possible input probabilities. The associated mutual informations are

$$I^{(0)}(A, B) = \sum_{k=1}^{n} \sum_{s=1}^{n} P(b_s \mid a_k) p_k^{(0)} \log \frac{P(b_s \mid a_k)}{P^{(0)}(b_s)}, \quad (4.3.1)$$

$$I^{(1)}(A, B) = \sum_{k=1}^{n} \sum_{s=1}^{r} P(b_s \mid a_k) p_k^{(1)} \log \frac{P(b_s \mid a_k)}{P^{(1)}(b_s)} \quad (4.3.2)$$

where $P^{(0)}(b_s)$ means the probability of b_s based on $p_1^{(0)}, \ldots, p_n^{(0)}$ and $P^{(1)}(b_s)$ has a similar significance in terms of $p_1^{(1)}, \ldots, p_n^{(1)}$.

Write $\mathbf{p}^{(0)}$ and $\mathbf{p}^{(1)}$ for the column vectors with components $p_1^{(0)}, \ldots, p_n^{(0)}$ and $p_1^{(1)}, \ldots, p_n^{(1)}$ respectively. Let $0 < \theta < 1$ and define

$$\mathbf{p} = \theta \mathbf{p}^{(0)} + (1 - \theta) \mathbf{p}^{(1)}.$$

Then $p_k = \theta p_k^{(0)} + (1 - \theta) p_k^{(1)} \geq 0$ since both θ and $1 - \theta$ are positive. Also $\sum_{k=1}^{n} p_k = 1$. Hence $\mathbf{p}$ provides another set of possible input probabilities. Its associated mutual information is

$$I(A, B) = \sum_{k=1}^{n} \sum_{s=1}^{r} P(b_s \mid a_k) p_k \log \frac{P(b_s \mid a_k)}{P(b_s)} \quad (4.3.3)$$

where

$$P(b_s) = \sum_{k=1}^{n} P(b_s \mid a_k) p_k$$

Now (4.3.2)–(4.3.3) differ only in their input probabilities and so the mutual information may be regarded as a function of the input probability. Accordingly, write

$$I(A, B) = I(\mathbf{p}), \qquad I^{(0)}(A, B) = I(\mathbf{p}^{(0)}), \qquad I^{(1)}(A, B) = I(\mathbf{p}^{(1)}).$$

THEOREM 4.3a. *The mutual information is a concave function of the input probability, i.e.*

$$\theta I(\mathbf{p}^{(0)}) + (1 - \theta) I(\mathbf{p}^{(1)}) \leq I\{\theta \mathbf{p}^{(0)} + (1 - \theta) \mathbf{p}^{(1)}\}$$

for $0 < \theta < 1$.

Proof. Let x be a random variable which can take only the values of 0 and 1 with probabilities

$$P(x=0)=\theta, \qquad P(x=1)=1-\theta. \qquad (4.3.4)$$

Define

$$P(a_k \mid x=0)=p_k^{(0)}, \qquad P(a_k \mid x=1)=p_k^{(1)}. \qquad (4.3.5)$$

From (4.3.5)

$$P(a_k) = P(a_k \mid x=0)P(x=0)+P(a_k \mid x=1)P(x=1)$$
$$= \theta p_k^{(0)}+(1-\theta)p_k^{(1)}$$

on account of (4.3.4). Thus the definitions imply that $\mathbf{p}$ gives the input probability resulting from the introduction of x.

Consider the three systems: S_1 with events $E_0(x=0)$ and $E_1(x=1)$; S_2 with events a_k, the probability being $\mathbf{p}$ as just demonstrated; S_3 with events b_s based on $\mathbf{p}$. Then

$$I(S_2, S_3) = \sum_{j=1}^{2} \sum_{k=1}^{n} \sum_{s=1}^{r} P(a_k \cap b_s \cap E_j)\log\frac{P(a_k \cap b_s)}{P(a_k)P(b_s)}$$
$$= \sum_{k=1}^{n} \sum_{s=1}^{r} P(a_k \cap b_s)\log\frac{P(a_k \cap b_s)}{P(a_k)P(b_s)}$$
$$= I(A, B)=I(\mathbf{p}) \qquad (4.3.6)$$

from (4.3.3).

Furthermore

$$I(S_2, S_3 \mid S_1) = \sum_{j=1}^{2} \sum_{k=1}^{n} \sum_{s=1}^{r} P(a_k \cap b_s \cap E_j)\log\frac{P(b_s \mid a_k \cap E_j)}{P(b_s \mid E_j)}$$

$$(4.3.7)$$

by virtue of Definition 2.4b. But

$$P(a_k \cap b_s \cap E_0)=P(a_k \cap b_s \mid E_0)P(E_0)$$
$$= \theta P(a_k \cap b_s \mid E_0)$$

by (4.3.4). Also

$$P(a_k \cap b_s \mid E_0)=P(b_s \mid a_k \cap E_0)P(a_k \mid E_0)$$
$$= P(b_s \mid a_k \cap E_0)p_k^{(0)}$$

from (4.3.5). The transition probabilities of the channel are fixed and are therefore totally independent of r, i.e.

$$P(b_s \mid a_k \cap E_j) = P(b_s \mid a_k) \tag{4.3.8}$$

for $j = 1, 2$, $k = 1, \ldots, n$, and $s = 1, \ldots, r$. Hence

$$P(a_k \cap b_s \cap E_0) = \theta P(b_s \mid a_k) p_k^{(0)} \tag{4.3.9}$$

In addition

$$P(b_s \mid E_0) = P^{(0)}(b_s). \tag{4.3.10}$$

Similarly

$$P(a_k \cap b_s \cap E_1) = (1 - \theta) P(b_s \mid a_k) p_k^{(1)}, \qquad P(b_s \mid E_1) = p^{(1)}(b_s). \tag{4.3.11}$$

The substitution of (4.3.8)–(4.3.11) in (4.3.7) gives

$$\begin{aligned}
I(S_2, S_3 \mid S_1) &= \sum_{k=1}^{n} \sum_{s=1}^{r} \left\{ \theta P(b_s \mid a_k) p_k^{(0)} \log \frac{P(b_s \mid a_k)}{P^{(0)}(b_s)} \right. \\
&\qquad \left. + (1 - \theta) P(b_s \mid a_k) p_k^{(1)} \log \frac{P(b_s \mid a_k)}{P^{(1)}(b_s)} \right\} \\
&= \theta I^{(0)}(A, B) + (1 - \theta) I^{(1)}(A, B) \\
&= \theta I(\mathbf{p}^{(0)}) + (1 - \theta) I(\mathbf{p}^{(1)}) \tag{4.3.12}
\end{aligned}$$

from (4.3.1) and (4.3.2).

Multiplication of (4.3.8) by $P(E_j \mid a_k)$ converts it to a form analogous to (2.4.5) so that S_1 and S_3 are statistically independent when conditioned on S_2. As a consequence of Theorem 2.4a, $I(S_1, S_3 \mid S_2) = 0$. Then the Convexity Theorem of Section 2.4 forces

$$I(S_2, S_3 \mid S_1) \leqslant I(S_2, S_3).$$

Insertion of (4.3.12) and (4.3.6) in this inequality leads to that of the theorem and the proof is finished.

Theorem 4.3a is the basis for demonstrating that (4.2.3) and (4.2.5) are necessary and sufficient conditions for the mutual information to be a maximum. Continuing to write $I(\mathbf{p})$ for the mutual information when the input probability is $\mathbf{p}$ we have the following theorem.

THEOREM 4.3b. *I*(**p**) *is a maximum* (*and therefore equal to the channel capacity*) *if, and only if,* **p** *is such that*

(a) $\dfrac{\partial}{\partial p_k} I(\mathbf{p}) = \lambda$ *for every k for which* $p_k \neq 0$,

(b) $\dfrac{\partial}{\partial p_k} I(\mathbf{p}) \leq \lambda$ *for every k for which* $p_k = 0$.

Proof. Suppose firstly that (a) and (b) are satisfied. It is then necessary to show that *I*(**p**) is a maximum, i.e. for any input probability **q**

$$I(\mathbf{q}) \leq I(\mathbf{p}). \tag{4.3.13}$$

With θ satisfying $0 < \theta < 1$ we obtain from Theorem 4.3a

$$\theta I(\mathbf{q}) + (1-\theta)I(\mathbf{p}) \leq I\{\theta\mathbf{q} + (1-\theta)\mathbf{p}\}$$

whence

$$I(\mathbf{q}) - I(\mathbf{p}) \leq [I\{\theta\mathbf{q} + (1-\theta)\mathbf{p}\} - I(\mathbf{p})]/\theta.$$

Proceeding to the limit as $\theta \to 0$ we derive

$$I(\mathbf{q}) - I(\mathbf{p}) \leq \sum_{k=1}^{n} (q_k - p_k) \frac{\partial}{\partial p_k} I(\mathbf{p}).$$

[How the right-hand side arises is elucidated in the Appendix to this chapter (p. 102).] Now, if $p_k \neq 0$, (a) ensures that $\partial I / \partial p_k = \lambda$ whereas, if $p_k = 0$, $q_k - p_k = q_k \geq 0$ and, from (b), $\partial I / \partial p_k \leq \lambda$. Hence

$$I(\mathbf{q}) - I(\mathbf{p}) \leq \lambda \sum_{k=1}^{n} (q_k - p_k) \leq 0$$

and (4.3.13) is confirmed.

Next, it has to be shown that *I*(**p**) being a maximum obliges (a) and (b) to hold. Let **q** be an arbitrary input probability. Then, as has been seen earlier, $\theta\mathbf{q} + (1-\theta)\mathbf{p}$ is also an input probability for $0 < \theta < 1$. Because *I*(**p**) is a maximum

$$I\{\theta\mathbf{q} + (1-\theta)\mathbf{p}\} \leq I(\mathbf{p}).$$

Divide by θ and take the limit as $\theta \to 0$; then

$$\sum_{k=1}^{n} (q_k - p_k) \frac{\partial}{\partial p_k} I(\mathbf{p}) \leq 0. \tag{4.3.14}$$

The fact that $\sum_{k=1}^{n} p_k = 1$ means that at least one p_k is non-zero. Suppose it is p_l. Choose **q**, which is arbitrary, so that

$$q_l = p_l - \varepsilon,$$
$$q_k = p_k \qquad (k \neq l, j), \qquad (4.3.15)$$
$$q_j = p_j + \varepsilon$$

where the only constraint on ε is that $-p_j \leq \varepsilon \leq p_l$ to guarantee that **q** has the properties of a probability. Then (4.3.14) takes the form

$$-\varepsilon \, \partial I/\partial p_l + \varepsilon \, \partial I/\partial p_j \leq 0$$

or

$$\varepsilon \, \partial I/\partial p_j \leq \lambda \varepsilon$$

on putting $\lambda = \partial I/\partial p_l$. Since $p_l > 0$, ε can always be selected to be positive and so

$$\partial I/\partial p_j \leq \lambda. \qquad (4.3.16)$$

If $p_j = 0$, we cannot assert more but (4.3.16) is still sufficient to establish (b).

If $p_j > 0$, ε may also be permitted to assume negative values and then

$$\partial I/\partial p_j \geq \lambda. \qquad (4.3.17)$$

Inequalities (4.3.16) and (4.3.17) can be consistent only if there is equality in both and so (a) is corroborated. The proof of the theorem is complete.

4.4. Solutions of the equations for capacity

Finding the capacity of a specific channel involves solving (4.2.3) for p_k, the unknowns being concealed inside the logarithm in $P(b_s)$. There is no general analytic method that is sure to result in a solution but one that sometimes works will be described.

For a given s look for those α_{jk} which satisfy

$$\sum_{k=1}^{n} \alpha_{jk} P(b_s \mid a_k) = 1 \qquad (j = s)$$
$$= 0 \qquad (j \neq s). \qquad (4.4.1)$$

Multiply (4.2.3) by α_{jk} and sum over k. Then

$$\sum_{k=1}^{n} \sum_{s=1}^{r} \alpha_{jk} P(b_s \mid a_k)\{\log P(b_s \mid a_k) - \log P(b_s)\} = (\lambda + \log e) \sum_{k=1}^{n} \alpha_{jk}$$

which becomes, on account of (4.4.1)

$$-\log P(b_j) = -\alpha_j$$

where

$$\alpha_j = \sum_{k=1}^{n} \sum_{s=1}^{r} \alpha_{jk} P(b_s \mid a_k)\log P(b_s \mid a_k) - (\lambda + \log e) \sum_{k=1}^{n} \alpha_{jk}.$$

Employing logarithms to the base 2 we obtain

$$\sum_{k=1}^{n} P(b_j \mid a_k)p_k = 2^{\alpha_i}.$$

If this be done for each s, there are r linear equations to be solved for the p_k. These equations may or may not possess a solution; suppose that they do. To ensure that this solution complies with $\sum_{k=1}^{n} p_k = 1$ the only unknown quantity in the α_j, namely λ, will have to be allotted a suitable value. The capacity is then known from (4.2.4).

Unfortunately, the method does not assure that the necessary conditions $p_k \geq 0$ are met. Therefore, even when the method does provide answers, they may not form an input probability distribution. For this reason, computational methods founded on the techniques of constrained optimization are generally to be preferred. Only simple cases are likely to be the exception.

One or two points about the behaviour of solutions, however obtained, of (4.2.3) and (4.2.5) are worthy of mention. The possibility that for some s the transition probabilities $P(b_s \mid a_k)$ vanish for $k = 1, \ldots, n$ may be dismissed as pathological because then (4.2.2) would force b_s never to appear and it should be deleted from the output alphabet right from the beginning.

With this understanding suppose that for some t solving (4.2.3) and (4.2.5) entailed $P(b_t) = 0$. Then, for any k for which $P(b_s \mid a_k) \neq 0$ it would be necessary that $p_k = 0$. For such a k (4.2.5) must hold; but the left-hand side is infinite. This contradiction prevents $P(b_t) = 0$, i.e. *for any input which achieves capacity* $P(b_s) \neq 0$ *for* $s = 1, \ldots, r$.

It might be argued against this conclusion that the proof of Theorem 4.3b tacitly assumed that the partial derivatives of I were finite whereas some of them might be infinite at the maximum. Such an argument is erroneous. Since the only terms which survive in a partial derivative are those in which $P(b_s \mid a_k) \neq 0$, $\partial I/\partial p_j$ can become infinite only as $p_j \to 0$. Define $\mathbf{q}$ by (4.3.15) with $p_j = 0$ and let $\mathbf{r}$ have every component zero except the jth which is ε. Then

$$\frac{1}{\varepsilon}\{I(\mathbf{q}) - I(\mathbf{p})\} = \frac{1}{\varepsilon}\{I(\mathbf{q}) - I(\mathbf{p}+\mathbf{r})\} + \frac{1}{\varepsilon}\{I(\mathbf{p}+\mathbf{r}) - I(\mathbf{p})\}.$$

Now assume that $\partial I/\partial p_j \to \infty$ as $p_j \to 0$. The last term on the right-hand side tends to infinity as $\varepsilon \to 0$ whereas the preceding term approaches the finite quantity $-\partial I/\partial p_l$. Hence, for small enough ε, $I(\mathbf{q}) > I(\mathbf{p})$, denying that $I(\mathbf{p})$ is a maximum. Thus our hypothesis is untenable and the partial derivatives of I are finite at its maximum.

4.5. Uniqueness

The answer to Example 4.2a shows that the input probabilities which achieve capacity need not be unique. Indeed, it is easy to construct any number of input probabilities which give the capacity of channel when two different ones are available. Suppose $\mathbf{p}^{(0)}$ and $\mathbf{p}^{(1)}$ are two different input probabilities satisfying (4.2.3) and (4.2.5), i.e. $I(\mathbf{p}^{(0)}) = C$ and $I(\mathbf{p}^{(1)}) = C$. Then, if $0 < \theta < 1$, Theorem 4.3a supplies

$$I\{\theta\mathbf{p}^{(0)} + (1-\theta)\mathbf{p}^{(1)}\} > \theta I(\mathbf{p}^{(0)}) + (1-\theta)I(\mathbf{p}^{(1)}) \geq C.$$

But the left-hand side cannot exceed C which is the maximum of I. Hence

$$I\{\theta\mathbf{p}^{(0)} + (1-\theta)\mathbf{p}^{(1)}\} = C,$$

i.e. $\theta\mathbf{p}^{(0)} + (1-\theta)\mathbf{p}^{(1)}$ is an input probability which results in capacity. The freedom of θ enables many input probabilities to be prepared.

The widespread lack of uniqueness which may exist for the input is in direct contrast to the situation for the output, which is dealt with in the following theorem.

THEOREM 4.5a. *The output probabilities which correspond to the capacity of the channel are unique.*

Proof. The theorem is trivial if the input is unique so suppose there are two different input probabilities $\mathbf{p}^{(0)}$ and $\mathbf{p}^{(1)}$ which achieve capacity. By what has been shown above

$$\theta I(\mathbf{p}^{(0)}) + (1-\theta)I(\mathbf{p}^{(1)}) - I\{\theta\mathbf{p}^{(0)} + (1-\theta)\mathbf{p}^{(1)}\} = 0.$$

Hence

$$\sum_{k=1}^{n} \sum_{s=1}^{r} P(b_s \mid a_k)\left[\theta p_k^{(0)} \log \frac{P(b_s \mid a_k)}{P^{(0)}(b_s)} + (1-\theta)p_k^{(1)} \log \frac{P(b_s \mid a_k)}{P^{(1)}(b_s)}\right.$$
$$\left. -\{\theta p_k^{(0)} + (1-\theta)p_k^{(1)}\}\log \frac{P(b_s \mid a_k)}{\theta P^{(0)}(b_s) + (1-\theta)P^{(1)}(b_s)}\right] = 0$$

or

$$\sum_{k=1}^{n} \sum_{s=1}^{r} P(b_s \mid a_k)\left[\theta p_k^{(0)} \log \frac{\theta P^{(0)}(b_s) + (1-\theta)P^{(1)}(b_s)}{P^{(0)}(b_s)}\right.$$
$$\left. + (1-\theta)p_k^{(1)} \log \frac{\theta P^{(0)}(b_s) + (1-\theta)P^{(1)}(b_s)}{P^{(1)}(b_s)}\right] = 0$$

whence

$$\sum_{s=1}^{r} \left[\theta P^{(0)}(b_s)\log \frac{\theta P^{(0)}(b_s) + (1-\theta)P^{(1)}(b_s)}{P^{(0)}(b_s)}\right.$$
$$\left. + (1-\theta)P^{(1)}(b_s)\log \frac{\theta P^{(0)}(b_s) + (1-\theta)P^{(1)}(b_s)}{P^{(1)}(b_s)}\right] = 0 \quad (4.5.1)$$

from (4.2.2).

Imagine that, for some s, $\theta P^{(0)}(b_s) + (1-\theta)P^{(1)}(b_s) \neq P^{(0)}(b_s)$. Then, by Theorem 2.2a, the left-hand side of (4.5.1) is less than

$$\log e \sum_{s=1}^{r} \theta(1-\theta)\{P^{(1)}(b_s) - P^{(0)}(b_s)\} + \theta(1-\theta)\{P^{(0)}(b_s) - P^{(1)}(b_s)\}$$

which is zero. This contravention of (4.5.1) means that the hypothesis is wrong. Accordingly

$$\theta P^{(0)}(b_s) + (1-\theta)P^{(1)}(b_s) = P^{(0)}(b_s)$$

for $s = 1, \ldots, r$. Hence $P^{(0)}(b_s) = P^{(1)}(b_s)$ and the theorem is proved.

The imposition of a mild restriction on the input is sufficient to remove some of the non-uniqueness there. It asks that the number of zero probabilities should be made as large as possible. The actual theorem is as follows.

THEOREM 4.5b. *In an input which achieves capacity with the largest number of zero probabilities, the non-zero probabilities are determined uniquely and their number does not exceed the number of output letters.*

Example 4.2c conforms to this theorem.

Proof. Let K be the smallest number of non-zero probabilities which can occur in inputs which achieve capacity. Let $\mathbf{p}$ be an input probability which attains capacity and has only K non-zero probabilities. Relabel the letters so that $p_k > 0$ $(1 \leq k \leq K)$ and $p_k = 0$ $(k > K)$. Then

$$P(b_s) = \sum_{k=1}^{K} P(b_s \mid a_k) p_k \qquad (s = 1, \ldots, r). \qquad (4.5.2)$$

Let $\mathbf{p}^{(1)}$ be another input in the same category as $\mathbf{p}$ and with the same letters. Then

$$P(b_s) = \sum_{k=1}^{K} P(b_s \mid a_k) p_k^{(1)} \qquad (s = 1, \ldots, r) \qquad (4.5.3)$$

the left-hand sides of (4.5.2) and (4.5.3) being identical because $P(b_s)$ is fixed uniquely at capacity. By subtraction of (4.5.2) and (4.5.3)

$$\sum_{k=1}^{K} P(b_s \mid a_k)(p_k - p_k^{(1)}) = 0 \qquad (s = 1, \ldots, r). \qquad (4.5.4)$$

Now consider $\mathbf{p} + \theta(\mathbf{p} - \mathbf{p}^{(1)})$. When $\theta = 0$ each component is positive. Increase θ until one at least of the components becomes zero; this is always possible if $\mathbf{p} \neq \mathbf{p}^{(1)}$ because one at least of $p_k - p_k^{(1)}$ must be negative to satisfy (4.5.4). Let $\theta = \theta_0$ be the value of θ when a component first vanishes. Every component of $\mathbf{p} + \theta_0(\mathbf{p} - \mathbf{p}^{(1)})$ is non-negative, $\sum_{k=1}^{K} \{p_k + \theta(p_k - p_k^{(1)})\} = 1$ and

$$\sum_{k=1}^{K} P(b_s \mid a_k)\{p_k + \theta(p_k - p_k^{(1)})\} = P(b_s)$$

because of (4.5.2) and (4.5.4). Thus $\mathbf{p} + \theta_0(\mathbf{p} - \mathbf{p}^{(1)})$ is an input probability which gives capacity and yet has at most $K - 1$ non-zero probabilities. This contradicts the definition of K and so we are forced to conclude that $\mathbf{p} = \mathbf{p}^{(1)}$, i.e. $\mathbf{p}$ is unique.

This also means that the solution of the r equations (4.5.4) can only be the trivial one. Such a statement would not be true if the number of unknowns K were greater than the number of equations r. Hence $K \leq r$, i.e. the number of non-zero probabilities is not higher than the number of output letters. The proof is finished.

Notice that the theorem does not assert that there is only one input with K non-zero probabilities. Indeed, two inputs of this type are feasible provided that one or more of the letters with zero probability are different in the two inputs. An illustration of how this can arise can be seen in the following considerations. Once an input giving capacity is known the $P(b_s)$ are determinate and will not be altered if the input is changed to another capacity input. In other words $\partial I / \partial p_k$ will not vary with the input at capacity. Some may be less than C and for these the corresponding p_k must always be zero. The remaining $\partial I / \partial p_k$ will be equal to C and the associated p_k may or may not be zero. For any given capacity input we can always try to increase the number of zero probabilities by solving the analogue of (4.5.4) and using the device immediately thereafter. However, if for some $j \neq k$, $P(b_s \mid a_k) = P(b_s \mid a_j)$ for $s = 1, \ldots, r$ only the sum $p_j + p_k$ occurs in equations of the form (4.5.2). Therefore, if in an input with the maximum number of zero probabilities $p_j > 0$ and $p_k = 0$ the exchange of p_j and p_k will provide a different capacity input with a like attribute. This counter-example prevents the assertion of a unique input with K non-zero probabilities in general.

4.6. Transmission properties

The purpose of a channel is to transmit the signals from the coder. The discussion of coding indicates that the typical situation will involve sequences of m symbols. So the behaviour of such sequences in the channel will now be examined, under the assumption that m is large.

The derivation of the Source Coding Theorem in Section 3.2 makes clear that the number of possible sequences which are available at the output is $2^{mH(B)}$ with high probability. An input sequence will generally be contaminated by noise in transmission; it may therefore generate any one of $2^{mH(B|A)}$ high probability signals at the output. Since the number of high probability input sequences is $2^{mH(A)}$ the total number of output sequences which can be produced may be as many as $2^{m\{H(A)+H(B|A)\}}$. The output can cope with this variety provided that $H(A)+H(B\mid A)\leqslant H(B)$. By (2.3.9), $H(B)-H(B\mid A)$ is the mutual information and so is bounded by the capacity C of the channel. Therefore it should be possible to eliminate errors in transmission if $H(A)\leqslant C$.

The organization of the coding, i.e. the channel input so as to keep errors to a minimum is not so much a matter of explicit construction as of being convinced of its existence. Let A_0 be an input or code which achieves capacity. Associate each of the $2^{mH(A)}$ high probability inputs when $H(A)<C$ with a different one of the $2^{mH(A_0)}$ inputs, the selection being carried out at random. Since $H(A)<C=H(A_0)-H(A_0\mid B)$ and $H(A_0\mid B)\geqslant 0$ there will be some of the A_0 inputs spare. In fact, the probability that an A_0 input is not an A signal is $1-2^{mH(A)}/2^{mH(A_0)}$. The coding is arranged so that when a sequence of A is generated its correspondent in A_0 is dispatched over the channel. Now, when a particular A signal is sent the actual output observed might have come from any one of $2^{mH(A_0|B)}A_0$-inputs. So long as only one of these inputs stems from an A signal the message will be correctly identified. The probability of this, in view of the largeness of m, is effectively the probability that none of the inputs is an A signal, i.e.

$$[1-2^{m\{H(A)-H(A_0)\}}]^{\mu}$$

where $\mu = 2^{mH(A_0|B)}$. If $H(A)=C-\eta$ where $\eta >0$

$$H(A)-H(A_0)=-H(A_0\mid B)-\eta.$$

Thus, as $m\to\infty$, the probability of correct identification

$$\sim 1-2^{-m\eta}\to 1$$

and the probability of error is negligibly small.

The quantity $H(A\mid B)$ is a measure of the uncertainty as to what was sent when observations are made on the output and so assesses the effect of noise during transmission; it may be called the *equivocation*. For coding in which the probability of correct identification is practically unity, the equivocation is small, signifying virtually noiseless conditions. In particular, if $H(A)=C$, the facts that $I(A,B)=H(A)-H(A\mid B)$ and C is the maximum of I force the equivocation to be zero and noiseless transmission is possible.

These points may be summarized as the following theorem.

SHANNON'S THEOREM I. *If $H(A) \leqslant C$, there is a code such that transmission over the channel is possible with an arbitrarily small number of errors, i.e. the equivocation is arbitrarily small.*

In contrast, if $H(A) = C + \eta$, then we must have $H(A \mid B) \geqslant \eta$ so that there is a lower bound beyond which the equivocation cannot be reduced whatever the coding. However, there is no necessity to do much worse. Split the source into two parts A_1 and A_2 with $H(A_1) = C$ and $H(A_2) = \eta$ and agree not to transmit any of the information from A_2. By Shannon's Theorem I the equivocation for A_1 can be made arbitrarily small and the absence of signals from A_2 cannot cause an uncertainty of more than $H(A_2)$ or $H(A) - C$. Thus we have the following.

SHANNON'S THEOREM II. *If $H(A) > C$ there is no code for which the equivocation is less than $H(A) - C$ but there is one for which the equivocation is less than $H(A) - C + \varepsilon$ where ε is an arbitrary positive quantity.*

The arguments leading to Shannon's Theorems are not, perhaps, strictly rigorous but they are plausible and persuasive. We shall accept the theorems without any attempt to set forth either the stricter proofs which are available or the estimates which show that, as $m \to \infty$, the probability of error in transmission is exponentially small in many important cases.

The drawbacks of Shannon's theorems should be mentioned. The theorems rely on $m \to \infty$, i.e. long symbol sequences must be encoded and they have to be received in their entirety before interpretation can be undertaken. To put it another way, error-free transmission is accomplished at the expense of long time delays. Each received message carries more information because it has a high level of correctness but, since the capacity sets a maximum to the rate of transmission, fewer messages can be handled per unit time. The trade-off between reliability and excessive time delay will form a substantial element in the judgement as to whether a particular system of operation is likely to be of value in practice.

Ways of structuring the coding to cut down the noise errors can be portrayed a little more explicitly than explained above. One method is to add symbols whose sole purpose is to confirm the accuracy or otherwise of the symbols in the original message. We shall have more say about this technique in Chapter 5. Another device, which is not unrelated to the first, is to have more letters present than are really necessary, i.e. *redundancy* is introduced. The English language is an example of this technique. Maybe as many as half the letters in a lengthy piece of English could be in error and still the original could be reconstructed from the context. In contrast, mathematical formulae have little or no redundancy because slight changes can alter the sense completely so that the original is irrecoverable without independent investigation.

4.7. Channels in cascade

One channel may be connected to another so that the output of the first becomes the input of the second. For example, the letters b_s would be both the output of Channel 1 and the input of Channel 2 in Fig. 4.7.1.

To deal with such circumstances let **a** be an n-vector with components $a_1, \ldots, a_n$ and **b** be an r-vector with components $b_1, \ldots, b_r$. Then the relations

$$P(b_s) = \sum_{k=1}^{n} P(b_s \mid a_k) P(a_k) \qquad (s = 1, \ldots, n)$$

can be combined into the matrix equation

$$P(\mathbf{b}) = P(\mathbf{b} \mid \mathbf{a}) P(\mathbf{a}) \qquad (4.7.1)$$

where $P(\mathbf{b} \mid \mathbf{a})$ is a $r \times n$ matrix whose sk element is $P(b_s \mid a_k)$.

Similarly, if the alphabet at C has l elements,

$$P(\mathbf{c}) = P(\mathbf{c} \mid \mathbf{b}) P(\mathbf{b}) \qquad (4.7.2)$$

where **c** is an l-vector and $P(\mathbf{c} \mid \mathbf{b})$ a $l \times r$ matrix.

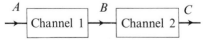

FIG. 4.7.1. Channels in cascade.

From (4.7.1) and (4.7.2)

$$P(\mathbf{c}) = P(\mathbf{c} \mid \mathbf{b})P(\mathbf{b} \mid \mathbf{a})P(\mathbf{a}). \qquad (4.7.3)$$

Thus the overall capacity from the input A to the output is determined by the transition probabilities which are elements of the product matrix $P(\mathbf{c} \mid \mathbf{b})P(\mathbf{b} \mid \mathbf{a})$. As such the problem becomes one for a single channel and therefore within the scope of the earlier theory of this chapter. Nothing further requires to be said about a few channels in cascade but when there are many there are some properties worthy of attention as will be seen in the next section.

*4.8. The infinite cascade

In communication over a great distance it is sometimes necessary in the effort to secure fidelity of transmission to have a fair number of channels connected in cascade by repeater stations. The purpose of the repeater station is to create a faithful replica of the output of one channel at an amplified level so as to mitigate the effects of noise in the next channel. As a simple model of this situation take M channels in cascade, each with the same transition probabilities and the same alphabet being used for both input and output. Write p_{sk} for the transition probability that the input letter a_k becomes the output letter a_s after one channel. With n letters in the common alphabet (4.2.1) becomes

$$\sum_{j=1}^{n} p_{jk} = 1. \qquad (k = 1, \ldots, n). \qquad (4.8.1)$$

Let $p_{jk}^{(m)}$ be the probability that a_k appears as a_j after m channels, so that $p_{jk}^{(1)} = p_{jk}$. From the analogue of (4.7.3)

$$p_{jk}^{(2)} = \sum_{i=1}^{n} p_{ji}p_{ik}$$

and, in general,

$$p_{jk}^{(m)} = \sum_{i=1}^{n} p_{ji}p_{ik}^{(m-1)}$$

which leads easily to

$$p_{jk}^{(m+r)} = \sum_{i=1}^{n} p_{ji}^{(m)}p_{ik}^{(r)}, \qquad (4.8.2)$$

as may be verified by induction. It follows from (4.8.1) that $\sum_{j=1}^{n} p_{jk}^{(?)} = 1$ and then induction gives

$$\sum_{j=1}^{n} p_{jk}^{(m)} = 1 \qquad (k = 1, \dots, n). \qquad (4.8.3)$$

If p_j is the probability that a_j appears at the input of the first channel, the probability that a_k appears at the output of the Mth channel is

$$p_k^{(M)} = \sum_{j=1}^{n} p_{kj}^{(M)} p_j. \qquad (4.8.4)$$

The question to which we address ourselves is whether the probability distribution of (4.8.4) is likely to bear some resemblance to the input or deviates widely from the input. In the former case messages may be expected to be transmitted with a fair degree of fidelity; in the latter case the input signal will be almost irrelevant to the output of the final channel. To allow for a large number of channels the behaviour as $M \to \infty$ will be considered.

Let $f_i^{(m)}$ be the probability that a_i appears as the input to the first channel and does not reappear until the output of the mth channel. Then

$$f_j^{(1)} = p_{jj}^{(1)} = p_{jj}.$$

The probability that a_j misses the output of the first channel, but not the second, is $p_{jj}^{(2)}$ minus the probability that a_j appears at the outputs of both the first and second channels, i.e.

$$f_j^{(2)} = p_{jj}^{(2)} - f_j^{(1)} p_{jj}.$$

For $f_j^{(3)}$ we must exclude a first reappearance after the first channel followed by a subsequent appearance after the third and a first reappearance after the second channel followed by an appearance after the third. These events are mutually exclusive and so

$$f_j^{(3)} = p_{jj}^{(3)} - f_j^{(1)} p_{jj}^{(2)} - f_j^{(2)} p_{jj}.$$

Clearly

$$f_j^{(m)} = p_j^{(m)} - \sum_{r=1}^{m-1} f_j^{(m-r)} p_{jj}^{(r)}. \qquad (4.8.5)$$

The sum

$$f_j = \sum_{m=1}^{\infty} f_j^{(m)} \qquad (4.8.6)$$

is the probability that, given a_j at the first input, a_j ever reappears at the output of any channel.

DEFINITION 4.8a. *The letter a_i is said to be transient if $f_i < 1$ and persistent if $f_i = 1$.*

The distinction between these possibilities is brought out by observing that f_j^r is the probability that a_j reappears at least r times. As $r \to \infty$, this tends to zero for a transient letter but not for a persistent. Thus we can assert *with probability one: a persistent letter appears infinitely often whereas a transient letter occurs only a finite number of times.* Thus transient letters tend to get lost in transmission whereas persistent ones survive.

The probability $f_{ij}^{(m)}$ that a_i appears after m channels when the input to the first was a_j satisfies a relation which can be derived in the same way as (4.8.5) and is

$$f_{ij}^{(m)} = p_{ij}^{(m)} - \sum_{r=1}^{m-1} f_{ij}^{(m-r)} p_{ii}^{(r)}. \qquad (4.8.7)$$

Then

$$f_{ij} = \sum_{m=1}^{\infty} f_{ij}^{(m)} \qquad (4.8.8)$$

is the probability that a_i ever appears after the first input was a_j.

It is desirable to have some criterion for deciding between transient and persistent letters in terms of the transition probabilities. One is given in the following theorem.

THEOREM 4.8a. *The letter a_j is transient if, and only if, $\sum_{m=1}^{\infty} p_{jj}^{(m)} < \infty$ and the probability that a_j ever reappears is*

$$1 - 1 \Big/ \sum_{m=1}^{\infty} p_{jj}^{(m)}.$$

Necessarily, $\sum_{m=1}^{\infty} p_{ji}^{(m)} < \infty$ for each i.
Proof. Let s be a real number and define

$$F(s) = \sum_{m=1}^{\infty} f_j^{(m)} s^m, \qquad Q(s) = \sum_{m=0}^{\infty} p_{jj}^{(m)} s^m$$

where $p_{jj}^{(0)}$ is understood to be unity. Since $f_j^{(m)}$ and $p_{jj}^{(m)}$ are both bounded, the series in $F(s)$ and $Q(s)$ certainly converge for $|s| < 1$. Also

$$F(s)Q(s) = \sum_{m=1}^{\infty} s^m \{f_j^{(m)} + f_j^{(m-1)}p_{jj}^{(1)} + \cdots + f_j^{(1)}p_{jj}^{(m-1)}\}$$

$$= Q(s) - 1 \qquad (4.8.9)$$

from (4.8.5).

Since $F(s) \to f_j$ as $s \to 1$, (4.8.9) implies that $Q(s) \to (1 - f_j)^{-1}$ when a_j is transient. Since $\sum_{m=1}^{M} p_{jj}^{(m)} \leqslant \lim_{s \to 1} Q(s)$, the 'only if' part of the theorem follows. Conversely,

$$\lim_{s \to 1} Q(s) \leqslant \sum_{m=0}^{\infty} p_{jj}^{(m)}$$

shows $Q(1)$ must be finite when the sum is and so $F(1) < 1$, i.e. the letter is transient.

The last part of the theorem follows from (4.8.7). In fact

$$\sum_{m=0}^{\infty} p_{ji}^{(m)} = f_{ji}(1 - f_j)^{-1};$$

the proof is complete.

The discussion of persistent letters is made awkward by the possibility of periodicity, i.e. a letter being prevented from appearing except after a number of channels. To be precise we introduce the following definition.

DEFINITION 4.8b. *A letter is said to have period* $t(>1)$ *if, after an appearance, it cannot reappear except, perhaps, after* $t, 2t, 3t, \ldots$ *channels, i.e.* $p_{jj}^{(m)} = 0$ *whenever* m *is not divisible by* t *and* t *is the smallest integer with this property.*

We can now state the following theorem.

THEOREM 4.8b. *A letter is persistent if, and only if,* $\sum_{m=1}^{\infty} p_{jj}^{(m)}$ *is divergent. If it is aperiodic then, as* $m \to \infty$,

$$p_{ji}^{(m)} \to f_{ji}/\mu_j, \qquad p_{jj}^{(m)} \to 1/\mu_j$$

where $\mu_j = \sum_{m=1}^{\infty} m f_j^{(m)}$. *If it is periodic*

$$p_{jj}^{(mt)} \to t/\mu_j.$$

In this theorem it is permitted that μ_j be infinite.

Proof. The first statement of the theorem is an immediate consequence of Theorem 4.8a. The remainder of the theorem will be
demonstrated in a plausible fashion since a completely rigorous
argument is lengthy.

When a_j is aperiodic, $F(s) = 1 + (s-1)F'(1) = 1 + (s-1)\mu_j$ when
s is near 1. Hence, from (4.8.9),

$$Q(s) \approx 1/(1-s)\mu_j \approx (1 + s + s^2 + \cdots)/\mu_j$$

and equating powers on the two sides we deduce $p_{jj}^{(m)} \sim 1/\mu_j$. A
similar approach to (4.8.7) gives the corresponding result for $p_{ij}^{(m)}$.

When a_j is periodic, $F(s)$ contains only powers of s^t. Put $u = s^t$
and $F_1(u) = F(u^{1/t})$; then $F_1(u)$ is a power series all of whose
coefficients are positive and $F_1(1) = 1$. By what has gone before
the coefficients in $\{1 - F_1(u)\}^{-1}$ approach $1/F_1'(1)$ and

$$F_1'(1) = \frac{1}{t} F'(1) = \mu_j/t,$$

i.e. $p_{jj}^{(mt)} \to t/\mu_j$.

Let a_j be a persistent letter which, after a number of channels,
becomes a_k. Let μ be the smallest number of channels in which a_j
can be converted to a_k; then $p_{kj}^{(\mu)} > 0$. If $p_{kj}^{(\mu)} = \alpha$ and the probability of a_j not appearing after a_k is zero, the probability that a_j
never reappears is at least α. Thus $f_j \leqslant 1 - \alpha < 1$ which, on account of Definition 4.8a, contradicts a_j being persistent. Therefore there is positive probability that a_j appears after a_k and so
there is a ν such that $p_{jk}^{(\nu)} > 0$; put $p_{jk}^{(\nu)} = \beta$. From (4.8.2)

$$p_{jj}^{(m+\mu+\nu)} \geqslant p_{jk}^{(\nu)} p_{kk}^{(m)} p_{kj}^{(\mu)} \geqslant \alpha\beta p_{kk}^{(m)}, \qquad (4.8.10)$$

$$p_{kk}^{(m+\mu+\nu)} \geqslant p_{kj}^{(\mu)} p_{jj}^{(m)} p_{jk}^{(\nu)} \geqslant \alpha\beta p_{jj}^{(m)}. \qquad (4.8.11)$$

Since $\sum_m p_{jj}^{(m)}$ is divergent, (4.8.11) implies that $\sum p_{kk}^{(m)}$ is and so,
from Theorem 4.8b, a_k is persistent. If $\mu_j = \infty$, $p_{jj}^{(m)} \to 0$ according
to Theorem 4.8b and then, from (4.8.10), $p_{kk}^{(m)} \to 0$ and a further
application of Theorem 4.8b gives $\mu_k = \infty$. If a_j has period t, $\mu + \nu$
must be an integral multiple of t; then (4.8.10) and (4.8.11) force
a_k to have period t. Thus we have demonstrated the following
theorem.

THEOREM 4.8c. *Once a persistent letter has appeared only persistent
letters can appear in later channels. Either all have μ_k infinite or all*

have μ_k finite. *If one letter which appears is periodic so are all the rest and with the same period.*

While this theorem prevents a transient letter appearing after a persistent one it is still possible for a transient one to be followed by a persistent one. However, we have the following theorem.

THEOREM 4.8d. *Not all the letters can be transient. If a_j is persistent then $\mu_j < \infty$.*

Proof. If a_j is transient, $p_{ji}^{(m)} \to 0$ for each i as a consequence of Theorem 4.8a. If this be true for $j = 1, \ldots, n$ then $\sum_{j=1}^{n} p_{ji}^{(m)} \to 0$ for $i = 1, \ldots, n$. But this violates (4.8.3) and so not all letters can be transient.

If a_j is persistent and $\mu_j = \infty$, then $p_{jj}^{(m)} \to 0$ for each i by Theorem 4.8b. For any a_k which can appear after a_j, $p_{kj}^{(m)} \to 0$ by Theorem 4.8c. For any a_k which cannot appear after a_j, $p_{kj}^{(m)} = 0$ and so, again, there is failure to meet (4.8.3). The proof is terminated.

On an infinite cascade the transient letters tend to be removed and the message becomes garbled unless the transient letters are few in number. It therefore pays to have as many persistent letters as possible. Unfortunately, the characterization of Theorem 4.8b is not an easy one to apply in practice so that an alternative criterion is desirable. In deriving it, the possibility of periodic letters will be ignored since one would wish to avoid periodicity in communication links, generally speaking.

Let a_j be persistent and let S be the set of letters (including a_j) which can appear subsequently. It is evident from Theorem 4.8c that any letter of S can be followed by any other letter of S but there is no escape from S once it has been entered. Any alphabet consisting entirely of persistent letters can be split into sets of the type S each of which is incommunicado with the others. It is therefore sufficient to obtain a criterion for a set of type S. An alphabet of the type S is called *irreducible*.

THEOREM 4.8e. *In an irreducible alphabet of aperiodic letters μ_j is the unique solution of*

$$1/\mu_j = \sum_{i=1}^{n} p_{ji}/\mu_i \qquad (j = 1, \ldots, n)$$

such that $\sum_{j=1}^{n} 1/\mu_j = 1$.

Proof. Irreducibility means that a_k must appear eventually after a_j and therefore $f_{kj} = 1$. Hence Theorem 4.8b asserts that $p_{kj}^{(m)} \to 1/\mu_k$ as $m \to \infty$ and $\mu_k < \infty$ by Theorem 4.8d. Substituting this result in (4.8.3) as $m \to \infty$ we obtain $\sum_{j=1}^{n} 1/\mu_j = 1$.

Put $m = 1$ in (4.8.2) and let $r \to \infty$. Then

$$1/\mu_j = \sum_{i=1}^{n} p_{ji}/\mu_i.$$

To confirm uniqueness let u_j be any solution of

$$u_j = \sum_{i=1}^{n} p_{ji} u_i \qquad (j = 1, \ldots, n)$$

such that $\sum_{j=1}^{n} u_j = 1$. Then

$$u_k = \sum_{j=1}^{n} p_{kj} u_j = \sum_{i=1}^{n} p_{ki}^{(2)} u_i$$

and, in general,

$$u_j = \sum_{i=1}^{n} p_{ji}^{(m)} u_i. \tag{4.8.12}$$

Letting $m \to \infty$ we have

$$u_j = \sum_{i=1}^{n} u_i/\mu_j = 1/\mu_j$$

and the proof is complete.

For an irreducible alphabet it is therefore only necessary to check that the equations of Theorem 4.8e have a non-trivial solution. Then transient letters can be excluded because they would require $p_{ji}^{(m)} \to 0$ which entails the trivial solution of (4.8.12).

The general alphabet can be split into irreducible sets and each set tested by Theorem 4.8e.

Note also that if $p_j = 1/\mu_j$ for an irreducible alphabet then $p_k^{(M)} = p_k$ from (4.8.4). In other words, the probability distribution does not alter as we move along the channels. So, from the point of view of fidelity, this represents an ideal to aim for.

The final question to be settled is whether only transient letters can appear. Let a_i be a transient letter and let $x_i^{(m)}$ be the probability that after m channels, and not before, a letter from S appears. (The existence of S is guaranteed by Theorem 4.8d.)

Then

$$x_i^{(1)} = \sum_S p_{ki}$$

the summation being over those k for which a_k is in S. If S is reached at the $(m+1)$th channel, then earlier letters must have been transient and

$$x_i^{(m+1)} = \sum_T p_{ti} x_t^{(m)} \tag{4.8.13}$$

summed over those t for which a_t is transient.

The probability x_i that a letter from S ultimately appears is given by $x_i = \sum_{m=1}^\infty x_i^{(m)}$. Hence, from (4.8.13),

$$x_i - \sum_T p_{ti} x_t = x_i^{(1)} \tag{4.8.14}$$

which constitutes a set of linear equations to determine x_i.

Let $y_i^{(m)}$ be the probability that a transient letter appears after m channels starting from a_i. Then

$$y_i^{(1)} = \sum_T p_{ti}, \qquad y_i^{(m+1)} = \sum_T p_{ti} y_t^{(m)}.$$

Thus $y_i^{(m+1)} \leqslant y_i^{(m)}$ and $y_i^{(1)} \leqslant 1$. Therefore $y_i = \lim_{m \to \infty} y_i^{(m)}$ exists and

$$y_i = \sum_T p_{ti} y_t.$$

There is no loss of generality in assuming $y_1 = y_2 = \cdots = y_r = M > y_{r+1} \geqslant y_{r+2} \cdots$ Then for $i \leqslant r$,

$$M = \sum_{t=1}^r p_{ti} M + \sum_{t=r+1} p_{ti} y_t$$

and this is possible only if $p_{ti} = 0$ for $t > r$. But this contravenes Theorem 4.8d and therefore $M = 0$. This also shows that the solution of (4.8.14) is unique and hence we have the following theorem.

THEOREM 4.8f. *The probability of only transient letters ever appearing is zero. The probability x_i of going from the transient letter a_i to S is the unique solution of* (4.8.14).

4.9. Channels in parallel

A user may have available more than one channel for transmission purposes. For instance, in Fig. 4.9.1, he might decide to send a number of letters from $A^{(1)}$ along Channel 1 and then several from $A^{(2)}$ along Channel 2 or he may elect to toss a coin at each letter to determine the channel to be used. By assigning a probability distribution to the selection of channels the problem can be treated as one of a single channel.

Let the letter of $A^{(1)}$ and $B^{(1)}$ be $a_1^{(1)}, \ldots, a_n^{(1)}$ and $b_1^{(1)}, \ldots, b_r^{(1)}$ respectively. Let those of $A^{(2)}$ and $B^{(2)}$ be $a_1^{(2)}, \ldots, a_N^{(1)}$ and $b_1^{(2)}, \ldots, b_R^{(2)}$ respectively. When Channel 1 has been selected let $p_k^{(1)}$ be the probability that $a_k^{(1)}$ is chosen and let $p_k^{(2)}$ be the probability of $a_k^{(2)}$ when Channel 2 has been picked. Let p_i be the probability of choosing Channel i. Then $P(a_k^{(1)}) = p_k^{(1)}p_1$ and $P(a_k^{(2)}) = p_k^{(2)}p_2$.

The mutual information of the parallel channels in combination is

$$\sum_{k=1}^{n} \sum_{s=1}^{r} P(b_s^{(1)} \mid a_k^{(1)}) p_k^{(1)} p_1 \log \frac{P(b_s^{(1)} \mid a_k^{(1)})}{p_1 P(b_s^{(1)})}$$

$$+ \sum_{k=1}^{N} \sum_{s=1}^{R} P(b_s^{(2)} \mid a_k^{(2)}) p_k^{(2)} p_2 \log \frac{P(b_s^{(2)} \mid a_k^{(2)})}{p_2 P(b_s^{(2)})}$$

where $P(b_s^{(1)}) = \sum_{k=1}^{n} P(b_s^{(1)} \mid a_k^{(1)}) p_k^{(1)}$ and likewise for $P(b_s^{(2)})$; that is, $P(b_s^{(1)})$ is the probability of $b_s^{(1)}$ occurring given that Channel 1 is in use. To find the capacity of the combination the mutual information has to be maximized for all possible $p_k^{(1)}$, all possible $p_k^{(2)}$ and all possible p_i subject to

$$\sum_{k=1}^{n} p_k^{(1)} = 1, \qquad \sum_{k=1}^{N} p_k^{(2)} = 1, \qquad p_1 + p_2 = 1.$$

Therefore, subtract from the mutual information $\lambda_1 \sum_{k=1}^{n} p_k^{(1)} +$

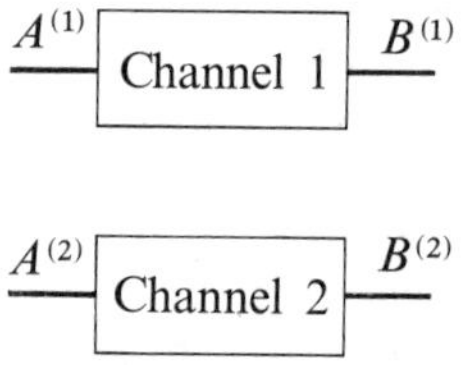

FIG. 4.9.1. Channels in parallel.

$\lambda_2 \sum_{k=1}^{N} p_k^{(2)} + \mu(p_1 + p_2)$ where λ_1, λ_2, and μ are Lagrange multipliers.

For variations in $p_k^{(1)}$ we obtain, analogous to (4.2.3),

$$\sum_{s=1}^{r} P(b_s^{(1)} \mid a_k^{(1)}) p_1 \log \frac{P(b_s^{(1)} \mid a_k^{(1)})}{p_1 P(b_s^{(1)})} - p_1 \log e = \lambda_1$$

for $k = 1, \ldots, n$. If $p_k^{(1)} = 0$ the $=$ sign is replaced by $\leqslant$ as in (4.2.5). Thus

$$\sum_{s=1}^{r} P(b_s^{(1)} \mid a_k^{(1)}) \log \frac{P(b_s^{(1)} \mid a_k^{(1)})}{P(b_s^{(1)})} = \log e + (\lambda_1 + p_1 \log p_1)/p_1.$$

$$(4.9.1)$$

But these are the same equations as would be derived for Channel 1 in isolation from (4.2.3) and (4.2.5) with λ replaced by $(\lambda_1 + p_1 \log p_1)/p_1$. Hence, from (4.2.4),

$$C_1 = \log e + \log p_1 + \lambda_1/p_1 \qquad (4.9.2)$$

where C_1 is the capacity Channel 1 alone.

Similarly, variations in $p_k^{(2)}$ supply

$$C_2 = \log e + \log p_2 + \lambda_2/p_2. \qquad (4.9.3)$$

Finally, a derivative with respect to p_1 gives

$$\sum_{k=1}^{n} \sum_{s=1}^{r} P(b_s^{(1)} \mid a_k^{(1)}) p_k^{(1)} \log \frac{P(b_s^{(1)} \mid a_k^{(1)})}{p_1 P(b_s^{(1)})} - \log e = \mu \quad (4.9.4)$$

or

$$C_1 - \log p_1 - \log e = \mu \qquad (4.9.5)$$

from (4.9.1) and (4.9.2). Note that $p_1 = 0$ does not need to be considered because that would correspond to Channel 1 never being operated and, in any case, would not allow C_1 to be finite on account of (4.9.2). Similarly,

$$C_2 - \log p_2 - \log e = \mu. \qquad (4.9.6)$$

Multiply (4.9.4) by p_1 and the corresponding equation with affix 2 by p_2 and add. The series amalgamate as the mutual information and so the capacity C of the combined channel is given by

$$C = \log e + \mu. \qquad (4.9.7)$$

Substitute (4.9.7) in (4.9.5) and (4.9.6); then

$$\log p_1 = C_1 - C, \qquad \log p_2 = C_2 - C.$$

But $p_1 + p_2 = 1$ and so

$$2^C = 2^{C_1} + 2^{C_2} \qquad (4.9.8)$$

with logarithms to the base 2.

The formula (4.9.8) gives the rule for finding the capacity of channels in parallel.

Appendix

$I(\mathbf{p})$ is a shorthand notation for a function of n variables, namely $I(p_1, p_2, \ldots, p_n)$. Hence

$$
\begin{aligned}
I(\mathbf{p} + \theta\mathbf{r}) - I(\mathbf{p}) &= I(p_1 + \theta r_1, p_2 + \theta r_2, \ldots, p_n + \theta r_n) \\
&\quad - I(p_1, p_2, \ldots, p_n) \\
&= I(p_1 + \theta r_1, p_2 + \theta r_2, \ldots, p_n + \theta r_n) \\
&\quad - I(p_1, p_2 + \theta r_2, \ldots, p_n + \theta r_n) \\
&\quad + I(p_1, p_2 + \theta r_2, \ldots, p_n + \theta r_n) \\
&\quad - I(p_1, p_2, p_3 + \theta r_3, \ldots, p_n + \theta r_n) \\
&\quad + \cdots + I(p_1, p_2, \ldots, p_{n-1}, p_n + \theta r_n) \\
&\quad - I(p_1, p_2, \ldots, p_n).
\end{aligned}
$$

Since

$$
\lim_{\theta \to 0} \frac{1}{\theta} \{ I(p_1, p_2, \ldots, p_k + \theta r_k, p_{k+1}, \ldots, p_n)
$$

$$
- I(p_1, p_2, \ldots, p_k, p_{k+1}, \ldots, p_n) \} = r_k \frac{\partial I}{\partial p_k}
$$

we obtain

$$
\lim_{\theta \to 0} \frac{1}{\theta} \{ I(\mathbf{p} + \theta\mathbf{r}) - I(\mathbf{p}) \} = r_1 \frac{\partial I}{\partial p_1} + r_2 \frac{\partial I}{\partial p_2} + \cdots + r_n \frac{\partial I}{\partial p_n}.
$$

On putting $\mathbf{r} = \mathbf{q} - \mathbf{p}$, we have the formula stated in Section 4.3.

Exercises

4.1. A channel transmits three symbols a, b, c. The symbol a is always received correctly while b and c each have probability p of coming through undisturbed and probability $q\ (=1-p)$ of being changed to c and b respectively. Show that the capacity of the channel is $\log(1+2/\alpha)$ where $\log \alpha = -p \log p - q \log q$.

   Discuss the cases $p = 1$ and $p = \frac{1}{2}$.

4.2. The input and output symbols of a channel are 0, 1, 2, 3. The input symbol i is converted with equal probability to i and $i+1$ (where $i+1$ means 0 when $i = 3$). Find the capacity of the channel.

4.3. A channel has input symbols 0, 1 and output symbols 0, 1, 2, 3. The transition probabilities are

Input	Output	T.P.	Input	Output	T.P.
0	0	1/3	1	0	1/6
	1	1/3		1	1/6
	2	1/6		2	1/3
	3	1/6		3	1/3

Determine the capacity of the channel.

4.4. The transition probabilities from each input of a channel to the r outputs form a permutation of the probabilities $p_1, \ldots, p_r$. The $p_1, \ldots, p_r$ are such that the permutations can be arranged so that the total transition probability attached to an output from all inputs does not vary from output to output.

   Show that, with this arrangement, the capacity of the channel is $\log r + \sum_{j=1}^{r} p_j \log p_j$.

4.5. With 0, 1 as both input and output, the transition probabilities for 0 to 0 and 1 are $1-\varepsilon$ and ε respectively while those for 1 to 1 and 0 are $1-\delta$ and δ respectively. Assuming that $0 < \varepsilon < 1$ and $0 < \delta < 1$, find the capacity of the channel.

4.6. A channel transmits two symbols. Noise affects them in blocks of seven symbols; a block of seven is either transmitted without error or exactly one symbol of the seven is incorrect. These eight possibilities are equally likely. Show that the capacity of the channel is 4/7 for logarithms to the base 2.

4.7. The input letters of a channel are $0, 1, \ldots, n-1$ and are denoted by $a_1, \ldots, a_n$. If

$$J(k) = \sum_{s=1}^{r} P(b_s \mid a_k) \log \frac{P(b_s \mid a_k)}{P(b_s)}$$

in the notation of this chapter prove that

$$\sum_{j=1}^{n} p_i J(j) \leqslant C \leqslant \max_{k} J(k).$$

Deduce that

$$C = \min \max_{k} J(k),$$

the minimum being taken over all possible input probabilities.

4.8. The binary symmetric channels $C_1, \ldots, C_m$ all have the same cross-over probability ε $(0 < \varepsilon < 1)$ and are connected in cascade with the output of C_i the input of C_{i+1}. Find the probability that a 0 appears at the output of C_m for any given probability distribution of the input of C_1.

Determine the capacity of the whole cascade and show that it tends to zero as $m \to \infty$.

4.9. The transition probabilities p_{ik} of an infinite cascade are given by

$$(i) \begin{bmatrix} 0 & \frac{1}{2} & \frac{1}{2} \\ \frac{1}{2} & 0 & \frac{1}{2} \\ \frac{1}{2} & \frac{1}{2} & 0 \end{bmatrix}, \quad (ii) \begin{bmatrix} \frac{1}{2} & \frac{1}{4} & \frac{1}{2} & 0 & 0 \\ 0 & \frac{1}{2} & 0 & 0 & 0 \\ \frac{1}{2} & \frac{1}{4} & \frac{1}{2} & 0 & 0 \\ 0 & 0 & 0 & \frac{1}{2} & \frac{1}{2} \\ 0 & 0 & 0 & \frac{1}{2} & \frac{1}{2} \end{bmatrix}, \quad (iii) \begin{bmatrix} 0 & 0 & \frac{1}{2} & 0 \\ 0 & 0 & \frac{1}{2} & 0 \\ 0 & 0 & 0 & 1 \\ 1 & 1 & 0 & 0 \end{bmatrix}.$$

Determine the persistent and transient letters in each case and examine the behaviour of $p_{ik}^{(m)}$ as $m \to \infty$.

4.10. In an infinite cascade $p_j = q_j$ and in all other columns the entries are zero except $p_{j-1,j}$ which is unity. Show that all letters are persistent and that

$$1/\mu_j = (q_j + q_{j+1} + \cdots + q_n) \Big/ \sum_{k=1}^{n} k q_k.$$

4.11. The letter a_k can appear after a_j in an infinite cascade with n letters. Show that it will appear after at most n channels.

If a_j is persistent, prove that there is $b < 1$ such that the probability of μ_j exceeding r where $r \geqslant n$ is smaller than b^r.

4.12. Solve Exercise 4.1 by treating it as two channels in parallel, one channel passing a and the other b and c.

4.13. A user has m channels in parallel and the probability of using the

ith is p_i. Prove from first principles that the capacity of the combination is given by

$$2^C = \sum_{i=1}^{m} 2^{C_i}$$

and that to achieve capacity $p_i = 2^{C_i - C}$.

Obtain the same result by means of (4.9.8).

5 Error correction

5.1. Block codes

The preceding chapters have brought to light the fact that reliable transmission can only be assured at the expense of lengthy sequences and long time delays. If this expense cannot be afforded then errors are inevitable. It is therefore advantageous to investigate methods of coping with errors and it is the aim of this chapter to study this matter.

Assume that there is an input source with the letters $a_1, \ldots, a_N$. Code the letters into binary sequences containing n digits. This is feasible provided that $2^n \geqslant N$. The ratio $2^n/N$, which gives an indication of the number of binary sequences available per input letter, is known as the *degeneracy*. For our coding, the degeneracy is to exceed unity and, indeed, the objective is to have the degeneracy much larger than unity so that many code words are at hand for each input letter.

When the code words are sent along a channel which can transmit 1 bit every second, the code word for an input letter will require n seconds for transmission. The information content of the input letter is $\log N$ if the input letters are equally probable. Hence, in this case,

$$T = \frac{\log N}{n} \tag{5.1.1}$$

can be regarded as the *transfer of information rate*. Increasing n to reduce the error rate results in a diminution of T, in harmony with previous observations that fidelity of transmission cuts down the rate at which information is transferred.

Divide the 2^n words into N *blocks* $B_1, B_2, \ldots, B_N$. Each block must contain at least one code word and will usually embrace several. Select one code word from each block, say u_i from B_i. When the input letter is a_i the code word u_i is despatched. The output code word y is checked; if it lies in B_j then y is decoded as a_j. If $a_j = a_i$ no error has been committed.

The idea is that if the blocks are chosen carefully several errors can be made in the digits of u_i without leaving the block B_i. In this way, some errors in transmission of the digits of u_i can be accepted without a consequent mistake in decoding. To some extent we do this in reading a text with misprints, the context providing a kind of block mechanism. Naturally, it must be recognized that the change of a single digit may switch the code word from one block to another but, on average, the system can be expected to do better than if blocks were not used.

Let $P(y \mid u_i)$ be the probability that y is received when the code word u_i is transmitted. Then, for the block system to work, it would be beneficial to impose the criterion that

$$P(y \mid u_i) \geqslant P(y \mid u_j) \qquad (5.1.2)$$

for every $y \in B_i$ (i.e. y is a member of B_i) and every $u_j \notin B_i$. In fact, it would be preferable to exclude the possibility of equality.

When the code word u_i is sent, the probability that it will be decoded correctly is $\sum_{y \in B_i} P(y \mid u_i)$ and incorrectly is $\sum_{y \notin B_i} P(y \mid u_i)$. On average, the probability of correct decoding P_c is given by

$$P_c = \sum_{i=1}^{N} p_i \sum_{y \in B_i} P(y \mid u_i) \qquad (5.1.3)$$

where p_i is the probability that the letter a_i will be picked from the input alphabet.

Our next objective is to derive a formula for P_c for a binary symmetric channel in which the cross-over probability is p. Suppose that y differs from u_i in k digits, i.e. k of the digits are incorrectly transmitted. Then

$$P(y \mid u_i) = p^k (1-p)^{n-k}.$$

Let a_{ik} be the number of sequence in B_i which differ from u_i in k digits. Then

$$\sum_{y \in B_i} P(y \mid u_i) = \sum_{k=0}^{n} a_{ik} p^k (1-p)^{n-k}$$

and

$$P_c = \sum_{i=1}^{N} p_i \sum_{k=0}^{n} a_{ik} p^k (1-p)^{n-k}. \qquad (5.1.4)$$

If n and N are not too large the calculation of (5.1.4) is tolerable. For greater values it becomes very tedious and some kind of approximation is desirable.

5.2. Upper bound for inputs of equal probability

The target of this section is the derivation of an upper bound for P_c which is easier to evaluate than (5.1.4). Only the special case in which the input letters are equally probable, i.e. $p_i = 1/N$ for $i = 1, \ldots, N$ will be considered. Thus

$$P_c = \frac{1}{N} \sum_{i=1}^{N} \sum_{k=0}^{n} a_{ik} p^k (1-p)^{n-k}. \tag{5.2.1}$$

The structure of the blocks is at our disposal so that adjustment of a_{ik} can be contemplated. However, there are limitations to the amount of movement that can be undertaken. Firstly, the number of y which can differ in k places from u_i is the same as the number of ways of choosing k objects from n and so is $n!/k!(n-k)!$. Not all of these variants need be in B_i but the figure sets a maximum to the number which can be. Hence

$$a_{ik} \leqslant \frac{n!}{k!(n-k)!}. \tag{5.2.2}$$

Moreover, $\sum_{k=0}^{n} a_{ik}$ is the total number of sequences in B_i and hence

$$\sum_{i=1}^{N} \sum_{k=0}^{n} a_{ik} \leqslant 2^n. \tag{5.2.3}$$

There will be equality if all available sequences are used in the blocks.

An upper bound for P_c is the objective and so the next manoeuvre is to vary the a_{ik} so as to make the right-hand side of (5.2.1) grow. It will be supposed that $p < \frac{1}{2}$ (in practical channels much smaller values of p are hoped for).

Imagine that for some particular i and k,

$$a_{ik} < \frac{n!}{k!(n-k)!}$$

and that, for some j, $a_{j,k+1} > 0$. Increase a_{ik} by 1 and decrease $a_{j,k+1}$ by 1; this procedure is not at variance with either (5.2.2) or

(5.2.3). The resulting change to the right hand side of (5.2.1) is

$$p^k(1-p)^{n-k} - p^{k+1}(1-p)^{n-k-1} = p^k(1-p)^{n-k}\left(1 - \frac{p}{1-p}\right) > 0$$

because $p < \frac{1}{2}$. Therefore the right-hand side of (5.2.1) is increased by making a_{ik} with the lower values of k as large as possible and those with the larger k zero, i.e. by concentrating in B_i those sequences which differ least from u_i.

At this stage it is not known where the subdivision between the two groups should be placed. So we leave it arbitrary for the moment and try

$$a_{ik} = \frac{n!}{k!(n-k)!} \qquad (0 \leqslant k \leqslant r-1)$$
$$= 0 \qquad (r+1 \leqslant k \leqslant n).$$

Notice that a_{ir} has not been specified and the maximum value of a_{ik} permitted by (5.2.2) has been adopted for the lower values of k. The choice of a_{ik} means that all sequences which differ from u_i in $0, 1, \ldots, r-1$ digits have been included in B_i and those with $r+1$ or greater digit changes have been left out. The total number of sequences in B_i is now

$$\sum_{k=0}^{r-1} \frac{n!}{k!(n-k)!} + a_{ir}.$$

Condition (5.2.3) can be met provided that r and a_{ir} satisfy

$$N \sum_{k=0}^{r-1} \frac{n!}{k!(n-k)!} + \sum_{i=1}^{N} a_{ir} \leqslant 2^n. \qquad (5.2.4)$$

If

$$N \sum_{k=0}^{r} \frac{n!}{k!(n-k)!} \geqslant 2^n \qquad (5.2.5)$$

a_{ir} cannot exceed its maximum value. Indeed, the highest it can aspire to is to make (5.2.4) as close to equality as possible. Therefore, the least value of r which satisfies (5.2.5) determines the choice of r that we need, in the sense that any larger value results in an unnecessary increase in the upper bound.

It has therefore been shown that, in general,

$$
\begin{aligned}
P_c \leqslant & \sum_{k=0}^{r-1} \frac{n!}{k!(n-k)!} p^k (1-p)^{n-k} \\
& + \frac{p^r (1-p)^{n-r}}{N} \sum_{i=1}^{N} a_{ir} \\
\leqslant & \sum_{k=0}^{r-1} \frac{n!}{k!(n-k)!} p^k (1-p)^{n-k} \\
& + \frac{p^r (1-p)^{n-r}}{N} \left\{ 2^n - N \sum_{k=0}^{r-1} \frac{n!}{k!(n-k)!} \right\}
\end{aligned} \tag{5.2.6}
$$

from (5.2.4). A rather simpler expression results from the observation that r has been chosen so that $\sum_{i=1}^{N} a_{ir} \leqslant n!N/r!(n-r)!$. Hence

$$
P_c \leqslant \sum_{k=0}^{r} \frac{n!}{k!(n-k)!} p^k (1-p)^{n-k}. \tag{5.2.7}
$$

In both (5.2.6) and (5.2.7) r is the least integer for which (5.2.5) is valid.

While the bound (5.2.7) is not so tight as (5.2.6) it is substantially easier to calculate and is the one which we shall adopt. It must be emphasized that (5.2.7), being an upper bound, is a guide only to the actual value of P_c and may differ appreciably from it. A lower bound would enable P_c to be bracketed; this matter will be deferred until later when upper bounds for the probability of error are discussed.

Example 5.2a. Let sequences of two digits be divided into three blocks so that $n = 2$ and $N = 3$. It is straightforward to check that the smallest value of r for which (5.2.5) holds is 1. Hence (5.2.7) gives

$$
P_c \leqslant (1-p)^2 + 2p(1-p) \leqslant 1 - p^2. \tag{5.2.8}
$$

Suppose the choice $u_1 = 00$, $u_2 = 10$, $u_3 = 11$ is made and the blocks are defined by

B_1	B_2	B_3
00	10	11
01		

Thus the output 00 or 01 will be decoded as a_1. In this case

$$P(\text{output } a_1 \mid u_1) = (1-p)^2 + p(1-p)$$

since u_1 must come through either unchanged or altered in one digit. Similarly

$$P(\text{output } a_2 \mid u_2) = (1-p)^2 = P(\text{output } a_3 \mid u_3).$$

Since $p_i = \frac{1}{3}$, (5.1.3) supplies

$$P_c = \tfrac{1}{3}\{3(1-p)^2 + p(1-p)\} = \tfrac{1}{3}(1-p)(3-2p). \qquad (5.2.9)$$

The upper bound of (5.2.8) is greater than the true value of (5.2.9) by the factor $(1+p)(1-\tfrac{2}{3}p)^{-1}$. This factor has its highest value of 6 when $p = 1$ but such a value of p would be intolerable in practice. For $p = 0.1$ the factor is 1.2 so that the upper bound is not out by an excessive margin. Indeed, the upper bound is 0.99 whereas (5.2.9) gives $P_c = 0.84$. Actually, even $p = 0.1$ would be regarded as quite noisy and levels of the order of 10^{-5} or 10^{-6} would be preferable. At such low values of p the disagreement between the upper bound and true value of P_c is virtually non-existent.

Example 5.2b. The effect of longer sequences can be seen by considering $n = 4$ and $N = 3$, i.e. sequences of four digits split into three blocks. Now $r = 2$ in order to comply with (5.2.5) and, from (5.2.7),

$$P_c \leqslant (1-p)^4 + 4p(1-p)^3 + 6p^2(1-p)^2 \leqslant (1-p)^2(1+2p+3p^2).$$
$$(5.2.10)$$

For $p = 0.1$, $P_c \leqslant 0.996$ which suggests, by comparison with Example 5.2a, that longer sequences will have more correct decoding. However, the rate of transfer of information T is, according to (5.1.1), $\tfrac{1}{2}\log 3$ or 0.8 for Example 5.2a and 0.4 for this example. So, the improvement in decoding is accompanied by a halving in the rate of transfer of information.

Suppose that $u_1 = 0000$, $u_2 = 1100$, $u_3 = 1111$. The 16 sequences available offers a fair amount of freedom in constructing the blocks. Trying to make the blocks have nearly equal size, we investigate

B_1	B_2	B_3
0000	1100	1111
0001	1010	1110
0010	0110	1101
0100	0101	1011
1000	0011	0111
1001		

Now

$$P(\text{output } a_1 \mid u_1) = (1-p)^4 + 4p(1-p)^3 + p^2(1-p)^2,$$
$$P(\text{output } a_2 \mid u_2) = (1-p)^4 + 3p^2(1-p)^2 + p^4,$$
$$P(\text{output } a_3 \mid u_3) = (1-p)^4 + 4p(1-p)^3$$

and

$$P_c = \tfrac{1}{3}\{3(1-p)^4 + 8p(1-p)^3 + 4p^2(1-p)^2 + p^4\}.$$

When $p = 0.1$, $P_c = 0.86$ so that the amelioration is not as significant as the upper bound might lead one to believe.

The interchange of 1001 and 0011 makes another block arrangement. In it $P_c = 0.89$ when $p = 0.1$; the probability of error is some $\tfrac{2}{3}$ of that for the shorter sequences.

The discussion in this section has been founded on equally probable input letters. When they are not equally probable the obvious strategy is to organize the block sizes so that they are in the ratios of the probabilities as near as may be. For instance, in Example 5.2a, suppose $P(a_1) = \tfrac{1}{2}$, $P(a_2) = \tfrac{1}{4}$, $P(a_3) = \tfrac{1}{4}$. Choose the same blocks; then

$$P_c = \tfrac{1}{2}\{(1-p)^2 + p(1-p)\} + 2. \qquad \tfrac{1}{4}(1-p)^2 = \tfrac{1}{2}(1-p)(2-p).$$

When $p = 0.1$, $P_c = 0.86$ revealing that the probability distribution of the input has some influence on P_c.

*5.3. Error bounds for a two letter alphabet

Let the input alphabet have two letters and let u_1, u_2 be code words of n digits allocated to them. The blocks are determined by imposing the rule that the output is decoded as a_1 if

$P(y \mid u_1) > P(y \mid u_2)$ and as a_2 otherwise. When u_1 is the input the probability of error in decoding is

$$P_{e1}(u_1, u_2) = \sum_{y \notin B_1} P(y \mid u_1).$$

If $y \notin B_1$, $P(y \mid u_1) \leqslant P(y \mid u_2)$ so that

$$P(y \mid u_1) \leqslant \{P(y \mid u_1)\}^{1-\sigma}\{P(y \mid u_2)\}^{\sigma}$$

for any σ satisfying $0 < \sigma < 1$, which is the only range which will be of interest here. By the addition of quantities which are non-negative we deduce that

$$P_{e1}(u_1, u_2) \leqslant \sum_{y} \{P(y \mid u_1)\}^{1-\sigma}\{P(y \mid u_2)\}^{\sigma} \qquad (5.3.1)$$

without any limitation on y.

Let u_{1j}, y_j be the jth letter of the code word u_1 and jth symbol of the output respectively. Then, for a memoryless channel,

$$P(y \mid u_1) = P(y_1 \mid u_{11})P(y_2 \mid u_{12}) \cdots P(y_n \mid u_{1n}). \qquad (5.3.2)$$

By means of (5.3.2) and (5.3.1) an upper bound to the probability of decoding error for a specific pair of code words from the blocks can be determined.

Example 5.3a. Let the channel be binary symmetric with cross-over probability ε ($0 \leqslant \varepsilon < \frac{1}{2}$). Select u_1 to consist entirely of zeros and u_2 to be composed wholly of units. Then

$$P(y_j = 0 \mid u_{1j} = 0) = 1 - \varepsilon, \qquad P(y_j = 1 \mid u_{1j} = 0) = \varepsilon,$$
$$P(y_j = 0 \mid u_{2j} = 1) = \varepsilon, \qquad P(y_j = 1 \mid u_{2j} = 1) = 1 - \varepsilon$$

and the other transition probabilities are zero. Hence

$$\sum_{y_j} \{P(y_j \mid u_{1j})\}^{1-\sigma}\{P(y_j \mid u_{2j})\}^{\sigma} = (1-\varepsilon)^{1-\sigma}\varepsilon^{\sigma} + \varepsilon^{1-\sigma}(1-\varepsilon)^{\sigma}.$$

It follows from (5.3.2) and (5.3.1) that

$$P_{e1}(u_1, u_2) \leqslant \{(1-\varepsilon)^{1-\sigma}\varepsilon^{\sigma} + \varepsilon^{1-\sigma}(1-\varepsilon)^{\sigma}\}^n.$$

The quantity inside the braces can be written as $\varepsilon(x^{1-\sigma} + x^{\sigma})$ where $x = (1-\varepsilon)/\varepsilon$; for variations in σ between 0 and 1 this has a minimum at $\sigma = \frac{1}{2}$. Therefore

$$P_{e1}(u_1, u_2) \leqslant \{2\varepsilon^{\frac{1}{2}}(1-\varepsilon)^{\frac{1}{2}}\}^n \leqslant \exp[\tfrac{1}{2}n \ln\{4\varepsilon(1-\varepsilon)\}]. \qquad (5.3.3)$$

Since $4\varepsilon(1-\varepsilon)<1$ for $0\leq\varepsilon<\tfrac{1}{2}$, P_{e1} decays exponentially as $n\rightarrow\infty$.

The result of Example 5.3a shows that the probability of decoding errors tends to zero exponentially as the length of the code words increases. On the other hand, each code word and its associated block is conveying only 1 bit of information so the improvement in decoding accuracy is achieved at the expense of a reduction in the rate of transfer of information. In an effort to maintain an undiminished rate of transfer let us consider the possibility of employing other code words as representatives of the blocks.

If a_k is a typical letter of the alphabet from which code words are constructed, introduce an arbitrary probability distribution in which $q(a_k)$ is the probability of selecting a_k. A code word is formed by making n statistically independent choices from the alphabet in accordance with this probability distribution. Thus the probability of selecting the particular code word u_1 is

$$Q(u_1)=q(u_{11})q(u_{12})\cdots q(u_{1n}) \qquad (5.3.4)$$

and of alighting on the pair u_1, u_2 is $Q(u_1)Q(u_2)$.

The probability of decoding error averaged over all possible code words that might arise is

$$\bar{P}_{e1}=\sum_{u_1}\sum_{u_2}Q(u_1)Q(u_2)P_{e1}(u_1,u_2). \qquad (5.3.5)$$

The inequality (5.3.1) can be inserted into the right-hand side of (5.3.5) and, if the special choice of $\sigma=\tfrac{1}{2}$ is made, there results

$$\bar{P}_{e1}\leq\sum_{u_1}\sum_{u_2}Q(u_1)Q(u_2)\sum_{y}\{P(y\mid u_1)P(y\mid u_2)\}^{\tfrac{1}{2}}$$

$$\leq\sum_{y}\left[\sum_{u_1}Q(u_1)\{P(y\mid u_1)\}^{\tfrac{1}{2}}\right]^2. \qquad (5.3.6)$$

For the memoryless channel (5.3.2) and (5.3.4) give

$$\sum_{u_1}Q(u_1)\{P(y\mid u_1)\}^{\tfrac{1}{2}}=\sum_{u_{11}}\sum_{u_{12}}\cdots\sum_{u_{1n}}q(u_{11})\cdots q(u_{1n})$$

$$\times\{P(y_1\mid u_{11})\cdots P(y_n\mid u_{1n})\}^{\tfrac{1}{2}}$$

$$=\prod_{j=1}^{n}\sum_{u_{1j}}q(u_{1j})\{P(y_j\mid u_{1j})\}^{\tfrac{1}{2}}.$$

Consequently

$$\bar{P}_{e1} \leqslant \prod_{j=1}^{n} \sum_{y_j} \left[\sum_{u_{1j}} q(u_{1j})\{P(y_j \mid u_{1j})\}^{\frac{1}{2}} \right]^2 \qquad (5.3.7)$$

from (5.3.6). Alternatively

$$\bar{P}_{e1} \leqslant \left\{ \sum_{y_j} \left[\sum_{u_{1j}} q(u_{1j})\{P(y_j \mid u_{1j})\}^{\frac{1}{2}} \right]^2 \right\}^n. \qquad (5.3.8)$$

Example 5.3b. For the binary symmetric channel take $q(0) = \frac{1}{2} = q(1)$. Then

$$\sum_{u_{1j}} q(u_{1j})P(y_j \mid u_{1j}) = \frac{1}{2}\{(1-\varepsilon)^{\frac{1}{2}} + \varepsilon^{\frac{1}{2}}\}$$

and hence

$$\bar{P}_{e1} \leqslant [\frac{1}{2}\{(1-\varepsilon)^{\frac{1}{2}} + \varepsilon^{\frac{1}{2}}\}^2]^n \qquad (5.3.9)$$

follows from (5.3.8).

It is simple to verify that the right-hand side of (5.3.9) is larger than that of (5.3.3) and that the ratio is worst as $\varepsilon \to 0$. Since (5.3.9) is an average of (5.3.3) over all possible choices of code word one might have expected otherwise. The reconciliation is that the codes in which P_{e1} is large must play an important part in the determination of the average. So, for reliable transmission, efforts should be concentrated on damping down the atypical codes with large associated errors in favour of the typical ones which are relatively error-free. This principle underlies the design of good transmission channels.

*5.4. Several code words

The theory enunciated in the preceding section can be extended to more than two code words. Let $P_e(\nu \to u_s, y)$ be the probability of a decoding error when the νth letter of the source is encoded as u_s and then appears at the output as y. To gain familiarity with this notation consider the case just discussed in Section 5.3. Then

$$P_e(1 \to u_1, y) = \sum{}' Q(u_2) \qquad (5.4.1)$$

where $\sum'$ means sum over all those u_2 for which $P(y \mid u_2) \geqslant P(y \mid u_1)$. Clearly

$$P_e(1 \to u_1, y) \leqslant \sum_{u_2} Q(u_2)\{P(y \mid u_2)/P(y \mid u_1)\}^\sigma. \qquad (5.4.2)$$

The average probability of decoding error for the first letter is

$$\bar{P}_{e1} \le \sum_{u_1} Q(u_1) \sum_y P(y \mid u_1) P_e(1 \rightarrow u_1, y)$$
$$\le \sum_{u_1} Q(u_1) \sum_y P(y \mid u_1) \sum_{u_2} Q(u_2)$$
$$\times \{P(y \mid u_2)/P(y \mid u_1)\}^\sigma \qquad (5.4.3)$$

on account of (5.4.2). The formula (5.4.3) is in agreement with (5.3.6) when $\sigma = \frac{1}{2}$.

In the more general case of N blocks the average probability of decoding error for the νth source letter is

$$\bar{P}_{e\nu} = \sum_{u_s} Q(u_s) \sum_y P(y \mid u_s) P_e(\nu \rightarrow u_s, y). \qquad (5.4.4)$$

For fixed ν, u_s, and y let E_r be the event that u_r is such that $P(y \mid u_r) \ge P(y \mid u_s)$ $(r \ne s)$. Then

$$P_e(\nu \rightarrow u_s, y) \le P\left(\bigcup_{r \ne s} E_r \right).$$

Now, if $\sum_{r \ne s} P(E_r) \ge 1$,

$$P\left(\bigcup_{r \ne s} E_r \right) \le 1 \le \left\{ \sum_{r \ne s} P(E_r) \right\}^\rho \qquad (0 < \rho \le 1)$$

and if $\sum_{r \ne s} P(E_r) < 1$

$$P\left(\bigcup_{r \ne s} E_r \right) \le \sum_{r \ne s} P(E_r) \le \left\{ \sum_{r \ne s} P(E_r) \right\}^\rho$$

so that, in either case,

$$P_e(\nu \rightarrow u_s, y) \le \left\{ \sum_{r \ne s} P(E_r) \right\}^\rho \qquad (5.4.5)$$

with $0 < \rho \le 1$. But

$$P(E_r) \le \sum_{u_t} Q(u_t)\{P(y \mid u_t)/P(y \mid u_s)\}^\sigma.$$

There are $N - 1$ possible choices for r and so (5.4.5) gives

$$P_e(\nu \rightarrow u_s, y) \le \left[(N-1) \sum_{u_t} Q(u_t)\{P(y \mid u_t)/P(y \mid u_s)\}^\sigma \right]^\rho.$$

Substitution in (5.4.4), followed by putting $\sigma = (1+\rho)^{-1}$, supplies the following theorem.

MANY CODE WORDS THEOREM. *The average probability of decoding error over an ensemble of codes satisfies*

$$\bar{P}_{ev} \leqslant (N-1)^\rho \sum_y \left[\sum_{u_s} Q(u_s)\{P(y \mid u_s)\}^{1/(1+\rho)} \right]^{1+\rho}$$

for $0 \leqslant \rho \leqslant 1$.

The additional point that the inequality is valid for $\rho = 0$ is trivial because then the right-hand side is equal to unity. When $N = 2$ and $\rho = 1$ the inequality coincides with that of (5.3.6) so that the theorem covers the theory of the preceding section.

For a memoryless channel the inequality transforms as in Section 5.3 to

$$\bar{P}_{ev} \leqslant (N-1)^\rho \left\{ \sum_{y_j} \left[\sum_{u_{1j}} q(u_{1j})\{P(y_j \mid u_{1j})\}^{1/(1+\rho)} \right]^{1+\rho} \right\}^n. \quad (5.4.6)$$

The theorem can also be expressed in terms of the rate of transfer of information T_0, defined in terms of natural logarithms by $T_0 = (\ln N)/n$, by specifying N to satisfy $N - 1 < e^{nT} \leqslant N$. Thus we have the following theorem.

RATE THEOREM. *In a memoryless channel with given n and T_0*

$$\bar{P}_{ev} \leqslant e^{n\{\rho T_0 - E(\rho)\}}$$

where

$$E(\rho) = -\ln \sum_{y_j} \left[\sum_{u_{1j}} q(u_{1j})\{P(y_j \mid u_{1j})\}^{1/(1+\rho)} \right]^{1+\rho}.$$

If $E(\rho) - \rho T_0$ is maximized with respect to q and ρ, the tightest bound on $\bar{P}_{ev}$ is attained. It is given by

$$\bar{P}_{ev} \leqslant e^{-nE_m} \quad (5.4.7)$$

where $E_m = \max\{E(\rho) - \rho T_0\}$, the maximum being taken over all probabilities q and over ρ in $0 \leqslant \rho \leqslant 1$.

The relationship between E_m and T is not at all simple even though E_m falls steadily as T_0 grows (Exercise 5.5). In general, parametric representation will be inevitable as is illustrated in the following example.

Example 5.4. For a binary symmetric channel with crossover probability ε $(0 \leqslant \varepsilon < \frac{1}{2})$ put $q(u_{11}) = p$ so that $q(u_{12}) = 1 - p$. Then

$$e^{-E(\rho)} = [p\{(1-\varepsilon)^{1/(1+\rho)} - \varepsilon^{1/(1+\rho)}\} + \varepsilon^{1/(1+\rho)}]^{1+\rho}$$
$$+ [(1-p)\{(1-\varepsilon)^{1/(1+\rho)} - \varepsilon^{1/(1+\rho)}\} + \varepsilon^{1/(1+\rho)}]^{1+\rho}.$$

As p increases from 0, the right-hand side diminishes to a minimum at $p = \frac{1}{2}$ and then grows steadily to its value at $p = 1$. Therefore, the greatest value of $E(\rho)$ occurs at $p = \frac{1}{2}$ and

$$E_m = \max_{0 \leqslant \rho \leqslant 1} [-\rho T_0 - \ln\{\varepsilon^{1/(1+\rho)} + (1-\varepsilon)^{1/(1+\rho)}\}^{1+\rho}/2^\rho]$$

$$= \max_{0 \leqslant \rho \leqslant 1} [\rho(\ln 2 - T_0) - (1+\rho)\ln(\varepsilon^{1/(1+\rho)}/\delta)] \qquad (5.4.8)$$

where

$$\delta = \frac{\varepsilon^{1/(1+\rho)}}{\varepsilon^{1/(1+\rho)} + (1-\varepsilon)^{1/(1+\rho)}}.$$

The derivative with respect to ρ of the quantity to be maximized in (5.4.8) is

$$\ln 2 - T_0 - \ln(\varepsilon^{1/(1+\rho)}/\delta) + \{\delta \ln \varepsilon + (1-\delta)\ln(1-\varepsilon)\}/(1+\rho)$$
$$= \ln 2 - T_0 + \delta \ln \delta + (1-\delta)\ln(1-\delta).$$

Now δ increases with ρ and so the derivative drops steadily from its value at $\rho = 0$ to that at $\rho = 1$. Since $\ln 2 > T_0$ because $2^n > N$ there is a range of ε for which the derivative has opposite signs at $\rho = 0$ and $\rho = 1$ so that the maximum occurs where

$$T_0 = \ln 2 + \delta \ln \delta + (1-\delta)\ln(1-\delta) \qquad (5.4.9)$$

which is an implicit equation to determine ρ in terms of T_0. Outside this range the maximum is at $\rho = 1$ for the lower ε and at $\rho = 0$ for the higher ε.

Insert (5.4.9) in (5.4.8) and then

$$E_m = \delta \ln \delta + (1-\delta)\ln(1-\delta) - \delta \ln \varepsilon - (1-\delta)\ln(1-\varepsilon). \quad (5.4.10)$$

There is no convenient way of combining (5.4.9) and (5.4.10) so that the parametric representation must be accepted as the way of calculating E_m. Plotting graphically the variation of T_0 and E_m against δ allows one to obtain some knowledge of the interrelation between E_m and T_0.

5.5. Error correcting codes

Block coding is one method of trying to ensure that errors in decoding are kept down. Another technique is to attempt to make a code word check and correct errors that have arisen due to transmission. This approach to controlling errors will be discussed for a channel passing binary digits.

The principle behind the method can be illustrated by a simple example. Take a particular code word and examine how many of its digits are unity. If the number of units is odd add a 1 at the end of the code word; if the number is even put a 0 at the end. The new code word always contains an even number of units. Therefore, if the code word received has an odd number of units it is certain that errors have been committed in transmission. The receipt of an even number of units gives more confidence in the correctness of the code word but by no means certainty because two digits may have been changed during transmission.

The above procedure does not offer much guidance as to the location of errors, so that more sophisticated versions have been designed. They are classed as *parity-check codes* and are widely used for storage on magnetic tapes because of their relative cheapness. Parity-check codes are made more powerful by employing more than one digit for checking purposes.

It is helpful to look at the mechanism in an example before proceeding to the general theory. Suppose that the original code word possesses three digits and that three checking digits are to be added, making a new code word of six digits. Let the given digits be u_1, u_2, u_3 and let the checking digits be $u_2 \oplus u_3$, $u_3 \oplus u_1$, $u_1 \oplus u_2$ where $\oplus$ means addition in modulo-2 arithmetic, i.e.

$$0 \oplus 0 = 0, \qquad 0 \oplus 1 = 1, \qquad 1 \oplus 0 = 1, \qquad 1 \oplus 1 = 0.$$

$$(5.5.1)$$

Thus the code word 000 has $u_1 = 0$, $u_2 = 0$, $u_3 = 0$ and, from (5.5.1), all the check digits are zero so that the code word 000000 is despatched.

Similarly, in the code word 001, $u_1 = 0$, $u_2 = 0$, $u_3 = 1$ so that (5.5.1) gives $u_2 \oplus u_3 = 1$, $u_3 \oplus u_1 = 1$, $u_1 \oplus u_2 = 0$. The new code word is 001110.

For the remaining code words we have

Original	New
011	011011
010	010101
100	100011
101	101101
110	110110
111	111000

Generally, the original code word will have r digits u_1, $u_2, \ldots, u_r$ and will be converted to a code word of n digits $x_1, x_2, \ldots, x_n$ with $n > r$. The conversion rule is

$$x_1 = u_1, \qquad x_2 = u_2, \ldots, x_r = u_r, \qquad (5.5.2)$$

$$x_m = \sum_{s=1}^{r} g_{ms} u_s \qquad (m = r+1, \ldots, n). \qquad (5.5.3)$$

In (5.5.3) each g_{ms} is either 1 or 0 (once the g_{ms} are chosen they remain unaltered for all messages) and the summation is carried out by modulo-2 arithmetic. A code based on (5.5.2) and (5.5.3) is called a *systematic parity-check code* and $x_{r+1}, \ldots, x_n$ are known as *check digits*.

There is no reason why the first r digits should not be modified also so that

$$x_m = \sum_{s=1}^{r} g_{ms} u_s \qquad (m = 1, \ldots, n). \qquad (5.5.4)$$

It is then a *parity-check code*. We shall concentrate on systematic parity-check codes but much of what is said is also applicable to parity-check codes.

Example 5.5. In the earlier illustration in which the check digits were $u_2 \oplus u_3$, $u_3 \oplus u_1$, $u_1 \oplus u_2$ a systematic parity-check code is obtained with $r = 3$, $n = 6$ and

$$g_{41} = 0, \qquad g_{42} = 1, \qquad g_{43} = 1,$$

$$g_{51} = 1, \qquad g_{52} = 0, \qquad g_{53} = 1,$$

$$g_{61} = 1, \qquad g_{62} = 1, \qquad g_{63} = 0.$$

The equations (5.5.3) (or (5.5.4) for that matter) can be expressed in matrix form. Let $\mathbf{x}$ be a column matrix with n elements $x_1, \ldots, x_n$ and $\mathbf{u}$ one with r elements $u_1, \ldots, u_r$. Define G as a matrix with n rows and r columns by

$$G = \begin{bmatrix} 1 & 0 & \cdots & 0 \\ 0 & 1 & \cdots & 0 \\ & & \cdot & \\ & & \cdot & \\ & & \cdot & \\ 0 & 0 & \cdots & 1 \\ g_{r+1,1} & & \cdots & g_{r+1,r} \\ & & \cdot & \\ & & \cdot & \\ & & \cdot & \\ g_{n1} & & \cdots & g_{nr} \end{bmatrix}.$$

Then

$$\mathbf{x} = G\mathbf{u} \tag{5.5.5}$$

covers both (5.5.2) and (5.5.3), provided that, in forming $G\mathbf{u}$, modulo-2 arithmetic is used. G is known as the *generator matrix*.

If $\mathbf{u}_1$ and $\mathbf{u}_2$ are two starting code words with elements $u_{11}, u_{12}, \ldots, u_{1r}$ and $u_{21}, u_{22}, \ldots, u_{2r}$ respectively, $\mathbf{u}_1 \oplus \mathbf{u}_2$ is defined by adding the separate components, i.e.

$$\mathbf{u}_1 \oplus \mathbf{u}_2 = \begin{bmatrix} u_{11} \oplus u_{21} \\ u_{12} \oplus u_{22} \\ \cdot \\ \cdot \\ \cdot \\ u_{1r} \oplus u_{2r} \end{bmatrix}. \tag{5.5.6}$$

In performing operations, the reader should remember that the associative laws

$$(a \oplus b) \oplus c = a \oplus (b \oplus c), \qquad (ab)c = a(bc), \tag{5.5.7}$$

the commutative laws

$$a \oplus b = b \oplus a, \qquad ab = ba \tag{5.5.8}$$

and the distributive law

$$(a \oplus b)c = ac \oplus bc \tag{5.5.9}$$

hold in modulo-2 arithmetic. Thus the mth element of $G\mathbf{u}_1 \oplus G\mathbf{u}_2$ is

$$\sum_{s=1}^{r} g_{ms} u_{1s} \oplus \sum_{t=1}^{r} g_{mt} u_{2t}$$

or

$$g_{m1} u_{11} \oplus g_{m2} u_{12} \oplus \cdots \oplus g_{mr} u_{1r} \oplus g_{m1} u_{21} \oplus \cdots \oplus g_{mr} u_{2r}$$
$$= g_{m1} u_{11} \oplus g_{m1} u_{21} \oplus g_{m2} u_{12} \oplus g_{m2} u_{22} \oplus \cdots$$

by repeated application of (5.5.7) and (5.5.8). An alternative form, on account of (5.5.9), is

$$g_{m1}(u_{11} \oplus u_{21}) \oplus g_{m2}(u_{12} \oplus u_{22}) \oplus \cdots$$

which is the mth element of $G(\mathbf{u}_1 \oplus \mathbf{u}_2)$. Hence

$$G\mathbf{u}_1 \oplus G\mathbf{u}_2 = G(\mathbf{u}_1 \oplus \mathbf{u}_2). \tag{5.5.10}$$

If $\mathbf{x}_1$ and $\mathbf{x}_2$ are the new code words corresponding to $\mathbf{u}_1$ and $\mathbf{u}_2$ respectively, (5.5.5) gives

$$\mathbf{x}_1 \oplus \mathbf{x}_2 = G\mathbf{u}_1 \oplus G\mathbf{u}_2 = G(\mathbf{u}_1 \oplus \mathbf{u}_2) \tag{5.5.11}$$

from (5.5.10). *Hence, the modulo-2 sum of two new code words is also a code word which corresponds to the starting code word* $\mathbf{u}_1 \oplus \mathbf{u}_2$.

Because of (5.5.2), (5.5.3) can be written as

$$x_m = \sum_{s=1}^{r} g_{ms} x_s \qquad (m = r+1, \ldots, n).$$

Hence

$$x_m \oplus \sum_{s=1}^{r} g_{ms} x_s = x_m \oplus x_m = 0 \qquad (m = r+1, \ldots, n).$$

$$\tag{5.5.12}$$

The equations (5.5.12) can be put in matrix form by means of a matrix F which is a simple modification of G, namely

$$F = \begin{bmatrix} g_{r+1,1} & \cdots & g_{r+1,r} & 1 & 0 & \cdots & 0 \\ & \bullet & & 0 & 1 & \cdots & 0 \\ & \bullet & & & & \cdots \\ & \bullet & & & & \cdots \\ g_{n1} & \cdots & g_{nr} & 0 & 0 & \cdots & 1 \end{bmatrix}$$

with $n - r$ rows and n columns. Consequently, (5.5.12) becomes

$$F\mathbf{x} = \mathbf{0} \tag{5.5.13}$$

the zero vector having $n - r$ elements.

Conversely, if $F\mathbf{x} = \mathbf{0}$,

$$x_m \oplus \sum_{s=1}^{r} g_{ms} x_s = 0 \qquad (m = r+1, \ldots, n)$$

so that

$$x_m = x_m \oplus x_m \oplus \sum_{s=1}^{r} g_{ms} x_s = \sum_{s=1}^{r} g_{ms} x_s \qquad (m = r+1, \ldots, n)$$

demonstrating that we have a code word in which the first r digits are given and the remaining $n - r$ are check digits.

We have thus proved the following theorem.

THEOREM 5.5. $F\mathbf{x} = \mathbf{0}$ *if and only if* $\mathbf{x}$ *is a code word with* $n - r$ *check digits.*

The matrix F is known as the *systematic parity-check matrix*.

In a parity-check code the upper part of the generator matrix G is not in general the unit matrix. Likewise the right-hand $(n-r) \times (n-r)$ matrix of F need not be the unit matrix.

5.6. Error sequences

The decoder has to decide when the output of the channel is the n-vector $\mathbf{y}$ what code word was sent or rather he must arrive at the best approximation to the original that he can. If he knew that $\mathbf{x}$ had been transmitted his difficulties would be resolved and, in fact, comparison of $\mathbf{x}$ and $\mathbf{y}$ would reveal the errors due to transmission. An easy way to do the comparison is to form $\mathbf{x} \oplus \mathbf{y}$. By virtue of (5.5.1) this will have a 1 in every position where $\mathbf{x}$ and $\mathbf{y}$ disagree. Therefore $\mathbf{x} \oplus \mathbf{y}$ can be regarded as an *error sequence*; generally, error sequences will be denoted by **e**. The number of units in a code word will be called the *weight*. Thus, the larger the weight of an error sequence the more errors are being committed.

Associated with the idea of an error sequence is the *syndrome* **s** of the output defined by

$$\mathbf{s} = F\mathbf{y}. \tag{5.6.1}$$

The syndrome is a column vector with $n-r$ components, the same number of elements as there are check digits. According to Theorem 5.5 $\mathbf{s} = \mathbf{0}$ if and only if **y** is a possible code word, i.e. there is some **u** for which $\mathbf{y} = G\mathbf{u}$. A syndrome of zero weight therefore corresponds precisely to the output being a permitted code word though not necessarily the code word which originated the message.

In general

$$s_k = \sum_{t=1}^{r} g_{r+k,t} y_t \oplus y_{r+k} \qquad (k = 1, \ldots, n-r).$$

It follows that $s_k \neq 0$ if

$$y_{r+k} \neq \sum_{t=1}^{r} g_{r+k,t} y_t,$$

i.e. y_{r+k} is not the check digit which should be calculated from $y_1, \ldots, y_r$. Thus the weight of **s** is some measure of the amount of error that has occurred. Note, however, that the check digits themselves may be in error even when $y_1, \ldots, y_r$ are not so that the weight of the syndrome is not an unambiguous indicator of error in the digits from the original code word.

When **e** is an error sequence

$$F\mathbf{e} = F(\mathbf{x} \oplus \mathbf{y}) = F\mathbf{x} \oplus F\mathbf{y}$$

from (5.5.10). By Theorem 5.5, $F\mathbf{x} = \mathbf{0}$ if and only if **x** is a code word. Therefore

$$F\mathbf{e} = F\mathbf{y} = \mathbf{s} \tag{5.6.2}$$

if and only if **e** is an error sequence.

In the decoding problem **y** is given and **x** has to be determined. From **y** the syndrome **s** is formed. Equation (5.6.2) is then solved for **e**. The solution may not be unique but supplies all possible error sequences which are appropriate to **y**. From these **e** select one $\mathbf{e}_{min}$ which has minimum weight and then construct $\mathbf{y} \oplus \mathbf{e}_{min}$.

Then
$$F'(y \oplus e_{min}) = Fy \oplus Fe_{min} = s \oplus s = 0$$

from (5.6.1) and (5.6.2). Theorem 5.5 shows that $y \oplus e_{min}$ is a possible code word and it is taken as the identifier in the input. In other words, it is being assumed that it is reasonable to imagine that the channel operates so that the input deviates as little as possible from the output. The code word $y \oplus e_{min}$ is called the *most likely estimate* of the input.

Example 5.6a. Let the systematic parity check matrix be
$$F = \begin{bmatrix} 0 & 1 & 1 & 1 & 0 & 0 \\ 1 & 0 & 1 & 0 & 1 & 0 \\ 1 & 1 & 0 & 0 & 0 & 1 \end{bmatrix}.$$

For the output in which y^T (the transpose of y) is given by $y^T = (0\ 0\ 1\ 1\ 1\ 0)$ the syndrome is
$$s = \begin{bmatrix} 1 \oplus 1 \\ 1 \oplus 1 \\ 0 \end{bmatrix} = \begin{bmatrix} 0 \\ 0 \\ 0 \end{bmatrix}.$$

If $e = 0$ then $Fe = 0 = s$ and since the weight of this e is zero there cannot be a smaller. Hence $e_{min} = 0$ and in this case the most likely estimate of x is y.

Usually, decoding tables are prepared which display the e_{min} for any given s. Since s has $n - r$ components the decoding table will have 2^{n-r} entries. The preparation of these tables commonly starts by assuming a given e (of which there are 2^n possibilities) and calculating the resulting s. To accomplish this in an orderly fashion the route that is traversed is:

(1) Take all e of zero weight and for each evaluate s from
   $s = Fe$;
(2) Take all e of unit weight and for each evaluate s from
   $s = Fe$; then delete all those e of unit weight which have the
   same s as in (1);
(3) Take all e of weight two and determine the corresponding
   s; delete those e for which s has appeared in (1) or (2);
(4) Continue in this way, steadily increasing the weight, until
   2^{n-r} different s have been generated. Stop at this point
   since all subsequent e will be deleted automatically.

Example 5.6b. Consider original code words of two symbols to which one check digit is added by the rule $x_3 = u_1 \oplus u_2$. In this case $r = 2$, $n = 3$, and the relevant matrices are

$$G = \begin{bmatrix} 1 & 0 \\ 0 & 1 \\ 1 & 1 \end{bmatrix}, \quad F = [1 \quad 1 \quad 1].$$

The only error sequence of zero weight is $\mathbf{e}^T = 000$ so that $F\mathbf{e} = 0$ and $\mathbf{s} = 0$.

A possibility for an error sequence of unit weight is $\mathbf{e}^T = 100$ with $F\mathbf{e} = 1$ and $\mathbf{s} = 1$. It is easily checked that the other sequences of unit weight, 010 and 001, also give $\mathbf{s} = 1$.

In fact, $2^{n-r} = 2$ so that no further $\mathbf{s}$ are possible and the process can be stopped. The reader should confirm for himself that the error sequences of weight two give $\mathbf{s} = 0$ and that of weight three $\mathbf{s} = 1$.

The decoding table is now

$\mathbf{s}$	$\mathbf{e}_{min}^T$
0	000
1	100

If the output is $\mathbf{y}^T = 111$ then $\mathbf{s} = F\mathbf{y} = 1$ and so $\mathbf{e}_{min}^T = 100$. Hence $(\mathbf{y} \oplus \mathbf{e}_{min})^T = 011$, i.e. the most likely estimate of $\mathbf{x}$ is 011 and of $\mathbf{u}$ is 01.

There is no obligation to fix on the $\mathbf{e}_{min}$ for $\mathbf{s} = 1$ as shown in the table (though once selected it must always be adhered to); the choice of $\mathbf{e}_{min}^T = 001$ also fulfils the condition. The most likely estimate of $\mathbf{u}$ would then be 11. With $\mathbf{e}_{min}^T = 010$ it would be 10.

So one check digit is not really sufficient to distinguish which of the digits is in error though, since all the estimates have one digit in common, we can be fairly sure that only one of them is wrong.

Example 5.6c. In the systematic parity-check code of Example 5.5, $r = 3$, $n = 6$, and

$$F = \begin{bmatrix} 0 & 1 & 1 & 1 & 0 & 0 \\ 1 & 0 & 1 & 0 & 1 & 0 \\ 1 & 1 & 0 & 0 & 0 & 1 \end{bmatrix}.$$

Since $2^{n-r} = 8$ the decoding table contains 8 entries and looks like

s^T	e_{min}^T
000	000000
011	100000
101	010000
110	001000
100	000100
010	000010
001	000001
111	100100

The only place where some arbitrariness of choice is available is in the last line; for example 010010 is also of weight two and give $s^T = 111$.

If the output $y^T = 010011$ is received, $s = Fy = (100)^T$ so that $e_{min}^T = 001000$. The most likely estimate of x is 011011 and of u is 011.

When the output differs from the input in one digit the error sequence is of unit weight. The decoding table contains all error sequences of unit weight so that all messages which are in error by a single digit will be decoded correctly by the most likely estimate. Only one output message with errors in two digits will be decoded as the right x and those with mistakes in more than two digits are bound to lead to most likely estimates of x which are in error.

The probability of the most likely estimate of x being wrong is the probability of the occurrence of an error sequence which is not in the decoding table. The easiest way of calculating this is to subtract from 1 the probability of the error sequences in the decoding table. When the channel is symmetric with cross-over probability p the probability that a sequence comes through unmodified is $(1-p)^6$ in Example 5.6c. The probability of one error is $p(1-p)^5$, of two $p^2(1-p)^4$ and so on. Hence the probability of decoding error is

$$P_e = 1 - (1-p)^6 - 6p(1-p)^5 - p^2(1-p)^4$$

for Example 5.6c.

5.7. Hamming codes

Consider an error sequence of unit weight, say $\mathbf{e}_k$ in which the component e_{kr} is zero if $r \neq k$ and unit if $r = k$. Then

$$F\mathbf{e}_k = \text{the } k\text{th column of } F.$$

Therefore, if the columns of F are all different and non-zero, the syndromes associated with $\mathbf{0}$ and $\mathbf{e}_k$ $(k = 1, \ldots, n)$ by (5.6.2) are all distinct from one another. Thus the decoding table will be able to find the correct input from all outputs which have no error or have an error in a single digit.

If the code has $n - r$ check digits there are $n - r$ rows in F. Hence there are 2^{n-r} different columns available for F. One of these consists entirely of zeros so there are $2^{n-r} - 1$ distinct non-zero columns which can be selected for F. Accordingly, if $n \leq 2^{n-r} - 1$ every column of F can be made different from every other one.

For instance, if a computer is based on a 48 bit word with 7 check digits, $n = 48$ and $r = 41$. So $2^{n-r} = 127 > 48 = n$ and the code can be arranged so that all errors in a single digit only are automatically corrected.

Hamming codes are those for which

$$n = 2^{n-r} - 1. \tag{5.7.1}$$

Solutions to (5.7.1) can be generated by specifying $n - r$ and calculating the right-hand side of (5.7.1). This gives n, and r follows at once. Thus values satisfying (5.7.1) are

$n - r$	2	3	4	5	6
n	3	7	15	31	63
r	1	4	11	26	57

For the case $n = 7$, $r = 4$ the form of F is

$$\begin{bmatrix} 0 & 1 & 1 & 1 & 1 & 0 & 0 \\ 1 & 0 & 1 & 1 & 0 & 1 & 0 \\ 1 & 1 & 0 & 1 & 0 & 0 & 1 \end{bmatrix}.$$

Exercises

5.1. Sequences of three digits are split into three blocks. Show that (5.2.7) gives $P_c \leq (1 - p)^2 (1 + 2p)$.

If the blocks are

	B_1	B_2	B_3
	000	001	111
	010	011	110
	100	101	

and $u_1 = 000$, $u_2 = 001$, $u_3 = 111$ prove that

$$P_c = (1-p)^2(1+\tfrac{5}{3}p).$$

Study the effect of rearranging the blocks.

5.2. Prove the statement made about the minimum of P_{e1} with respect to σ in Example 5.3a.

5.3. Prove that, in Example 5.3a,

$$P_{e1} = \sum_{r=\frac{1}{2}n}^{n} \frac{n!}{r!(n-r)!} (1-\varepsilon)^{n-r}\varepsilon^r$$

when n is even.

If n is large, use the fact that $n!/j!(n-j)!$ is slowly varying relative to $\varepsilon^j(1-\varepsilon)^{n-j}$ when j is near $\frac{1}{2}n$ to demonstrate that

$$P_{e1} \approx \left(\frac{2}{\pi n}\right)^{\frac{1}{2}}\left(\frac{1-\varepsilon}{1-2\varepsilon}\right)\{4\varepsilon(1-\varepsilon)\}^{\frac{1}{2}n}.$$

[Advantage can be taken of *Stirling's approximation* that $m! \approx (2\pi m)^{\frac{1}{2}}(m/e)^m$ for large m.]

5.4. Some inequalities which are sometimes useful for binary symmetric channels can be derived from the fact that

$$m! = (2\pi m)^{\frac{1}{2}}(m/e)^m e^a$$

where a is a function of m which decreases as m increases; it is always true that $0 < ma < 1/12$.

In (a), (b), and (c), n, j are integers such that $j \geq 1$, $n-j \geq 1$.

(a)
$$\left\{\frac{n}{8j(n-j)}\right\}^{\frac{1}{2}} \leq \frac{n!}{j!(n-j)!}e^{-\alpha n} < \left\{\frac{n}{2\pi j(n-j)}\right\}^{\frac{1}{2}}$$

where

$$\alpha = -\frac{j}{n}\ln\frac{j}{n} - \left(1-\frac{j}{n}\right)\ln\left(1-\frac{j}{n}\right);$$

(b) $(2n)^{-\frac{1}{2}} \le n!e^{-\alpha n}/j!(n-j)! < 1;$

(c) $(2n-1)!/n!(n-1)! \ge 2^{2n-2}/n^{\frac{1}{2}};$

(d)   if $0 < p < 1$ and $np < j < n$

$$\frac{n!}{j!(n-j)!}p^j(1-p)^{n-j} \le \sum_{m=j}^{n} \frac{n!}{m!(n-m)!}p^m(1-p)^{n-m}$$

$$\le \frac{j(1-p)}{j(1-p)-(n-j)p}\frac{n!}{j!(n-j)!}p^j(1-p)^{n-j}.$$

5.5. After $E(\rho)$ in the Rate Theorem has been maximized with respect to q its stationary values satisfy $dE/d\rho = T_0$. Assuming that this has a solution in the required range of ρ show that $dE_m/dT_0 = -\rho$ and deduce that E_m is a decreasing function of T_0.

5.6. Sequences of two digits are converted to code words of length 4 by the following rule:

$$00 \to 0000, \quad 01 \to 0111, \quad 10 \to 1010, \quad 11 \to 1101.$$

Show that the rule gives a systematic parity-check code and find a decoding table which yields the most likely estimate. Determine the probability of the occurrence of an error sequence not in the decoding table for a binary symmetric channel.

5.7. If sequences are transformed by the following rule:

$$00 \to 00000, \quad 01 \to 01101, \quad 10 \to 10111, \quad 11 \to 11010$$

show that it is a systematic parity-check code and determine the generator and parity-check matrices. Find a decoding table and the probability of an error sequence not in the table.

5.8. The *distance* $d(\mathbf{x}, \mathbf{y})$ between two binary sequences $\mathbf{x}$ and $\mathbf{y}$ of n digits is defined as the number of digits at which $\mathbf{x}$ and $\mathbf{y}$ disagree. The distance of every $\mathbf{x}$ from a given output $\mathbf{y}$ is examined and then, in a *minimum-distance decoder*, the output is decoded as any code word $\mathbf{x}$ for which $d(\mathbf{x}, \mathbf{y})$ is a minimum. If there are m code words $\mathbf{x}_1, \ldots, \mathbf{x}_m$ altogether and

$$d(\mathbf{x}_i, \mathbf{x}_j) \ge 2k+1 \qquad (i \ne j)$$

with k a positive integer, show that if $\mathbf{y}$ is in error by a single digit, or by two digits, . . . , or by k digits the mistakes are automatically corrected by a minimum-distance decoder.

5.9. If a minimum-distance decoder corrects all single digit, double digit, . . . , k digit errors prove that it is necessary that

$$m \sum_{j=0}^{k} \frac{n!}{j!(n-j)!} \leqslant 2^n.$$

5.10. If the code word composed entirely of zeros is denoted by $\mathbf{x}_0$ prove that the number of code words at a distance k ($\leqslant n$) from a given code word $\mathbf{x}$ is the same as the number of code words at a distance k from $\mathbf{x}_0$.

If $d_{\min}$ is the minimum distance between pairs of code words show that it is the minimum distance between pairs of code words excluding $\mathbf{x}_0$. Prove that it is possible to correct all outputs which contain fewer than $\frac{1}{2}d_{\min}$ errors in their digits.

5.11. Prove that the most likely estimate of a systematic parity-check code gives the same decoding as a minimum-distance decoder. Prove also that outputs with errors in not more than k digits are correctly decoded by the most likely estimate if and only if every set of $2k$ columns of the parity-check matrix are linearly independent.

5.12. Prove that, for the most likely estimate to correct all outputs with errors in not more than k digits, it is necessary that the number N of check digits satisfies

$$2^N \geqslant \sum_{j=0}^{k} \frac{n!}{j!(n-j)!}$$

and sufficient that

$$2^N > \sum_{j=0}^{2k-1} \frac{(n-1)!}{j!(n-1-j)!}.$$

5.13. In a systematic parity-check code prove that either all the code words contain an even number of units or half the code words have an odd number of units and half an even number.

If x_{mr} is the rth digit of the mth code word show that, for fixed r, either exactly half or all of the x_{mr} are zero.

5.14. Code A is a systematic parity-check code with the rules

$$x_1 = u_1, \qquad x_2 = u_2, \qquad x_3 = u_3, \qquad x_4 = u_1 \oplus u_2,$$
$$x_5 = u_1 \oplus u_3, \qquad x_6 = u_2 \oplus u_3, \qquad x_7 = u_1 \oplus u_2 \oplus u_3.$$

Code B differs from Code A only in that $x_6 = u_2$.

Find the probability of decoding error for the two codes on a binary symmetric channel with cross-over probability p and determine which code is preferable when $p < \frac{1}{2}$.

5.15. If the columns of the generator matrix of a parity-check code are not linearly independent prove that some non-zero sequence is converted into the code word consisting entirely of zeros.

5.16. F_1 and F_2 are two parity-check matrices. For every $\mathbf{a}_1$ there is an $\mathbf{a}_2$ such that $\mathbf{a}_1{}^T F_1 = \mathbf{a}_2{}^T F_2$ and for every $\mathbf{a}_2$ there is an $\mathbf{a}_1$ such that the same relation holds. Show that $F_2 \mathbf{x} = \mathbf{0}$ if and only if $F_1 \mathbf{x} = \mathbf{0}$. [$\mathbf{a}_1$ and $\mathbf{a}_2$ have as many components as F_1 and F_2 have rows.]

Prove that two output sequences have different syndromes with respect to F_2 if and only if they have different syndromes with respect to F_1.

If F_1 has r rows and m ($<r$) is the largest number of linearly independent rows prove that the code has 2^{n-m} code words and that the decoding table has 2^m entries.

6 *Continuous signals

The preceding chapters have discussed systems in which both the input and output alphabets are composed of a finite number of letters. Not all communication systems fall into this category. For instance, the variations in time of the signals in television, radio, or speech are continuous rather than discrete. It is therefore desirable to examine how the theory can cope with continuously varying messages. For this purpose it is necessary to say something about the theory of continuous probability.

6.1. Continuous distributions

Imagine that the outcome of an experiment is the real number x. It may be that repeat performances of the experiment produce a variety of values of x. Associating a probability with x is a natural step and then x may be called a *random variable.*

Actually, it is convenient to begin by defining the *distribution function F* of a random variable by means of

$$F(x_0) = P(x \leq x_0). \qquad (6.1.1)$$

In other words, $F(x_0)$ gives the probability that, on making a choice of x, a value is selected which does not exceed x_0.

There are various properties of the distribution function which intuitive considerations suggest. Firstly, we do not expect x to be less than $-\infty$ ever and so we take $F(-\infty) = 0$. Secondly, some value of x must be chosen so that $F(+\infty) = 1$ is appropriate. Finally, as x_0 increases we anticipate that it will be more likely that a value of x lower than x_0 can be secured, i.e. $F(x_0)$ must not decrease as x_0 grows. Thus the distribution function of a random variable starts from 0 at $-\infty$ and grows, without ever decreasing, to 1 at $+\infty$. Conversely, any function with these attributes can be regarded as the distribution function of some random variable.

It is evident from (6.1.1) that

$$P(x_1 < x \leq x_2) = F(x_2) - F(x_1). \qquad (6.1.2)$$

Allow x_2 to approach x_1 and then

$$P(x = x_1) = F(x_1 + 0) - F(x_1). \qquad (6.1.3)$$

If $F(x_1+0) = F(x_1)$ for every x_1, the distribution is said to be *continuous*.

If there are x_1 for which $F(x_1+0) \neq F(x_1)$ and F does not change except for the discontinuous jumps at these points the distribution is called *discrete*. Behaviour of this type has formed the basis of earlier chapters.

Distributions in which there are x_1 for which $F(x_1+0) \neq F(x_1)$ and places where F increases continuously are a mixture of discrete and continuous. Such distributions will not concern us subsequently. Discrete distributions will also be excluded because they have already been treated. We shall concentrate wholly on continuous distributions.

In a continuous distribution (6.1.3) indicates that $P(x = x_1) = 0$ for every x_1. Yet in making a choice of x some value must be chosen. Consequently, zero probability in a continuous distribution does not firmly prevent the possibility.

The *probability density* $f_X(x)$ is defined by

$$f_X(x) = \frac{d}{dx} F(x). \qquad (6.1.4)$$

The suffix X is added to tell us what set of values x is being drawn from. It is not really essential when dealing with probability in one variable but serves as a useful identifier when there are more variables. The monotonicity of F is sufficient to guarantee the existence of the derivative in (6.1.4) almost everywhere but, instead of appealing to this result from analysis, we shall assume that the distribution functions of information theory are so well-behaved that they have a finite derivative everywhere. More precisely, the probability density will be assumed to be piecewise continuous.

Because F is monotone (6.1.4) implies that

$$f_X(x) \geq 0. \qquad (6.1.5)$$

Also the inverse of (6.1.4) is

$$F(x) = \int_{-\infty}^{x} f_X(t)\, dt \qquad (6.1.6)$$

the lower limit of integration being fixed by the requirement that

$F(-\infty) = 0$. Since $F(\mid \infty) - 1$, it follows from (6.1.6) that

$$\int_{-\infty}^{\infty} f_X(t)\, dt = 1. \tag{6.1.7}$$

Any function satisfying (6.1.5) and (6.1.7) can be deemed the probability density of some random variable whose distribution function can be taken from (6.1.6).

It is important to realize that neither (6.1.5) nor (6.1.7) forces the probability density to be less than unity. Abundant counterexamples demonstrate that the probability density can exceed unity and one will be found in Example 6.1b below.

Example 6.1a. If $a > 0$, the function

$$f_X(x) = 0 \qquad (x < 0)$$
$$= e^{-ax} \qquad (x > 0)$$

satisfies (6.1.5) and is a candidate for a probability density if (6.1.7) can be verified. To comply with (6.1.7) we must have

$$\int_0^{\infty} e^{-at}\, dt = 1$$

or $1/a = 1$. Thus $f_X(x) = e^{-x}$ in $x > 0$ will be a probability density and, from (6.1.6), the corresponding distribution function is given by

$$F(x) = 0 \qquad\qquad (x < 0)$$
$$= \int_0^x e^{-t}\, dt = 1 - e^{-x} \qquad (x \geqslant 0).$$

Example 6.1b. The probability density defined for all x by

$$f_X(x) = \frac{1}{(2\pi)^{\frac{1}{2}}\sigma}\, e^{-(x-\mu)^2/2\sigma^2}$$

is known as the *Gaussian (or normal) distribution* with *mean* μ and *variance* σ^2 (or *standard deviation* σ). The constant σ is required to be positive so that (6.1.5) is confirmed. Also the substitution $t - \mu = 2^{\frac{1}{2}}\sigma u$ gives

$$\int_{-\infty}^{\infty} \frac{1}{(2\pi)^{\frac{1}{2}}\sigma}\, e^{-(t-\mu)^2/2\sigma^2}\, dt = \frac{1}{\pi^{\frac{1}{2}}} \int_{-\infty}^{\infty} e^{-u^2}\, du.$$

Quoting the result (which can be deduced from Euler's integral for the factorial function)

$$\int_{-\infty}^{\infty} e^{-u^2} \, du = \pi^{\frac{1}{2}} \qquad (6.1.8)$$

we see that (6.1.7) is satisfied.

Extensive tables of the distribution function, which can be written down from (6.1.6), have been prepared.

Putting $x = \mu$ demonstrates that the probability density of the Gaussian distribution can exceed unity whenever $(2\pi)^{\frac{1}{2}}\sigma < 1$.

6.2. Entropy

Comparison of discrete and continuous distributions suggests that one might go from the former to the latter by replacing probability by probability density and by substituting integration for summation. In line with this idea we introduce the following definition.

DEFINITION 6.2. *The entropy of X is defined by*

$$H(X) = -\int_{-\infty}^{\infty} f_X(x) \log f_X(x) \, dx$$

whenever the integral exists.

The contrast between continuous and discrete distributions is worth emphasizing. Firstly, the entropy of a continuous distribution need not exist. Secondly, when it does exist there is nothing to ensure that the entropy is positive because f_X can exceed unity.

The third feature is tied to the fact that the definition is in terms of a probability density rather than a probability. The entropy may not, therefore, be invariant to a change of variables. To illustrate this let $y = g(x)$ where g is a steadily increasing function of x. Since the mapping from X to Y is $1-1$

$$P(y \leqslant y_0) = P(g(x) \leqslant y_0) = P(x \leqslant x_0)$$

where $g(x_0) = y_0$. Hence

$$F_Y(y_0) = F_X(x_0)$$

and

$$f_Y(y_0) = \frac{\mathrm{d}}{\mathrm{d}y_0} F_Y(y_0) = \frac{\mathrm{d}}{\mathrm{d}x_0} F_X(x_0) \cdot \frac{\mathrm{d}x_0}{\mathrm{d}y_0} = \frac{f_X(x_0)}{g'(x_0)}.$$

Accordingly

$$H(Y) = -\int_{-\infty}^{\infty} f_Y(y)\log f_Y(y)\,\mathrm{d}y$$

$$= -\int_{-\infty}^{\infty} \frac{f_X(x)}{g'(x)} \log \frac{f_X(x)}{g'(x)}\,\mathrm{d}xg'(x)$$

$$= H(X) + \int_{-\infty}^{\infty} f_X(x)\log g'(x)\,\mathrm{d}x.$$

In general, the last integral will be non-zero and $H(Y)$ will not be the same as $H(X)$.

These important differences between the discrete and continuous cases are a warning that results for discrete distributions cannot be translated to continuous distributions without independent verification. Fortunately, some of the significant concepts rely upon differences between entropies and for these the difficulties disappear.

Example 6.2. The entropy of the Gaussian distribution.

The probability density of the Gaussian distribution is given in Example 6.1b so that, by Definition 6.2, its entropy is

$$-\int_{-\infty}^{\infty} \frac{1}{(2\pi)^{\frac{1}{2}}\sigma} e^{-\frac{1}{2}(x-\mu)^2/\sigma^2} \left[\log \frac{1}{(2\pi)^{\frac{1}{2}}\sigma} - \frac{1}{2}\frac{(x-\mu)^2}{\sigma^2}\log e\right]\mathrm{d}x$$

$$= \frac{1}{\pi^{\frac{1}{2}}}\int_{-\infty}^{\infty} e^{-t^2}[\log\{(2\pi)^{\frac{1}{2}}\sigma\} + t^2\,\log e]\,\mathrm{d}t$$

on making the substitution $x - \mu = 2^{\frac{1}{2}}\sigma t$.

Now, by integration by parts,

$$\int_{-\infty}^{\infty} t^{2n}e^{-t^2}\,\mathrm{d}t = [-\tfrac{1}{2}t^{2n-1}e^{-t^2}]_{-\infty}^{\infty} + (n-\tfrac{1}{2})\int_{-\infty}^{\infty} t^{2n-2}e^{-t^2}\,\mathrm{d}t$$

$$= (n-\tfrac{1}{2})\int_{-\infty}^{\infty} t^{2n-2}e^{-t^2}\,\mathrm{d}t.$$

Carrying on in this way we shall eventually reach the integrand

e^{-t^2} when n is a positive integer. The deduction from (6.1.8) is that

$$\int_{-\infty}^{\infty} t^{2n}e^{-t^2}\,dt = (n-\tfrac{1}{2})(n-\tfrac{3}{2})\cdots\tfrac{1}{2}\pi^{\frac{1}{2}} \qquad (6.2.1)$$

for positive integral n. Observe that

$$\int_{-\infty}^{\infty} t^{2n+1}e^{-t^2}\,dt = 0 \qquad (6.2.2)$$

because the integrand is an odd function of t.

By means of (6.1.8) and (6.2.1) we conclude that the entropy is $\log\{(2\pi)^{\frac{1}{2}}\sigma\} + \tfrac{1}{2}\log e$. In other words *the entropy of the Gaussian distribution is* $\log\{(2\pi e)^{\frac{1}{2}}\sigma\}$.

It will be noted that increasing σ makes the entropy larger, i.e. the bigger the scatter of the data the more the uncertainty is.

Discrete systems have the characteristic that the entropy has a maximum which can be attained (Theorem 2.2b). If we attempt to move towards a continuous system by allowing the number of events to grow without limit we find that maximum ($\log n$) tends to infinity. This means that we can expect that there are probability densities of continuous distributions for which the entropy is larger than any specified finite number. Maximization of the entropy with respect to the probability density is therefore impossible unless additional constraints are introduced. When there are constraints there can be a maximum as is demonstrated by the following theorem.

THEOREM 6.2. *The probability density which gives the greatest entropy subject to the restriction* $\int_{-\infty}^{\infty} x^2 f_X(x)\,dx = \sigma^2$ *is the Gaussian distribution with zero mean and variance* σ^2.

Proof. The behaviour of $H(X)$ has to be considered for all f_X which satisfy (6.1.7) and the stated restriction. Instead of considering f_X restricted in this way we can, by bringing in Lagrange multipliers, convert to an unconstrained problem, i.e. the behaviour of

$$J(f) = -\int_{-\infty}^{\infty} f(x)\log f(x)\,dx - \alpha\int_{-\infty}^{\infty} f(x)\,dx - \beta\int_{-\infty}^{\infty} x^2 f(x)\,dx$$

is examined for constant α, β and unrestricted f (other than a requirement that J exists).

Let f_0 be a function which makes J an extremum. Let g be an arbitrary continuous function and let ε be a parameter. If we prescribe g to be zero outside some finite interval $J(f_0 + \varepsilon g)$ will exist. That $J(f_0)$ is an extremum signifies that, for small ε, it differs from $J(f_0 + \varepsilon g)$ by a quantity of the second order, i.e.

$$\frac{\partial}{\partial \varepsilon} J(f_0 + \varepsilon g) = 0 \qquad (6.2.3)$$

when $\varepsilon = 0$.

Now

$$\frac{\partial}{\partial \varepsilon} J(f_0 + \varepsilon g) = -\int_{-\infty}^{\infty} \{g \log(f_0 + \varepsilon g) + g \log e + \alpha g + \beta x^2 g\} \, dx$$

and so (6.2.3) is satisfied at $\varepsilon = 0$ when

$$\int_{-\infty}^{\infty} g(\log f_0 + \log e + \alpha + \beta x^2) \, dx = 0. \qquad (6.2.4)$$

But, for any given finite interval, g may be selected arbitrarily and the interval may be placed anywhere convenient. So (6.2.4) can hold only if

$$\log f_0 + \log e + \alpha + \beta x^2 = 0$$

or

$$f_0 = e^{-(A + Bx^2)}$$

when $A \log e = \alpha + \log e$, $B \log e = \beta$.

The constraint

$$\int_{-\infty}^{\infty} f_0(x) \, dx = 1$$

has to be satisfied. To secure convergence $B > 0$ and then

$$e^{-A}(\pi/B)^{\frac{1}{2}} = 1 \qquad (6.2.5)$$

from (6.1.8). There is also the restriction

$$\int_{-\infty}^{\infty} x^2 f_0(x) \, dx = \sigma^2$$

which supplies

$$\tfrac{1}{2} e^{-A} \pi^{\frac{1}{2}} / B^{\frac{3}{2}} = \sigma^2 \qquad (6.2.6)$$

from (6.2.1). Division of (6.2.5) and (6.2.6) gives $B = 1/2\sigma^2$ and then (6.2.5) provides $\mathrm{e}^{-A} = 1/(2\pi)^{\frac{1}{2}}\sigma$. Thus

$$f_0 = \frac{1}{(2\pi)^{\frac{1}{2}}\sigma}\,\mathrm{e}^{-\frac{1}{2}x^2/\sigma^2}$$

confirming the statement of the theorem.

Theorem 6.2 may be interpreted as saying that, of all distributions with a given variance, the Gaussian possesses the most uncertainty.

6.3. Two random variables

When there are two random variables to be considered it is natural to generalize the notions of one dimension. Thus, if the variables are x and y, the *probability density* is a piecewise continuous function $f_{X,Y}(x, y)$ such that

$$f_{X,Y}(x, y) \geq 0, \qquad \int_{-\infty}^{\infty}\int_{-\infty}^{\infty} f_{X,Y}(x, y)\,\mathrm{d}x\,\mathrm{d}y = 1. \quad (6.3.1)$$

The probability that the point (x, y) falls in the domain D of the plane is then

$$P\{(x, y) \in D\} = \int\!\!\int_D f_{X,Y}(x, y)\,\mathrm{d}x\,\mathrm{d}y \qquad (6.3.2)$$

provided, of course, that D is sufficiently regular for the integral to exist. In particular, if D is a rectangle,

$$P\{a_1 < x \leq b_1, a_2 < y \leq b_2\} = \int_{a_1}^{b_1}\int_{a_2}^{b_2} f_{X,Y}(x, y)\,\mathrm{d}x\,\mathrm{d}y.$$

Allowing a_1 and a_2 to tend to $-\infty$ we obtain the *distribution function*

$$F(x_0, y_0) = P(x \leq x_0, y \leq y_0)$$

$$= \int_{-\infty}^{x_0}\int_{-\infty}^{y_0} f_{X,Y}(x, y)\,\mathrm{d}x\,\mathrm{d}y. \qquad (6.3.3)$$

If the distribution function is given the probability density can be deduced, via (6.3.3), as

$$f_{X,Y}(x, y) = \frac{\partial^2}{\partial x\,\partial y}\,F(x, y). \qquad (6.3.4)$$

However, the concept of distribution function is much less significant in the plane than it is on the line and so it will generally be more valuable to visualize probabilities in the plane as being assigned by probability densities.

The probability that the single variable x does not exceed x_0 can be derived from (6.3.2) by taking D as the domain $x \leqslant x_0$. Thus

$$P(x \leqslant x_0) = \int_{-\infty}^{x_0} \int_{-\infty}^{\infty} f_{X,Y}(x, y) \, dx \, dy.$$

Thus the probability density assigned to x alone by this plane distribution is (cf. (6.1.4) and (6.1.6))

$$f_X(x) = \int_{-\infty}^{\infty} f_{X,Y}(x, y) \, dy. \tag{6.3.5}$$

Similarly, the probability density for y only is

$$f_Y(y) = \int_{-\infty}^{\infty} f_{X,Y}(x, y) \, dx. \tag{6.3.6}$$

Both f_X and f_Y comply with (6.1.7) by virtue of (6.3.1).

A further feature which can arise with two variables is conditional probability. Let $f_{X,Y}$ be continuous and suppose that f_X is positive. Then the conditional probability of the event $y \leqslant y_0$ given that $x_0 < x \leqslant x_0 + h$ can be written

$$P(y \leqslant y_0 \mid x_0 < x \leqslant x_0 + h) = \frac{\displaystyle\int_{x_0}^{x_0+h} \int_{-\infty}^{y_0} f_{X,Y}(x, y) \, dx \, dy}{\displaystyle\int_{x_0}^{x_0+h} f_X(x) \, dx}. \tag{6.3.7}$$

Making $h \to 0$ in (6.3.7) we have

$$P(y \leqslant y_0 \mid x = x_0) = \frac{\displaystyle\int_{-\infty}^{y_0} f_{X,Y}(x_0, y) \, dy}{f_X(x_0)}. \tag{6.3.8}$$

Formula (6.3.8) can be thought of as specifying the distribution function of y when it is given that $x = x_0$. It will therefore have a probability density which can be expressed as

$$f_Y(y \mid x = x_0) = f_{X,Y}(x_0, y)/f_X(x_0) \tag{6.3.9}$$

and may be called *the conditional probability density of y given that $x = x_0$*.

Similarly, the conditional probability density of x given that $y = y_0$ is

$$f_X(x \mid y = y_0) = f_{X,Y}(x, y_0)/f_Y(y_0). \qquad (6.3.10)$$

Two distributions are said to be *statistically independent* when

$$f_{X,Y}(x, y) = f_X(x)f_y(y) \qquad (6.3.11)$$

on every rectangle of non-zero area. It follows from (6.3.9) and (6.3.10) that, in the case of statistical independence,

$$f_X(x) = f_X(x \mid y = y_0), \qquad f_Y(y) = f_Y(y \mid x = x_0)$$

revealing that conditioning has no effect when there is statistical independence. Equivalent to (6.3.11) is that the distribution functions satisfy $F(x, y) = F_X(x)F_Y(y)$.

By analogy with Chapter 2 we can introduce the following definition.

DEFINITION 6.3. *The entropies $H(X \cap Y)$ and $H(X \mid Y)$ are defined by*

$$H(X \cap Y) = -\int_{-\infty}^{\infty} \int_{-\infty}^{\infty} f_{X,Y}(x, y)\log f_{X,Y}(x, y) \, dx \, dy,$$

$$H(X \mid Y) = -\int_{-\infty}^{\infty} \int_{-\infty}^{\infty} f_{X,Y}(x, y)\log \frac{f_{X,Y}(x, y)}{f_Y(y)} \, dx \, dy.$$

The mutual information $I(X, Y)$ is given by

$$I(X, Y) = H(X) - H(X \mid Y).$$

In all these definitions it is assumed that the probability densities are such that the integrals exist.

From Definition 6.3

$$H(X \cap Y) = H(X \mid Y) - \int_{-\infty}^{\infty} \int_{-\infty}^{\infty} f_{X,Y}(x, y)\log f_Y(y) \, dx \, dy$$

$$= H(X \mid Y) - \int_{-\infty}^{\infty} f_Y(y)\log f_Y(y) \, dy$$

from (6.3.6). Invoking Definition 6.2 we have

$$H(X \cap Y) = H(Y) + H(X \mid Y) \qquad (6.3.12)$$

in formal agreement with (2.3.6). Interchanging the roles of X and Y we obtain the analogue of (2.3.7) namely

$$H(X \cap Y) = H(X) + H(Y \mid X). \qquad (6.3.13)$$

Substitution from (6.3.12) in $I(X, Y)$ gives

$$I(X, Y) = H(X) + H(Y) - H(X \cap Y) \qquad (6.3.14)$$
$$= H(Y) - H(Y \mid X) \qquad (6.3.15)$$

from (6.3.13). Once again the harmony with the results of Section 2.3 will be observed.

An explicit formula for the mutual information is

$$I(X, Y) = \int_{-\infty}^{\infty} \int_{-\infty}^{\infty} f_{X,Y}(x, y) \log \frac{f_{X,Y}(x, y)}{f_X(x) f_Y(y)} \, dx \, dy \quad (6.3.16)$$

since

$$H(X) = -\int_{-\infty}^{\infty} \int_{-\infty}^{\infty} f_{X,Y}(x, y) \log f_X(x) \, dx \, dy$$

from (6.3.5). On account of Theorem 2.2a

$$-I(X, Y) \le \int_{-\infty}^{\infty} \int_{-\infty}^{\infty} \{ f_X(x) f_Y(y) - f_{X,Y}(x, y) \} \, dx \, dy$$
$$\le 1 - 1 \le 0. \qquad (6.3.17)$$

If $f_{X,Y}/f_X f_Y \ne 1$ on a rectangle of non-zero area there must be strict inequality in (6.3.17). Thus there is equality only when X and Y are statistically independent.

We can thus state the following theorem.

THEOREM 6.3. $I(X, Y) \ge 0$ and $H(X) \ge H(X \mid Y)$ *with equality if and only if X and Y are statistically independent.*
Remark that Theorem 6.3 implies that conditioning does not increase entropy so that this property is common to both continuous and discrete distributions.

Example 6.3. Consider the distribution in which

$$f_X(x) = \frac{1}{(2\pi)^{\frac{1}{2}} \sigma} e^{-\frac{1}{2} x^2 / \sigma^2},$$

$$f_Y(y \mid x = x_0) = \frac{1}{(2\pi)^{\frac{1}{2}} \tau} e^{-\frac{1}{2}(y - x_0)^2 / \tau^2}.$$

From (6.3.9)

$$f_{X,Y}(x, y) = \frac{1}{2\pi\sigma\tau} e^{-\frac{1}{2}(x^2/\sigma^2)-\frac{1}{2}(y-x)^2/\tau^2}$$

and so (6.3.6) gives

$$f_Y(y) = \frac{1}{2\pi\sigma\tau} \int_{-\infty}^{\infty} e^{-\frac{1}{2}(x^2/\sigma^2)-\frac{1}{2}(y-x)^2/\tau^2} \, \mathrm{d}x.$$

Now

$$\frac{x^2}{\sigma^2} + \frac{(y-x)^2}{\tau^2} = \left(\frac{1}{\sigma^2}+\frac{1}{\tau^2}\right)\left(x - \frac{\sigma^2 y}{\sigma^2+\tau^2}\right)^2 + \frac{y^2}{\sigma^2+\tau^2}.$$

Hence the substitution

$$x - \sigma^2 y/(\sigma^2+\tau^2) = 2^{\frac{1}{2}} t\sigma\tau/(\sigma^2+\tau^2)^{\frac{1}{2}}$$

followed by (6.1.8) gives

$$f_Y(y) = \frac{e^{-\frac{1}{2}y^2/(\sigma^2+\tau^2)}}{\{2\pi(\sigma^2+\tau^2)\}^{\frac{1}{2}}}.$$

Thus y is Gaussian with mean zero and variance $\sigma^2+\tau^2$. Hence, from Example 6.2,

$$H(Y) = \log\{2\pi e(\sigma^2+\tau^2)\}^{\frac{1}{2}}.$$

Also

$$H(Y \mid X) = -\int_{-\infty}^{\infty} \int_{-\infty}^{\infty} f_{X,Y}(x, y)$$

$$\times \left\{\log \frac{1}{(2\pi)^{\frac{1}{2}}\tau} - \frac{1}{2\tau^2}(y-x)^2 \log e\right\} \mathrm{d}x \, \mathrm{d}y$$

$$= \log(2\pi)^{\frac{1}{2}}\tau + \frac{1}{2}\log e \int_{-\infty}^{\infty} \frac{e^{-\frac{1}{2}x^2/\sigma^2}}{(2\pi)^{\frac{1}{2}}\sigma} \mathrm{d}x$$

from (6.3.1) and the integration with respect to y using (6.2.1). After an application of (6.1.8) we obtain

$$H(Y \mid X) = \log(2\pi e\tau^2)^{\frac{1}{2}}.$$

Definition 6.3 now supplies

$$I(X, Y) = \frac{1}{2}\log(1+\sigma^2/\tau^2).$$

The effect of a change of variable on entropy has been remarked in Section 6.2. The corresponding behaviour in two dimensions is now to be examined. Make a $1-1$ mapping from the (x, y)-plane to the (ξ, η)-plane and let $g(\xi, \eta)$ be the probability density in the second plane. The connection between g and f is arrived at by considering an arbitrary domain D of the (x, y)-plane. Suppose that D is mapped to D' in the (ξ, η)-plane. Then

$$P\{(x, y) \in D\} = P\{(\xi, \eta) \in D'\}$$

or

$$\int\int_D f_{X,Y}(x, y) \, dx \, dy = \int\int_{D'} g(\xi, \eta) \, d\xi \, d\eta$$

by virtue of (6.3.2). Transforming back from the (ξ, η)-plane to the (x, y)-plane we have

$$\int\int_D f_{X,Y}(x, y) \, dx \, dy = \int\int_D g(\xi, \eta) \frac{\partial(\xi, \eta)}{\partial(x, y)} \, dx \, dy \quad (6.3.18)$$

where $\partial(\xi, \eta)/\partial(x, y)$ is the Jacobian of the mapping, i.e.

$$\frac{\partial(\xi, \eta)}{\partial(x, y)} = \begin{vmatrix} \partial\xi/\partial x & \partial\eta/\partial x \\ \partial\xi/\partial y & \partial\eta/\partial y \end{vmatrix}.$$

Since (6.3.18) is valid for arbitrary D

$$f_{X,Y}(x, y) = g(\xi, \eta) \frac{\partial(\xi, \eta)}{\partial(x, y)} \quad (6.3.19)$$

or, equally well,

$$g(\xi, \eta) = f_{X,Y}(x, y) \frac{\partial(x, y)}{\partial(\xi, \eta)}. \quad (6.3.20)$$

The presence of the Jacobian in (6.3.19) and (6.3.20) means that entropy will not in general be invariant under a mapping of the plane. However, quantities which depend upon the difference between entropies such as the mutual information may have a structure which cancels out the effect of the Jacobian. Consider, in particular, the mapping in which $x \to \xi$ and $y \to \eta$ so that

$\partial\xi/\partial y = 0$ and $\partial\eta/\partial x = 0$. Then

$$g_\Xi(\xi) = \int_{-\infty}^{\infty} g(\xi, \eta)\, \mathrm{d}\eta = \int_{-\infty}^{\infty} f_{X,Y}(x, y)\frac{\mathrm{d}x}{\mathrm{d}\xi}\frac{\mathrm{d}y}{\mathrm{d}\eta}\, \mathrm{d}\eta$$

$$= f_X(x)\frac{\mathrm{d}x}{\mathrm{d}\xi}.$$

Similarly

$$g_H(\eta) = f_Y(y)\frac{\mathrm{d}y}{\mathrm{d}\eta}.$$

Consequently

$$\frac{g(\xi, \eta)}{g_\Xi(\xi)g_H(\eta)} = \frac{f_{X,Y}(x, y)}{f_X(x)f_Y(y)}.$$

It follows from (6.3.16) that

$$I(\Xi, H) = I(X, Y),$$

i.e. the mutual information is invariant under a change of variables of the type described.

6.4. Addition of random variables

When x and y are random variables the probability of their sum $x + y$ can be found from a consideration of Fig. 6.4.1. For

$$P(x + y \leqslant z) = P\{(x, y)\ \text{in shaded area}\}$$

$$= \int_{-\infty}^{\infty} \int_{-\infty}^{z-x} f_{X,Y}(x, y)\, \mathrm{d}x\, \mathrm{d}y.$$

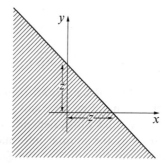

FIG. 6.4.1. $x + y \leqslant z$ in the shaded area.

But the left-hand side is the distribution function of the sum. Therefore, from (6.1.4), the probability density of $z = x + y$ is given by

$$f_Z(z) = \frac{d}{dz} \int_{-\infty}^{\infty} \int_{-\infty}^{z-x} f_{X,Y}(x, y) \, dx \, dy$$

$$= \int_{-\infty}^{\infty} f_{X,Y}(x, z - x) \, dx. \tag{6.4.1}$$

For statistically independent variables (6.4.1) reduces to

$$f_Z(z) = \int_{-\infty}^{\infty} f_X(x) f_Y(z - x) \, dx \tag{6.4.2}$$

$$= \int_{-\infty}^{\infty} f_X(z - y) f_Y(y) \, dy \tag{6.4.3}$$

on making the change of variable $x = z - y$.

Example 6.4. The two variables are statistically independent and Gaussian, their respective means being μ_1, μ_2 and their variances σ_1^2, σ_2^2. The probability density of the sum is, by (6.4.2),

$$\int_{-\infty}^{\infty} \frac{1}{2\pi\sigma_1\sigma_2} \exp\left\{ -\frac{1}{2\sigma_1^2}(x - \mu_1)^2 - \frac{1}{2\sigma_2^2}(z - x - \mu_2)^2 \right\} dx.$$

But

$$\frac{1}{\sigma_1^2}(x - \mu_1)^2 + \frac{1}{\sigma_2^2}(z - x - \mu_2)^2 = \left(\frac{1}{\sigma_1^2} + \frac{1}{\sigma_2^2} \right)$$

$$\times \left\{ x + \frac{\sigma_1^2(\mu_2 - z) - \sigma_2^2\mu_1}{\sigma_1^2 + \sigma_2^2} \right\}^2$$

$$+ \frac{(z - \mu_1 - \mu_2)^2}{\sigma_1^2 + \sigma_2^2}.$$

Hence, after the integration has been carried out, the probability density is

$$\frac{1}{\{2\pi(\sigma_1^2 + \sigma_2^2)\}^{\frac{1}{2}}} \exp\left\{ -\frac{1}{2} \frac{(z - \mu_1 - \mu_2)^2}{\sigma_1^2 + \sigma_2^2} \right\}$$

which is Gaussian. Thus, *the sum of two statistically independent*

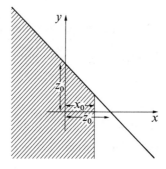

FIG. 6.4.2. Shaded region supplies the distribution function for x and z.

Gaussian variables is also Gaussian; its mean is the sum of the two individual means and its variance is the sum of the variances. Note that it is the variances which are additive and not the standard deviations.

The joint distribution between x and z is also of interest. The distribution function of x and z is obtained from

$$F(x_0, z_0) = P(x \leqslant x_0, x + y \leqslant z_0)$$

so that the points (x, y) in the shaded domain of Fig. 6.4.2 are relevant. Thus

$$F(x_0, z_0) = \int_{-\infty}^{x_0} \int_{-\infty}^{z_0-x} f_{X,Y}(x, y) \, dx \, dy.$$

From (6.3.4) the probability density of x and z is given by

$$f_{X,Z}(x_0, z_0) = \frac{\partial^2}{\partial x_0 \, \partial z_0} F(x_0, z_0)$$

so that

$$f_{X,Z}(x, z) = f_{X,Y}(x, z - x). \qquad (6.4.4)$$

When x and y are statistically independent (6.4.4) becomes

$$f_{X,Z}(x, z) = f_X(x) f_Y(z - x). \qquad (6.4.5)$$

For the case of statistical independence (6.4.5) and Definition 6.3 provide

$$H(X \cap Z) = -\int\int f_X(x) f_Y(z - x) \log\{f_X(x) f_Y(z - x)\} \, dx \, dz$$

$$= -\int\int f_X(x) f_Y(y) \{\log f_X(x) + \log f_Y(y)\} \, dx \, dy$$

on replacing z by $y \mid x$. Consequently,

$$H(X \cap Z) = H(X) + H(Y)$$

when X and Y are statistically independent. From (6.3.12)

$$H(Z) + H(X \mid Z) = H(X) + H(Y)$$

or

$$I(X, Z) = H(X) - H(X \mid Z) = H(Z) - H(Y) \qquad (6.4.6)$$

when X and Y are statistically independent. There will be an important application of this result in the discussion of continuous signals on channels (Section 6.9).

6.5. More than two variables

The changes that are required to cope with more than two variables are mainly notational. With a point $(x_1, \ldots, x_n)$ of n-dimensional space is associated a *probability density* $f_{X_1,\ldots,X_n}(x_1, \ldots, x_n)$ which is a piecewise continuous function such that

$$f_{X_1,\ldots,X_n}(x_1, \ldots, x_n) \geq 0,$$

$$\int_{-\infty}^{\infty} \cdots \int_{-\infty}^{\infty} f_{X_1,\ldots,X_n}(x_1, \ldots, x_n) \, dx_1 \cdots dx_n = 1. \qquad (6.5.1)$$

For brevity, $(x_1, \ldots, x_n)$ will be denoted by $\mathbf{x}$ and the probability density by $f_{\mathbf{X}}(\mathbf{x})$. Then (6.5.1) reads as

$$f_{\mathbf{X}}(\mathbf{x}) \geq 0, \qquad \int_{-\infty}^{\infty} f_{\mathbf{X}}(\mathbf{x}) \, d\mathbf{x} = 1. \qquad (6.5.2)$$

The probability that the point $\mathbf{x}$ falls in the domain D of the space is given by

$$P(\mathbf{x} \in D) = \int_{D} f_{\mathbf{X}}(\mathbf{x}) \, d\mathbf{x} \qquad (6.5.3)$$

so long as D is regular enough for the integral to exist.

It is sometimes convenient to think of an $(n + m)$-dimensional space as composed of an n-dimensional space $\mathbf{X}$ and an m-dimensional space $\mathbf{Y}$. Such a split may be indicated by writing the probability density as $f_{\mathbf{X},\mathbf{Y}}(\mathbf{x}, \mathbf{y})$. The probability density for the space $\mathbf{X}$ is, by analogy with (6.3.5),

$$f_{\mathbf{X}}(\mathbf{x}) = \int_{-\infty}^{\infty} f_{\mathbf{X},\mathbf{Y}}(\mathbf{x}, \mathbf{y}) \, d\mathbf{y}, \qquad (6.5.4)$$

the integral being, of course, an m-dimensional one. Similarly

$$f_{\mathbf{Y}}(\mathbf{y}) = \int_{-\infty}^{\infty} f_{\mathbf{X},\mathbf{Y}}(\mathbf{x}, \mathbf{y}) \, d\mathbf{y}, \qquad (6.5.5)$$

Both $f_{\mathbf{X}}(\mathbf{x})$ and $f_{\mathbf{Y}}(\mathbf{y})$ will satisfy (6.5.2).

Conditional probability densities can be derived in a similar way to those in (6.3.9) and (6.3.10). Thus

$$f_{\mathbf{Y}}(\mathbf{y} \mid \mathbf{x} = \mathbf{x}_0) = f_{\mathbf{X},\mathbf{Y}}(\mathbf{x}_0, \mathbf{y})/f_{\mathbf{X}}(\mathbf{x}_0), \qquad (6.5.6)$$

$$f_{\mathbf{X}}(\mathbf{x} \mid \mathbf{y} = \mathbf{y}_0) = f_{\mathbf{X},\mathbf{Y}}(\mathbf{x}, \mathbf{y}_0)/f_{\mathbf{Y}}(\mathbf{y}_0). \qquad (6.5.7)$$

$\mathbf{X}$ and $\mathbf{Y}$ are said to be *statistically independent* when

$$f_{\mathbf{X},\mathbf{Y}}(\mathbf{x}, \mathbf{y}) = f_{\mathbf{X}}(\mathbf{x})f_{\mathbf{Y}}(\mathbf{y}) \qquad (6.5.8)$$

on any domain of non-zero measure.

DEFINITION 6.5. *The entropies* $H(\mathbf{X})$, $H(\mathbf{X} \cap \mathbf{Y})$, *and* $H(\mathbf{X} \mid \mathbf{Y})$ *are defined by*

$$H(\mathbf{X}) = -\int_{-\infty}^{\infty} f_{\mathbf{X}}(\mathbf{x}) \log f_{\mathbf{X}}(\mathbf{x}) \, d\mathbf{x},$$

$$H(\mathbf{X} \cap \mathbf{Y}) = -\int_{-\infty}^{\infty} \int_{-\infty}^{\infty} f_{\mathbf{X},\mathbf{Y}}(\mathbf{x}, \mathbf{y}) \log f_{\mathbf{X},\mathbf{Y}}(\mathbf{x}, \mathbf{y}) \, d\mathbf{x} \, d\mathbf{y},$$

$$H(\mathbf{X} \mid \mathbf{Y}) = -\int_{-\infty}^{\infty} \int_{-\infty}^{\infty} f_{\mathbf{X},\mathbf{Y}}(\mathbf{x}, \mathbf{y}) \log \frac{f_{\mathbf{X},\mathbf{Y}}(\mathbf{x}, \mathbf{y})}{f_{\mathbf{Y}}(\mathbf{y})} \, d\mathbf{x} \, d\mathbf{y}$$

and the mutual information $I(\mathbf{X}, \mathbf{Y})$ *is specified by*

$$I(\mathbf{X}, \mathbf{Y}) = H(\mathbf{X}) - H(\mathbf{X} \mid \mathbf{Y}).$$

It will be observed that if $\mathbf{X}$ is two-dimensional $H(\mathbf{X})$ can be written as $H(X_1 \cap X_2)$, the entropy of Definition 6.3. Also

$$H(\mathbf{X} \cap \mathbf{Y}) = H(X_1 \cap \cdots \cap X_n \cap Y_1 \cap \cdots \cap Y_m).$$

Formally, Definition 6.5 differs from Definition 6.3 only in having $\mathbf{x}, \mathbf{y}$ for x, y. So we can anticipate the following results from Section 6.3:

$$H(\mathbf{X} \cap \mathbf{Y}) = H(\mathbf{Y}) + H(\mathbf{X} \mid \mathbf{Y}) \tag{6.5.9}$$

$$= H(\mathbf{X}) + H(\mathbf{Y} \mid \mathbf{X}), \tag{6.5.10}$$

$$I(\mathbf{X}, \mathbf{Y}) = H(\mathbf{X}) + H(\mathbf{Y}) - H(\mathbf{X} \cap \mathbf{Y}) \tag{6.5.11}$$

$$= H(\mathbf{Y}) - H(\mathbf{Y} \mid \mathbf{X}). \tag{6.5.12}$$

The proof that $I(\mathbf{X}, \mathbf{Y})$ is invariant under a change of variables is left for the reader (see Exercise 6.17).

In addition we have the following theorem.

THEOREM 6.5. $I(\mathbf{X},\mathbf{Y}) \geq 0$ *and* $H(\mathbf{X}) \geq H(\mathbf{X} \mid \mathbf{Y})$ *with equality if and only if* $\mathbf{X}$ *and* $\mathbf{Y}$ *are statistically independent.*
Once again, conditioning does not increase entropy.

Example 6.5. The *n-dimensional Gaussian distribution* has probability density

$$f_{\mathbf{X}}(\mathbf{x}) = \frac{\Delta^{\frac{1}{2}}}{(2\pi)^{\frac{1}{2}n}} \exp\left\{ -\frac{1}{2} \sum_{i=1}^{n} \sum_{j=1}^{n} a_{ij}(x_i - \mu_i)(x_j - \mu_j) \right\} \tag{6.5.13}$$

where the matrix (a_{ij}) is real symmetric $(a_{ij} = a_{ji})$ and positive definite. The constant Δ is the determinant of the matrix, i.e.

$$\Delta = \det(a_{ij}) \tag{6.5.14}$$

To verify (6.5.2) for the Gaussian distribution make the transformation $x_i - \mu_i = u_i$ $(i = 1, \ldots, n)$. Then

$$\int_{-\infty}^{\infty} f_{\mathbf{X}}(\mathbf{x})\, d\mathbf{x} = \frac{\Delta^{\frac{1}{2}}}{(2\pi)^{\frac{1}{2}n}} \int_{-\infty}^{\infty} \exp(-\tfrac{1}{2}\mathbf{u}^T A \mathbf{u})\, d\mathbf{u}$$

where A is the matrix (a_{ij}). Since A is real symmetric there is an orthogonal matrix L such that

$$L^T A L = \Lambda \tag{6.5.15}$$

where Λ is a diagonal matrix whose only non-zero entries $\lambda_1, \ldots, \lambda_n$ lie on the diagonal. In fact, $\lambda_1 > 0, \ldots, \lambda_n > 0$ because A is positive definite. Since L is orthogonal the mapping $\mathbf{u} = L\mathbf{v}$

corresponds to a rotation of axes and so

$$\int_{-\infty}^{\infty} f_{\mathbf{X}}(\mathbf{x})\, d\mathbf{x} = \frac{\Delta^{\frac{1}{2}}}{(2\pi)^{\frac{1}{2}n}} \int_{-\infty}^{\infty} \exp(-\tfrac{1}{2}\mathbf{v}^T L^T A L \mathbf{v})\, d\mathbf{v}$$

$$= \frac{\Delta^{\frac{1}{2}}}{(2\pi)^{\frac{1}{2}n}} \int_{-\infty}^{\infty} \exp(-\tfrac{1}{2}\mathbf{v}^T \Lambda \mathbf{v})\, d\mathbf{v}$$

$$= \frac{\Delta^{\frac{1}{2}}}{(2\pi)^{\frac{1}{2}n}} \int_{-\infty}^{\infty} \cdots \int_{-\infty}^{\infty} \exp\{-\tfrac{1}{2}(\lambda_1 v_1{}^2 + \lambda_2 v_2{}^2$$
$$+ \cdots + \lambda_n v_n{}^2)\}\, dv_1 \cdots dv_n$$

from (6.5.15). The integrations with respect to $v_1, v_2, \ldots$ may each be carried out separately, the positivity of $\lambda_1, \ldots, \lambda_n$ warranting convergence. From (6.1.8)

$$\int_{-\infty}^{\infty} f_{\mathbf{X}}(\mathbf{x})\, d\mathbf{x} = \Delta^{\frac{1}{2}}/(\lambda_1 \cdots \lambda_n)^{\frac{1}{2}}.$$

But

$$\lambda_1 \cdots \lambda_n = \det \Lambda = \det A$$

from (6.5.15) and so (6.5.2) has been checked.

The device of the orthogonal mapping also enables one to show that

$$H(\mathbf{X}) = \log\{(2\pi e)^{\frac{1}{2}n}/\Delta^{\frac{1}{2}}\} \tag{6.5.16}$$

for the n-dimensional Gaussian distribution.

6.6. Ensembles of functions

The discussion of propagation along discrete channels was formulated in terms of sequences of letters drawn from a source according to some probability law. The natural analogue for the continuous case is to consider families of continuous waveforms. For example, one possibility might be the family of functions which vary sinusoidally with the time t. A typical member of the family will have the form

$$g(t) = a \sin(\omega t + \phi).$$

The whole family is obtained by allowing a, ω, and ϕ to run through their different values.

It may happen that the selection of values for a, ω, and ϕ is governed by probabilistic considerations, e.g. there is a probability $P(\omega)$ of choosing the particular value ω. In that case ω is a random variable. Such a family, in which the choice of members is dictated by random variables, is known as an *ensemble*. For instance, if it is known that a is always 1 and ϕ is always 0, $P(\omega)$ is the probability that the particular function $\sin \omega t$ will be selected from the ensemble of functions of the form $\sin \omega t$.

If a, ω, and ϕ are all random variables, the three-dimensional $P(a, \omega, \phi)$ will need to be known to specify the probability of g. When a is fixed but ω and ϕ are random variables, knowledge of $P(\omega, \phi)$ will be sufficient and $P(\phi)$ will be enough if both a and ω are fixed.

More elaborate ensembles can be constructed. For example

(i)
$$g(t) = \sum_{k=1}^{r} a_k \sin(kt + \phi_k)$$

where a_k and ϕ_k are random variables. The joint probability of the $2r$ variables $a_1, \ldots, a_r$, $\phi_1, \ldots, \phi_r$ will be required.

(ii)
$$g(t) = \sum_{k=-\infty}^{\infty} a_k \frac{\sin \pi(2Wt - k)}{\pi(2Wt - k)} \qquad (6.6.1)$$

where W is a constant and the a_k are random variables.

(iii)
$$g(t) = \sum_{k=-\infty}^{\infty} h(t + t_k)$$

where h is a specified function whose argument contains the random variable t_k.

(iv) English speech with probability according to the frequency of occurrence in ordinary usage.

6.7. Bandwidth

An important concept which arises in connection with signal transmission is that of *bandwidth* which is specified by the following definition.

DEFINITION 6.7. *If $g(t)$ is a signal varying with time t and, for real ω,*

$$G(\omega) = \int_{-\infty}^{\infty} g(t)e^{-i\omega t}\, dt$$

is such that $G(\omega) = 0$ for $|\omega| > 2\pi W$ the signal is said to have bandwidth W.

The units of bandwidth are *Hertz* (Hz).

When g has finite bandwidth, there is the possibility of expanding G in its non-zero interval by a Fourier series. For later development the complex form of the expansion is the most convenient. Let

$$\Theta_k(\omega) = \frac{1}{2(W\pi)^{\frac{1}{2}}} e^{-ik\omega/2W} \qquad (|\omega| \leqslant 2\pi W)$$

$$= 0 \qquad (|\omega| > 2\pi W).$$

Then

$$\int_{-2\pi W}^{2\pi W} \Theta_k(\omega)\Theta_j(\omega)\, d\omega = \frac{1}{4W\pi} \int_{-2\pi W}^{2\pi W} e^{-i\omega(k+j)/2W}\, d\omega.$$

If $k + j \neq 0$, the right-hand side is

$$\frac{1}{2\pi} \left[\frac{e^{-i\omega(k+j)/2W}}{-i(k+j)} \right]_{-2\pi W}^{2\pi W} = 0$$

whereas, if $k + j = 0$, the right-hand side is 1. Hence

$$\left. \begin{aligned} \int_{-2\pi W}^{2\pi W} \Theta_k(\omega)\Theta_j(\omega)\, d\omega &= 0 \\ &= 1 \end{aligned} \right\} \quad \left. \begin{aligned} (k+j \neq 0) \\ (k+j = 0) \end{aligned} \right\} \qquad (6.7.1)$$

Thus, when g has finite bandwidth, the Fourier series expansion for G is

$$G(\omega) = \sum_{k=-\infty}^{\infty} G_k \Theta_k(\omega) \qquad (|\omega| < 2\pi W) \qquad (6.7.2)$$

$$= 0 \qquad (|\omega| > 2\pi W).$$

In (6.7.2)

$$G_k = \int_{-2\pi W}^{2\pi W} G(\omega)\Theta_{-k}(\omega)\, d\omega \qquad (6.7.3)$$

as may be checked by multiplying (6.7.2) by Θ_{-j} and using (6.7.1), assuming that summation and integration may be interchanged.

There is a theorem, known as the Fourier Inversion Theorem, which states that, when suitable conditions are satisfied,

$$g(t) = \frac{1}{2\pi} \int_{-\infty}^{\infty} G(\omega) e^{i\omega t} \, d\omega \qquad (6.7.4)$$

when

$$G(\omega) = \int_{-\infty}^{\infty} g(t) e^{-i\omega t} \, dt.$$

No attempt will be made to lay down conditions here; it will merely be assumed that the signals we have to handle are such that (6.7.4) is satisfied.

If the signal has bandwidth W, (6.7.4) reduces to

$$g(t) = \frac{1}{2\pi} \int_{-2\pi W}^{2\pi W} G(\omega) e^{i\omega t} \, d\omega. \qquad (6.7.5)$$

Substitution of (6.7.2), followed by interchange of summation and integration (assumed legitimate), leads to

$$g(t) = \sum_{k=-\infty}^{\infty} (G_k/2\pi) \int_{-2\pi W}^{2\pi W} \Theta_k(\omega) e^{i\omega t} \, d\omega.$$

Now

$$\int_{-2\pi W}^{2\pi W} e^{i\omega(t-k/2W)} \, d\omega = 4W \frac{\sin \pi(2Wt-k)}{2Wt-k}.$$

Hence

$$g(t) = \sum_{k=-\infty}^{\infty} \left(\frac{W}{\pi}\right)^{\frac{1}{2}} G_k \frac{\sin \pi(2Wt-k)}{\pi(2Wt-k)}.$$

But, from (6.7.5) with $t = k/2W$ and (6.7.3),

$$g\left(\frac{k}{2W}\right) = \left(\frac{W}{\pi}\right)^{\frac{1}{2}} G_k.$$

Hence we have the following theorem.

SAMPLING THEOREM. *If* $g(t)$ *has finite bandwidth* W, *then*

$$g(t) = \sum_{k=-\infty}^{\infty} g\left(\frac{k}{2W}\right) \frac{\sin \pi(2Wt-k)}{\pi(2Wt-k)}.$$

One consequence of the Sampling Theorem is that a signal of bandwidth W is known for all time if its values at the times $k/2W$ (k integer) are available. Such a signal can be determined fully by sampling its values at intervals of $1/2W$. In communication the coefficients $g(k/2W)$ are often random variables so that a signal of limited bandwidth can be regarded as one from the ensemble of type (ii) (6.6.1) in Section 6.6.

The time interval $(0, T)$ may be such that $g(t)$ is small outside of it. Then, to a first approximation, only points within $(0, T)$ need be considered for the expansion of the Sampling Theorem. Since the sampling points are separated by $1/2W$ there will be about $2WT$ of them. Therefore the series can be restricted to $2WT$ terms and our consideration can be limited to signals which possess $2WT$ random variables. The estimate improves as $T \to \infty$.

Strictly, a signal of finite bandwidth cannot be zero also for all times outside a finite interval. For, although the terms in the series in the Sampling Theorem become small as t increases, they are never exactly zero. Nevertheless, most communication signals have a finite bandwidth and have most of their energy concentrated into a finite time interval. So any practical signal will be determined to a high degree of accuracy by its values at $2WT$ sampling points provided that $2WT \gg 1$.

6.8. Continuous channels

The input to a continuous channel will be denoted by $x(t)$, the t signifying its variation with respect to time. It will be a representative from an ensemble of functions. The structure of the expansion in the Sampling Theorem suggests that we should try to place the probability in coefficients multiplying functions which are deterministic.

Let $T > 0$ and let $\theta_1(t), \theta_2(t), \ldots$ be a set of *fixed* real functions, i.e. they contain no probability element. Further, suppose that

$$\left. \begin{aligned} \int_0^T \theta_r(t)\theta_s(t)\, \mathrm{d}t &= 0 \qquad (r \neq s) \\ &= 1 \qquad (r = s) \end{aligned} \right\}. \tag{6.8.1}$$

An example of a possible set is

$$\frac{1}{T^{\frac{1}{2}}}, \frac{2}{T^{\frac{1}{2}}}\cos\frac{2\pi t}{T}, \frac{2}{T^{\frac{1}{2}}}\cos\frac{4\pi t}{T}, \ldots, \frac{2}{T^{\frac{1}{2}}}\sin\frac{2\pi t}{T}, \frac{2}{T^{\frac{1}{2}}}\sin\frac{4\pi t}{T}, \ldots$$

as may be readily verified.

Under appropriate conditions, which will be assumed to be satisfied, it is known that

$$x(t) = \sum_{k=1}^{\infty} x_k \theta_k(t) \qquad (0 < t < T). \tag{6.8.2}$$

On multiplying (6.8.2) by $\theta_j(t)$ and integrating from 0 to T we see from (6.8.1) that

$$x_j = \int_0^T x(t)\theta_j(t)\,\mathrm{d}t. \tag{6.8.3}$$

The formulae (6.8.2) and (6.8.3) constitute a generalized form of Fourier series.

The output $y(t)$ of the channel can be dealt with likewise. Let $\psi_1(t), \psi_2(t), \dots$ have similar properties to the θ_k. It is permissible to put $\psi_k = \theta_k$ (all k) if desired. Then

$$y(t) = \sum_{k=1}^{\infty} y_k \psi_k(t) \qquad (0 < t < T) \tag{6.8.4}$$

where

$$y_k = \int_0^T y(t)\psi_k(t)\,\mathrm{d}t. \tag{6.8.5}$$

The series (6.8.2) and (6.8.4) reveal that the random variables in $x(t)$ are $x_1, x_2, \dots$ and in $y(t)$ are $y_1, y_2, \dots$ In line with the discussion of the preceding section a reasonably good estimate should be obtained if a series is truncated after the first n terms, provided that n is large. The eventual identification $n = 2TW$ is a natural follow-on from the Sampling Theorem. With a representation by means of a truncated series the input can be characterized by the n-dimensional $\mathbf{x}$ with components $x_1, \dots, x_n$ and has an associated probability density $f_{\mathbf{X}}(\mathbf{x})$. Similarly, the output characteristics come from $\mathbf{y}$ with components $y_1, \dots y_n$ and $f_{\mathbf{Y}}(\mathbf{y})$. The conditional probability $f_{\mathbf{Y}}(\mathbf{y} \mid \mathbf{x} = \mathbf{x}_0)$ controls the transitions from input to output and so describes the statistics of any noise on the channel.

The mutual information $I(\mathbf{X}, \mathbf{Y})$ conveys knowledge of the amount of information conveyed from input to output as in the discrete case. Since this occurs in a time interval T, a quantity relevant to unit time is

$$C_T = \frac{1}{T} \sup I(\mathbf{X}, \mathbf{Y}) \tag{6.8.6}$$

where the supremum is taken over all input probability distributions *consistent with any input constraints*. C_T may thus be thought of as a capacity per unit time for truncated inputs and outputs. There is an extra condition on the input, as compared with the discrete case, because it must be recognized that inputs which demand unlimited power must be excluded by practical considerations.

Theoretically, the limit as $n \to \infty$ with T fixed should now be considered. However, the discussion of Section 6.7 suggests that n can be taken effectively as $2WT$ in many practical situations. Therefore, we shall not examine what happens as $n \to \infty$ independent of T. Instead, we shall suppose that n and T go to infinity together and define

$$C = \lim_{T \to \infty} C_T \qquad (6.8.7)$$

as the *channel capacity per unit time*, when the limit exists.

Existence of C may not be guaranteed but when C can be found one assertion can be made. For $\lim_{T \to \infty} H(\mathbf{X})/T$, when it exists, can be regarded as the entropy per unit time of the source. When this entropy exceeds C, (6.8.6), (6.8.7), and Definition 6.5 show that the equivocation cannot be less than $\lim_{T \to \infty} H(\mathbf{X})/T - C$. Thus there is an analogue of Shannon's Theorem II (Section 4.6) and there is no coding which is error free. In general, the analogue of Shannon's Theorem I is false because there are channels which transmit below capacity but the probability of error in the data cannot be made arbitrarily small.

6.9. Additive noise

One particular case in which progress can be achieved is that in which the output differs from the input only by the addition of noise, i.e.

$$y(t) = x(t) + z(t)$$

where z is due to noise.

Choose $\psi_k = \theta_k$ and then, from (6.8.5),

$$y_k = \int_0^T y(t)\theta_k(t)\,\mathrm{d}t = \int_0^T \{x(t) + z(t)\}\theta_k(t)\,\mathrm{d}t$$

$$= x_k + z_k \qquad (6.9.1)$$

where $x_k = \int_0^T x(t)\theta_k(t)\,dt$. Keeping to the truncated versions of series we may express (6.9.1) as

$$\mathbf{y} = \mathbf{x} + \mathbf{z}.$$

Although this is a vector we may proceed in a similar manner to Section 6.4 so that

$$f_{\mathbf{Y}}(\mathbf{y}) = \int_{-\infty}^{\infty} f_{\mathbf{X},\mathbf{Z}}(\mathbf{x}, \mathbf{y} - \mathbf{x})\,d\mathbf{x} \tag{6.9.2}$$

the integral, of course, being in n-dimensions.

If $\mathbf{X}$ and $\mathbf{Z}$ are statistically independent, i.e. $f_{\mathbf{X},\mathbf{Z}}(\mathbf{x}, \mathbf{z}) = f_{\mathbf{X}}(\mathbf{x})f_{\mathbf{Z}}(\mathbf{z})$ (6.9.2) becomes

$$f_{\mathbf{Y}}(\mathbf{y}) = \int_{-\infty}^{\infty} f_{\mathbf{X}}(\mathbf{x})f_{\mathbf{Z}}(\mathbf{y} - \mathbf{x})\,d\mathbf{x} \tag{6.9.3}$$

and

$$f_{\mathbf{X},\mathbf{Y}}(\mathbf{x}, \mathbf{y}) = f_{\mathbf{X}}(\mathbf{x})f_{\mathbf{Z}}(\mathbf{y} - \mathbf{z}). \tag{6.9.4}$$

Thus, as in (6.4.6),

$$I(\mathbf{X}, \mathbf{Y}) = H(\mathbf{Y}) - H(\mathbf{Z}) \tag{6.9.5}$$

Consequently, when the noise is statistically independent of the input (as it frequently is), (6.9.5) demonstrates that I varies with input only via $H(\mathbf{Y})$ because the value of $H(\mathbf{Z})$ is set by the noise alone. The problem of finding capacity in an additive noise channel therefore becomes that of finding the largest $H(\mathbf{Y})$ subject to the input constraints.

The constraint to be considered is that in which the input is *power limited*. Specifically

$$\int_{-\infty}^{\infty} f_{\mathbf{X}}(\mathbf{x}) \int_0^T \{x(t)\}^2\,dt\,d\mathbf{x} \leqslant PT \tag{6.9.6}$$

with $x(t)$ represented by its truncated series. The quantity P is known as the *average power* available. Since

$$\int_0^T \{x(t)\}^2\,dt = \int_0^T \sum_{r=1}^n x_r\theta_r(t) \sum_{s=1}^n x_s\theta_s(t)\,dt$$

$$= \sum_{r=1}^n x_r^2$$

from (6.8.1), the limitation (6.9.6) can be rewritten as

$$\sum_{k=1}^{n} \int_{-\infty}^{\infty} f_{\mathbf{X}}(\mathbf{x}) x_k^2 \, d\mathbf{x} \leq PT. \tag{6.9.7}$$

Also

$$\int_{-\infty}^{\infty} f_{\mathbf{X}}(\mathbf{x}) x_k^2 \, d\mathbf{x} = \int_{-\infty}^{\infty} f_{X_k}(x_k) x_k^2 \, dx_k = \sigma_k^2 \text{ (say)};$$

σ_k^2 is connected to the variance of the random variable x_k. An alternative version of (6.9.7) is accordingly

$$\sum_{k=1}^{n} \sigma_k^2 \leq PT. \tag{6.9.8}$$

The question of finding capacity can be answered if the mutual information can be maximized subject to (6.9.7) or (6.9.8). The analysis for a special form of noise will be developed in the next section.

6.10. Additive white Gaussian noise

The noise is said to be *white Gaussian* when all the random variables $z_1, \ldots, z_n$ are mutually statistically independent Gaussian distributions. Each Gaussian distribution has zero mean and variance σ^2. In other words

$$f_{\mathbf{Z}}(\mathbf{z}) = \frac{1}{(2\pi\sigma^2)^{\frac{1}{2}n}} \exp\left(-\frac{1}{2\sigma^2} \sum_{k=1}^{n} z_k^2\right) \tag{6.10.1}$$

for white Gaussian noise. Expressed another way

$$f_{\mathbf{Z}}(\mathbf{z}) = f_Z(z_1) f_Z(z_2) \cdots f_Z(z_n) \tag{6.10.2}$$

where

$$f_Z(z) = \frac{1}{(2\pi)^{\frac{1}{2}}\sigma} e^{-\frac{1}{2}z^2/\sigma^2}. \tag{6.10.3}$$

To begin with, our deliberations will deal with a more general class of noise namely that in which (6.10.2) is valid but (6.10.3) is not imposed. However, it is required that

$$\int_{-\infty}^{\infty} z f_Z(z) \, dz = 0. \qquad \int_{-\infty}^{\infty} z^2 f_Z(z) \, dz = \sigma^2. \tag{6.10.4}$$

Noise of this type is called *white*. Obviously, white Gaussian noise is one example in this category.

The formula for the mutual information is

$$I(\mathbf{X}, \mathbf{Y}) = \int_{-\infty}^{\infty} f_{\mathbf{X}, \mathbf{Y}}(\mathbf{x}, \mathbf{y}) \log \frac{f_{\mathbf{X}, \mathbf{Y}}(\mathbf{x}, \mathbf{y})}{f_{\mathbf{X}}(\mathbf{x}) f_{\mathbf{Y}}(\mathbf{y})} \, d\mathbf{x} \, d\mathbf{y}.$$

Now

$$\frac{f_{\mathbf{X}, \mathbf{Y}}(\mathbf{x}, \mathbf{y})}{f_{\mathbf{X}}(\mathbf{x}) f_{\mathbf{Y}}(\mathbf{y})} = \prod_{r=1}^{n} \frac{f_{\mathbf{X}, Y_1, \ldots, Y_r}(\mathbf{x}, y_1, \ldots, y_r) f_{Y_1, \ldots, Y_{r-1}}(y_1, \ldots, y_{r-1})}{f_{Y_1, \ldots, Y_r}(y_1, \ldots, y_r) f_{X, Y_1, \ldots, Y_{r-1}}(\mathbf{x}, y_1, \ldots, y_{r-1})}$$

because of cancellation of terms in the numerator and denominator in adjacent factors of the product. Hence

$$I(\mathbf{X}, \mathbf{Y}) = \sum_{r=1}^{n} \int_{-\infty}^{\infty} f_{\mathbf{X}, \mathbf{Y}}(\mathbf{x}, \mathbf{y})$$
$$\times \log \frac{f_{\mathbf{X}, Y_1, \ldots, Y_r}(\mathbf{x}, y_1, \ldots, y_r) f_{Y_1, \ldots, Y_{r-1}}(y_1, \ldots, y_{r-1})}{f_{Y_1, \ldots, Y_r}(y_1, \ldots, y_r) f_{\mathbf{X}, Y_1, \ldots, Y_{r-1}}(\mathbf{x}, y_1, \ldots, y_{r-1})} \, d\mathbf{x} \, d\mathbf{y}.$$

From (6.9.4)

$$f_{\mathbf{X}, \mathbf{Y}}(\mathbf{x}, \mathbf{y}) = f_{\mathbf{X}}(\mathbf{x}) f_{\mathbf{Z}}(\mathbf{y} - \mathbf{x})$$

and integration from $-\infty$ to ∞ over $y_{r+1}, \ldots, y_n$ gives, (6.10.2) being borne in mind,

$$f_{\mathbf{X}, Y_1, \ldots, Y_r}(\mathbf{x}, y_1, \ldots, y_r) = f_{\mathbf{X}}(\mathbf{x}) f_Z(y_1 - x_1) \cdots f_Z(y_r - x_r). \quad (6.10.5)$$

Thus

$$\frac{f_{\mathbf{X}, Y_1, \ldots, Y_r}(\mathbf{x}, y_1, \ldots, y_r)}{f_{\mathbf{X}, Y_1, \ldots, Y_{r-1}}(\mathbf{x}, y_1, \ldots, y_{r-1})} = f_Z(y_r - x_r). \quad (6.10.6)$$

Integration of (6.10.5) with respect to $y_1, \ldots, y_{r-1}$ supplies

$$f_{\mathbf{X}, Y_r}(\mathbf{x}, y_r) = f_{\mathbf{X}}(\mathbf{x}) f_Z(y_r - x_r). \quad (6.10.7)$$

Further integration over all components of $\mathbf{x}$ except x_r results in

$$f_{X_r Y_r}(\mathbf{x}, y_r) = f_{X_r}(x_r) f_Z(y_r - x_r). \quad (6.10.8)$$

Combining (6.10.6) and (6.10.8) we obtain

$$I(\mathbf{X}, \mathbf{Y}) = \sum_{r=1}^{n} \int_{-\infty}^{\infty} f_{\mathbf{X}, \mathbf{Y}}(\mathbf{x}, \mathbf{y})$$
$$\times \log \frac{f_{X_r Y_r}(x_r, y_r) f_{Y_1, \ldots, Y_{r-1}}(y_1, \ldots, y_{r-1})}{f_{X_r}(x_r) f_{Y_1, \ldots, Y_r}(y_1, \ldots, y_r)} \, d\mathbf{x} \, d\mathbf{y}.$$

Next

$$\int_{-\infty}^{\infty} f_{\mathbf{X},\mathbf{Y}}(\mathbf{x}, \mathbf{y}) \log \frac{f_{Y_r}(y_r) f_{Y_1,\ldots,Y_{r-1}}(y_1,\ldots,y_{r-1})}{f_{Y_1,\ldots,Y_r}(y_1,\ldots,y_r)} \, d\mathbf{x} \, d\mathbf{y}$$

$$= \int_{-\infty}^{\infty} \cdots \int_{-\infty}^{\infty} f_{Y_1,\ldots,Y_r}(y_1,\ldots,y_r)$$

$$\times \log \frac{f_{Y_r}(y_r) f_{Y_1,\ldots,Y_{r-1}}(y_1,\ldots,y_{r-1})}{f_{Y_1,\ldots,Y_r}(y_1,\ldots,y_r)} \, dy_1 \cdots dy_r$$

$$\leq \log e \int_{-\infty}^{\infty} \cdots \int_{-\infty}^{\infty} \{ f_{Y_1,\ldots,Y_{r-1}}(y_1,\ldots,y_{r-1})$$

$$\times f_{Y_r}(y_r) - f_{Y_1,\ldots Y_r}(y_1,\ldots,y_r) \} \, dy_1 \cdots dy_r$$

$$\leq 0 \qquad\qquad (6.10.9)$$

since both integrands lead to the value of unity when integrated. Equality occurs in (6.10.9) for

$$f_{Y_1,\ldots,Y_r}(y_1,\ldots,y_r) = f_{Y_1,\ldots,Y_{r-1}}(y_1,\ldots,y_{r-1}) f_{Y_r}(y_r). \quad (6.10.10)$$

It follows that

$$I(\mathbf{X}, \mathbf{Y}) \leq \sum_{r=1}^{n} \int_{-\infty}^{\infty} f_{\mathbf{X},\mathbf{Y}}(\mathbf{x}, \mathbf{y}) \log \frac{f_{X_r, Y_r}(x_r, y_r)}{f_{X_r}(x_r) f_{Y_r}(y_r)} \, d\mathbf{x} \, d\mathbf{y}$$

$$(6.10.11)$$

with equality only when (6.10.10) holds for every r. Putting $r = 2$ in (6.10.10) shows that y_1 and y_2 are statistically independent. The further substitution $r = 3$ reveals that y_1, y_2, and y_3 are mutually statistically independent. Step-by-step we arrive at the conclusion that there is equality in (6.10.11) only when the output random variables $y_1,\ldots,y_n$ are mutually statistically independent.

All the integrations in (6.10.11) except those over x_r and y_r may be carried out with the result that

$$I(\mathbf{X}, \mathbf{Y}) \leq \sum_{r=1}^{n} I(X_r, Y_r) \qquad\qquad (6.10.12)$$

equality obtaining only when the outputs are statistically independent.

Since X_r and Z_r are statistically independent (an immediate consequence of the statistical independence of $\mathbf{X}$ and $\mathbf{Z}$) another form of (6.10.12) is

$$I(\mathbf{X}, \mathbf{Y}) \le \sum_{r=1}^{n} \{H(Y_r) - H(Z_r)\}. \qquad (6.10.13)$$

The next aim is to make the right-hand side of (6.10.13) as large as possible which means, in essence, maximizing $H(Y_r)$ since $H(Z_r)$ is not at our disposal. Now

$$\int_{-\infty}^{\infty} f_{Y_r}(y_r) y_r^2 \, dy_r = \int_{-\infty}^{\infty} y_r^2 \int_{-\infty}^{\infty} f_{X_r}(x_r) f_Z(y_r - x_r) \, dx_r \, dy_r$$

$$= \int_{-\infty}^{\infty} \int_{-\infty}^{\infty} (x_r + z_r)^2 f_{X_r}(x_r) f_Z(z_r) \, dx_r \, dz_r$$

$$= \sigma_r^2 + \sigma^2 \qquad (6.10.14)$$

on account of (6.10.4). Thus $H(Y_r)$ has to be maximized subject to (6.10.14). By Theorem 6.2 the maximum is $\log(2\pi e)^{\frac{1}{2}}(\sigma^2 + \sigma_r^2)^{\frac{1}{2}}$ and is achieved when the distribution is Gaussian. Hence

$$I(\mathbf{X}, \mathbf{Y}) \le \sum_{r=1}^{n} [\tfrac{1}{2} \log\{2\pi e(\sigma^2 + \sigma_r^2)\} - H(Z_r)] \quad (6.10.15)$$

with equality only when the outputs are statistically independent and Gaussian.

The values of σ_r^2 can still be allocated, provided that (6.9.8) is satisfied. The objective is to adjust them so as to make the right-hand side of (6.10.15) have its largest possible value. Write $\sigma_r^2 = e_r$; then $\sum_{r=1}^{n} \tfrac{1}{2} \log(\sigma^2 + e_r)$ is to be maximized subject to $e_r \ge 0$ $(r = 1, \ldots, n)$ and $\sum_{r=1}^{n} e_r \le PT$. Introducing the Lagrange multiplier λ we have

$$\frac{\partial}{\partial e_s} \left\{ \sum_{r=1}^{n} \tfrac{1}{2} \log(\sigma^2 + e_r) - \frac{\lambda}{PT} e_r \right\} = \frac{1}{2} \frac{\log e}{\sigma^2 + e_s} - \frac{\lambda}{PT}$$

which vanishes if $e_s = \dfrac{1}{2} \dfrac{PT}{\lambda} \log e - \sigma^2$. This implies that $\sum_{r=1}^{n} e_r = PT$ if

$$\lambda = \frac{\tfrac{1}{2} nPT \log e}{PT + n\sigma^2}.$$

We infer that $e_s = PT/n$ $(s = 1, \ldots, n)$ satisfies the constraint and gives the desired maximum. That it is a maximum can be deduced from the inequality

$$\sum_{r=1}^{n} \tfrac{1}{2} \log(\sigma^2 + e_r) = \sum_{r=1}^{n} \tfrac{1}{2} \log\left(\sigma^2 + \frac{PT}{n} + e_r - \frac{PT}{n}\right)$$

$$\leqslant \sum_{r=1}^{n} \tfrac{1}{2} \log\left(\sigma^2 + \frac{PT}{n}\right)$$

$$+ \frac{1}{2} \frac{n \log e}{n\sigma^2 + PT} \left(e_r - \frac{PT}{n}\right)$$

$$\leqslant \sum_{r=1}^{n} \tfrac{1}{2} \log(\sigma^2 + PT/n).$$

Consequently

$$I(\mathbf{X}, \mathbf{Y}) \leqslant \tfrac{1}{2} n \log\{2\pi e(\sigma^2 + PT/n)\} - \sum_{r=1}^{n} H(Z_r) \quad (6.10.16)$$

with equality only when the outputs are statistically independent and Gaussian with the same variance.

In view of the Sampling Theorem we put $n = 2WT$. Also, because of (6.10.2), $H(Z_r)$ is independent of r and can be written as $H(Z)$. Then (6.8.6) and (6.10.16) give

$$C_T \leqslant W\left[\log\left\{2\pi e\left(\sigma^2 + \frac{P}{2W}\right)\right\} - 2H(Z)\right].$$

The right-hand side does not vary with T and so, by (6.8.7), C satisfies the same inequality. Calling σ^2 the *spectral density* of the noise we can enunciate the following theorem.

CAPACITY BOUND THEOREM. *Let the output be the sum of the input and statistically independent white noise of spectral density $\tfrac{1}{2}N$. Let the input be limited to average power P. Then the capacity per unit time of a channel of bandwidth W satisfies*

$$C \leqslant W[\log\{\pi e(N + P/W)\} - 2H(Z)],$$

equality occurring only when the output components are statistically independent and Gaussian with the same variance.

The phrase 'channel of bandwidth W' is a shorthand way of describing the fact that only signals with $2WT$ components in the time interval T are considered.

When the white noise is also Gaussian

$$H(Z) = \tfrac{1}{2} \log \pi e N.$$

Moreover, the outputs can be arranged to be Gaussian by making the inputs Gaussian because Example 6.4 shows that the sum of two statistically independent Gaussian variables is also Gaussian. By giving the inputs the same variance (PT/n) and making them statistically independent we can comply with the conditions for equality in the Capacity Bound Theorem. Hence we have the following theorem.

SHANNON'S CONTINUOUS CHANNEL THEOREM. *Let the output be the sum of the input and statistically independent white Gaussian noise of spectral density $\frac{1}{2}N$. Let the input be limited to average power P. Then the capacity per unit time of a channel of bandwidth W is*

$$C = W \log(1 + P/WN).$$

Let $n \to \infty$ in (6.10.16) when the signals are distorted by white Gaussian noise. Then by an argument similar to that just foregoing, we can deduce the

FREE CHANNEL THEOREM. *Under the conditions of Shannon's Continuous Channel Theorem the capacity per unit time of a channel of unlimited bandwidth is* $(P/N)\log e$.

It will be remarked that the same capacity can be obtained from Shannon's Continuous Channel Theorem by allowing $W \to \infty$, an agreement which is very pleasing.

If the noise is white but not Gaussian it is advantageous to supplement the upper bound of the Capacity Bound Theorem by one which sets a lower limit to the capacity. This is provided by the following theorem.

THEOREM 6.10. *Let the output be the sum of the input and statistically independent white noise with the input limited to average power P. Then the capacity per unit time of a channel of bandwidth W satisfies*

$$C \geq W[\log\{e^{2H(Z)/\log e} + \pi e P/W\} - 2H(Z)].$$

If the noise is also Gaussian equality holds in both Theorem 6.10 and the Capacity Bound Theorem. The common value for the capacity coincides with that of Shannon's Continuous Channel Theorem.

Proof. We are at liberty to select a special input and we shall make the x_k statistically independent Gaussian variables all of zero mean and variance σ_1^2 which will be taken as PT/n at the end. It follows from (6.9.4) that the y_k are statistically independent random variables all with the same density

$$f_Y(y) = \frac{1}{(2\pi)^{\frac{1}{2}}\sigma_1} \int_{-\infty}^{\infty} e^{-\frac{1}{2}x^2/\sigma_1^2} f_Z(y - x) \, dx. \qquad (6.10.17)$$

For this input

$$I(\mathbf{X}, \mathbf{Y}) = n\{H(Y) - H(Z)\}$$

and so (6.8.6) and (6.8.7) give

$$C \geq 2W\{H(Y) - H(Z)\}. \qquad (6.10.18)$$

To secure the lower bound of the theorem we seek to minimize $H(Y)$ while keeping $H(Z)$ constant. The introduction of two Lagrange multipliers will enable the constraint on $H(Z)$ to be met as well as the requirement that f_Z is a probability density. Therefore consider

$$-\int_{-\infty}^{\infty} f_Y(y)\log f_Y(y) \, dy + \lambda \int_{-\infty}^{\infty} f_Z(z)\log f_Z(z) \, dz + \mu \int_{-\infty}^{\infty} f_Z(z) \, dz$$

with f_Y given by (6.10.17). Replace f_Z by $f_Z + \varepsilon g$ where g is arbitrary. Then the derivative with respect to ε vanishes at $\varepsilon = 0$ if

$$\int_{-\infty}^{\infty} f_X(y - x)\log\{ef_Y(y)\} \, dy - \lambda \log\{ef_Z(x)\} - \mu = 0. \qquad (6.10.19)$$

Try as a solution to (6.10.19)

$$f_Z(z) = \frac{1}{(2\pi)^{\frac{1}{2}}\sigma_0} e^{-\frac{1}{2}z^2/\sigma_0^2}$$

where, to make sure that the entropy is correct,

$$\sigma_0^2 = \frac{1}{2\pi e} e^{2H(Z)/\log e}. \qquad (6.10.20)$$

Then y is Gaussian with zero mean and variance $\sigma_0^2 + \sigma_1^2$. Hence

$$\int_{-\infty}^{\infty} f_X(y - x)\log\{ef_Y(y)\} \, dy = \frac{1}{2} \log \frac{e^2}{2\pi(\sigma_0^2 + \sigma_1^2)} - \frac{1}{2} \frac{\sigma_1^2 + x^2}{\sigma_0^2 + \sigma_1^2} \log e.$$

Thus the terms involving x in (6.10.19) cancel if $\lambda = \sigma_0^2/(\sigma_0^2 + \sigma_1^2)$ and the remaining terms are removed by adjusting

μ appropriately. Since the constraints are already satisfied all the conditions for an extremum are met. But for this choice of z, $H(Y) = \frac{1}{2}\log 2\pi e(\sigma_0^2 + \sigma_1^2)$ and so

$$H(Y) \geq \frac{1}{2}\log\{e^{2H(Z)/\log e} + 2\pi e\sigma_1^2\} \qquad (6.10.21)$$

by (6.10.20). Substitution in (6.10.18) with $\sigma_1^2 = PT/n$ supplies the result of the theorem.

Actually it should be verified that the extremum for $H(Y)$ is a minimum rather than a maximum. This can be done by showing that for some particular z which is not Gaussian the inequality in (6.10.21) is the right way round. Choose

$$f_Z(z) = 1/2b \qquad (|z| < b)$$
$$= 0 \qquad (|z| > b).$$

From (6.10.17)

$$f_Y(y) = \frac{1}{2b(2\pi)^{\frac{1}{2}}} \int_{(y-b)/\sigma_1}^{(y+b)/\sigma_1} e^{-\frac{1}{2}t^2}\,dt \qquad (6.10.22)$$

and $f_Y(-y) = f_Y(y)$.

Now

$$H(Z) = \log 2b$$

and, if we take σ_1 small, we have to show

$$H(Y) \geq \log 2b + O(\sigma_1^2)$$

or, in view of the evenness of f_Y,

$$-2\int_0^\infty f_Y(y)\log f_Y(y)\,dy \geq \log 2b + O(\sigma_1^2) \qquad (6.10.23)$$

with f_Y given by (6.10.22).

Let $\eta = \sigma_1^\alpha$ where $0 < \alpha < 1$. Then for $0 \leq y \leq b - \eta$,

$$f_Y(y) = \frac{1}{2b(2\pi)^{\frac{1}{2}}}\left\{(2\pi)^{\frac{1}{2}} - \left(\int_{(y+b)/\sigma_1}^\infty + \int_{-\infty}^{(y-b)/\sigma_1}\right)e^{-\frac{1}{2}t^2}\,dt\right\}.$$

But

$$\int_y^\infty e^{-\frac{1}{2}t^2}\,dt \leq e^{-\frac{1}{4}y^2}\int_y^\infty e^{-\frac{1}{4}t^2}\,dt = O(e^{-\frac{1}{4}y^2})$$

and so

$$f_Y(y) \geq \frac{1}{2b} - Ke^{-\frac{1}{4}(y-b)^2/\sigma_1^2}.$$

Since $f_Y(y) \leqslant 1/2b$ for all y it follows that

$$f_Y(y) = 1/2b + O(\sigma_1^2)$$

in $0 \leqslant y \leqslant b - \eta$. Hence

$$-2 \int_0^{b-\eta} f_Y(y) \log f_Y(y) \, dy = \log 2b + O(\sigma_1^2). \quad (6.10.24)$$

Now $f_Y(y)$ is a decreasing function of y and therefore $-f_Y(y) \ln f_Y(y)$ is a decreasing function of y if we insist that $-\ln 2b < -1$; there is no difficulty in arranging this since b is at our disposal. Hence

$$-2 \int_{b-\eta}^{\infty} f_Y(y) \log f_Y(y) \, dy \geqslant -2 \int_{b-\eta}^{b} f_Y(y) \log f_Y(y) \, dy$$

$$\geqslant -2\eta f_Y(b) \log f_Y(b)$$

$$\geqslant K_1 \eta \quad (6.10.25)$$

where $K_1 \neq 0$ since $f_Y(b) \to 1/2^{\frac{3}{2}}b$ as $\sigma_1 \to 0$. Combining (6.10.24) and (6.10.25) we see, because $0 < \alpha < 1$, that (6.10.23) is verified and we have consistency with (6.10.21).

6.11. Discussion

In order to achieve the capacity of Shannon's Continuous Channel Theorem both the input and output have to be constructed of independent Gaussian distributions with zero mean and common variance. Therefore, at capacity, both input and output resemble white Gaussian noise. Disentangling the required signal from the added noise which is also white Gaussian may therefore not be exactly straightforward, which implants the idea that continuous channels will rarely be used near capacity. The obligation to have a large number of waveforms θ_k available (since $WT \to \infty$ as $T \to \infty$) is another feature which has to be borne in mind. Nevertheless, the theorem implies that it should be possible to transmit, by a sufficiently intricate coding, binary digits at the rate $W \log_2(1 + P/WN)$ bits per second with an arbitrarily small frequency of errors.

A possible system is to prepare M samples of white noise each of duration T. These samples are assigned the binary numbers from 0 to $M-1$. The message to be transmitted is split into groups of $\log_2 M$ and for each group the corresponding sample is dispatched as the signal. At the output the received signal $y(t)$ is compared with each of the samples (call them $X_m(t)$) and identified with that X_m for which

$$\int_0^T \{y(t) - X_m(t)\}^2 \, dt$$

is least for $m = 1, \ldots, M$. The corresponding binary number is then taken as the output. The size of M will determine the frequency of errors but so long as M is large enough the frequency can be kept tolerably low.

However, any coding which allows the transmission to approach a rate which is near to the channel capacity is subject to a sudden large increase in error rate if the noise becomes slightly bigger. This *threshold effect* is due to the increase in noise reducing the channel capacity. If the channel capacity falls below the signalling rate the information output is limited to that dictated by the capacity by the introduction of errors. As an illustration, suppose that $W = 10^6$ Hz (which is a rough approximation to the transmission of television signals) and that $P/WN = 1$. Then

$$C = 10^6 \text{ bits/s.}$$

Imagine that a code has been devised which allows signals to be sent at 8×10^5 bits/s with a very small error rate, i.e. the channel is operating near capacity. Now suppose that the spectral density of the noise doubles; the new capacity becomes

$$10^6 \log_2(3/2) = 5.85 \times 10^5 \text{ bits/s}$$

which will force errors if the previous code is retained. Comparison with a binary symmetric channel in which the cross-over probability is ε is enlightening. This has a capacity of

$$1 + \varepsilon \log_2 \varepsilon + (1 - \varepsilon)\log_2(1 - \varepsilon)$$

bits per symbol (Section 4.2), which matches our situation when it is 0.73, i.e. $\varepsilon = 0.045$. An error rate of such magnitude makes the channel virtually useless for digital signals such as teletype or data transmission. The only remedy is to recode the input so that the transmission rate is below capacity.

Other calculations have been made that indicate why operation near capacity is impractical. For instance, it might well be desirable to have the probability of error no worse than 10^{-5}. To signal at the rate of $0.95C$ would require about 25 000 bits per message element or about 10^{7500} code signals. Such a number is quite out of the question. Lowering the signal rate gives the following figures

Rate	Bits/message	Code signals
$0.5C$	100	10^{30}
$0.25C$	17	10^{5}

Thus at a quarter capacity we are approaching a situation which can be realized practically but the channel is not being operated anywhere near capacity.

It is of interest to see how various channels compare. Firstly, consider a discrete channel in which teletype letters are sent at the rate of 10 characters per second. Since the maximum information associated with each character is 5 bits the capacity of the channel is 50 bits/s.

Most speech can be encompassed by a bandwidth $W = 4500$ Hz; actually, telephone circuits have a narrower bandwidth. If $P/WN = 4000$ the channel capacity is 54 000 bits/s approximately.

Similarly, in television $W = 5 \times 10^6$ Hz and, if $P/WN = 4000$ again, the channel capacity is about 6×10^7 bits/s.

So a speech circuit has about 1000 times the capacity of the teletype channel and a video circuit has about 1000 times the capacity of a speech circuit. It might be inferred that a voice circuit would carry the output of 1000 teletype channels or that the output of 1000 speech channels could be accommodated by a single video circuit but this would be false in practice. Most telephone lines are subject to distortion and a level of errors which the human ear can circumvent but which could be intolerable for discrete signals. For discrete signals the error rate must be very low and that demands a signalling rate well below capacity (perhaps less than $0.1C$) as we have seen. At a rate of $0.1C$ the voice circuit could cope with only 100 teletype channels. Moreover, when a channel is divided into sub-channels there has to be enough separation between the sub-channels to prevent them interfering with one another and this is a further factor which reduces the number of sub-channels which can be accommodated.

The parameter PW/C or

$$P/\log_2(1 + P/WN)$$

is a guide to the amount of energy involved in transmitting one bit of information. The parameter rises from WN when $P/WN = 1$ to $100WN$ when $P/WN = 1000$. Thus the energy required to send one bit of information is 100 times greater when the signal-to-noise ratio P/WN is 1000 than when the signal-to-noise ratio is unity. Since communication systems customarily employ signal-to-noise ratios of 1000 or higher, it is evident that practical systems use more energy than is strictly necessary to transmit information. The reason is that channels are rarely used efficiently. Most audio and visual signals contain a good deal of unnecessary detail so as to reduce the error in decoding. But this redundant detail has usually been incorporated in an *ad hoc* fashion and, despite its improvement of accuracy, has not been planned on an efficient basis.

It is of interest to compare the human being with other channels. If it is assumed that a human can read 500 words per minute and that each word has 5 letters, one letter containing 3 bits (which is probably an overestimate), the information rate is 125 bits/s. But it is doubtful if the reader is totally absorbing all this information except possibly over short periods. So it seems likely that 100 bits/s is the maximum and that 50 bits/s is closer to the mark.

Concentration over long periods brings down the rate significantly. In chess, for example, a player has, on average a choice of about 8 equally probable moves. (Some situations will offer less opportunity, especially if there is a check, and some more but 8 seems a reasonable average.) So chess involves about 3 bits per move. The number of moves per unit of time depends upon tournament rules and psychological considerations but an upper limit can be set by a Grand Master playing simultaneous boards. He can cope with a move every 15 seconds or so, giving a rate of 1/5 bits/s.

It would therefore appear that, at best, a human being cannot process fully more than $\frac{1}{2}$ bit/s over long periods. For short periods he can aspire to 50 bits/s but it is unlikely to process it completely.

Exercises

6.1. For a continuous distribution prove that

$$\int_{-\infty}^{\infty} F(x)f_X(x)\, dx = \tfrac{1}{2}.$$

6.2. In a continuous distribution x can take values only between $-a$ and a. Show that the probability density which gives maximum entropy is $f_X(x) = 1/2a$ ($|x| \le a$) and that the maximum entropy is $\log 2a$.

6.3. In a continuous distribution x can take only positive values and $\int_0^\infty f_X(x)x\, dx = 1/b$. Prove that the probability density which gives maximum entropy is $f_X(x) = be^{-bx}$ for $x \ge 0$ and find the maximum entropy.

6.4. Prove that, in a continuous distribution,

$$\int_{-\infty}^{\infty} x^2 f_X(x)\, dx \ge \frac{1}{2\pi e} \exp\left\{ \frac{2H(X)}{\log e} \right\}.$$

6.5. By considering the terms of order ε^2 in $J(f_0 + \varepsilon g)$ demonstrate that the extremum in Theorem 6.2 is a maximum.

6.6. The probability density of y is defined from that of x by

$$f_Y(y) = \int_{-\infty}^{\infty} h(y, x)f_X(x)\, dx$$

where $h(y, x) \ge 0$, $\int_{-\infty}^{\infty} h(y, x)\, dx = 1 = \int_{-\infty}^{\infty} h(y, x)\, dy$. By considering

$$\int_{-\infty}^{\infty} \int_{-\infty}^{\infty} h(y, x)f_X(x)\log\left\{ f_Y(y) \bigg/ \int_{-\infty}^{\infty} h(z, x)f_Y(z)\, dz \right\} dx\, dy$$

show that $H(Y) \ge H(X)$.

6.7. A probability density is subject to the constraints

$$\int_{-\infty}^{\infty} xf_X(x)\, dx = \mu, \qquad \int_{-\infty}^{\infty} (x-\mu)^2 f_X(x)\, dx = \sigma^2.$$

Show that for all such distributions the entropy has a maximum of $\tfrac{1}{2}\log(2\pi e\sigma^2)$ which occurs when x is Gaussian with mean μ and variance σ^2.

6.8. The function $f(x, y)$ is defined by

$$f(x, y) = \{(1+ax)(1+ay) - a\}e^{-x-y-axy}$$

with $0 \leq a \leq 1$ for $x > 0$, $y > 0$ and by $f(x, y) = 0$ elsewhere. Show that f is a probability density in two dimensions and that $f_X(x) = e^{-x}$ for $x > 0$, $= 0$ for $x < 0$.

6.9. The continuous function $g(x)$ is odd, i.e. $g(x) = -g(-x)$ and vanishes outside $(-1, 1)$. If $|g| < (2\pi e)^{-\frac{1}{2}}$ prove that

$$\frac{1}{2\pi} e^{-\frac{1}{2}(x^2+y^2)} + g(x)g(y)$$

is a two-dimensional probability density which is not Gaussian. Show that both $f_X(x)$ and $f_Y(y)$ are Gaussian.

6.10. If $f_X(x)$, $g_Y(y)$ are the probability densities of the distribution functions $F(x)$, $G(y)$ respectively, prove that, for $|a| \leq 1$,

$$f_X(x)g_Y(y)[1 + a\{1 - 2F(x)\}\{1 - 2G(y)\}]$$

is a probability density whose density for x is $f_X(x)$.

6.11. The variables x, y are converted to ξ, η by the linear transformation

$$x = a_{11}\xi + a_{12}\eta, \qquad y = a_{21}\xi + a_{22}\eta.$$

Prove that

$$f_{\Xi,H}(\xi, \eta) = f_{X,Y}(a_{11}\xi + a_{12}\eta, a_{21}\xi + a_{22}\eta)(a_{11}a_{22} - a_{12}a_{21})$$

when $a_{11}a_{22} > a_{12}a_{21}$.

6.12. The variables x, y are statistically independent and have the same distributions, namely $f_X(x) = ae^{-ax}$ with $a > 0$ for $x > 0$ and $f_X(x) = 0$ for $x < 0$. Find the probability density of $(x, x+y)$ and prove that

$$f_X(x \mid x + y = z) = 1/z$$

for $0 < x < z$. [Hint: see Exercise 6.11.] This demonstrates that the knowledge that $x + y = z$ gives no clue to the location of x in $(0, z)$.

6.13. For two-dimensional probability densities which vanish outside a finite domain of area A show that the maximum entropy is $\log A$, achieved when the probability density has the constant value $1/A$.

6.14. The variables $x_1, x_2, \ldots, x_n$ are mutually statistically independent, each with the same distribution function F. If $x = \max(x_1, \ldots, x_n)$ and $y = \min(x_1, \ldots, x_n)$ prove that

$$P(x \leq x_0, y > y_0) = \{F(x_0) - F(y_0)\}^n \quad \text{for} \quad y_0 < x_0,$$

and

$$P(x_1 \leqslant x_0 \mid x = t) = \frac{n-1}{n} \frac{F(x_0)}{F(t)} \quad \text{for} \quad x_0 < t$$

$$= 1 \qquad \text{for} \quad x_0 \geqslant t.$$

6.15. From an n-dimensional distribution another is formed by the transformation

$$y_i = \sum_{j=1}^{n} a_{ij} x_j \qquad (i = 1, \ldots, n)$$

where $\det(a_{ij}) \neq 0$. Find the probability density of $\mathbf{y}$ and prove that

$$H(\mathbf{Y}) = H(\mathbf{X}) + \log \det(a_{ij}).$$

6.16. Prove (6.5.16).

6.17. A one-to-one mapping is made in which $\mathbf{x} \to \mathbf{x}'$ and $\mathbf{y} \to \mathbf{y}'$. Show that

$$H(\mathbf{Y}') - H(\mathbf{Y}' \mid \mathbf{X}') = H(\mathbf{Y}) - H(\mathbf{Y} \mid \mathbf{X}).$$

6.18. For n-dimensional probability densities which are zero outside a finite domain of 'volume' v show that the maximum entropy is $\log v$.

6.19. Prove that, among probability densities which satisfy

$$\int_{-\infty}^{\infty} x_i x_j f_{\mathbf{X}}(\mathbf{x}) \, d\mathbf{x} = a_{ij}$$

where (a_{ij}) is a symmetric positive definite matrix, the entropy is a maximum when

$$f_{\mathbf{X}}(\mathbf{x}) = \frac{\exp\{-\frac{1}{2} \sum_{i=1}^{n} \sum_{j=1}^{n} A_{ij} x_i x_j / \det(a_{ij})\}}{(2\pi)^{\frac{1}{2}n} \{\det(a_{ij})\}^{\frac{1}{2}}}$$

where A_{ij} is the cofactor of a_{ij} in $\det(a_{ij})$.

6.20. Show that, for fixed WN, the energy required to transmit one bit of information has a minimum of $0.693\,WN$. If P/WN exceeds 4000, as is desirable in good quality television, show that the energy required is at least 490 times the minimum so that the system is less efficient than the ideal by a factor of some hundreds.

6.21. In frequency modulation $P = 3P_0 M^2(M+1)$ where M is the modulation index and P_0 is related to the carrier power, The energy required to transmit one bit of information is $2P_0(1+M)W/C$ and for practical reasons $P_0/WN \geqslant 16$. Show that, when $P_0/WN = 16$, the optimal value of

M is 2 when the system is about 13 times less efficient than the ideal minimum of $0.693WN$ in Exercise 6.20. The efficiency is not very sensitive to variations of M between 1 and 4 which is of importance in voice transmission by frequency modulation.

Answers

CHAPTER 4

4.2. $\log 2$.

4.3. $\frac{5}{3}\log 2 - \log 3$.

4.5. $\log_2(1+2^\mu) - \nu$ where

$$(1-\delta-\varepsilon)\mu = (1-\delta)\log_2(1-\delta)$$
$$+ \delta\log_2\delta - (1-\varepsilon)\log_2(1-\varepsilon) - \varepsilon\log_2\varepsilon,$$
$$(1-\delta-\varepsilon)\nu = (1-\delta)\varepsilon\log_2\{(1-\delta)/\varepsilon\}$$
$$+ \delta\varepsilon\log_2\delta - (1-\varepsilon)(1-\delta)\log_2(1-\varepsilon).$$

4.8. $1 + \frac{1}{2}(2p_0 - 1)(1-2\varepsilon)^m$ where p_0 is the probability of 0 at the input of C_1.

4.9.   (i) All persistent and $p_{jk}^{(m)} \to \frac{1}{3}$. (ii) a_2 is transient, the rest persistent but a_1 and a_3 are never followed by a_4, a_5 or vice versa. $p_{jk}^{(m)} \to \frac{1}{2}$ for j, $k = 1, 3$ or j, $k = 4, 5$; $p_{2j}^{(m)} \to 0$; $p_{k2}^{(m)} \to \frac{1}{2}$ for $k = 1, 3$ and $p_{k2}^{(m)} \to 0$ for $k = 2, 4, 5$. (iii) All persistent with period 3.

CHAPTER 5

5.6.

$\mathbf{s}^T$	$\mathbf{e}_{min}^T$
00	0000
10	1000
11	0100
01	0001

$P_e = 1 - (1-p)^4 - 3p(1-p)^3$.

5.7.

$$G = \begin{bmatrix} 10 \\ 01 \\ 11 \\ 10 \\ 11 \end{bmatrix} \quad F = \begin{bmatrix} 11100 \\ 10010 \\ 11001 \end{bmatrix}$$

$\mathbf{s}^T$	$\mathbf{e}_{min}^T$
000	00000
111	10000
101	01000
100	00100
010	00010
001	00001
011	10100
110	10001

$P_e = 1 - (1-p)^5 - 5p(1-p)^4 - 2p^2(1-p)^3$

5.14.   B.

CHAPTER 6

6.3. log(e/b).

6.12. The probability density is $a^2 e^{-az}$ for $z > x > 0$ and zero elsewhere.

Index